SYSTEMS ANALYSIS AND DESIGN: PEOPLE, PROCESSES, AND PROJECTS

SYSTEMS ANALYSIS AND DESIGN: PEOPLE, PROCESSES, AND PROJECTS

KENG SIAU
ROGER H.L. CHIANG
BILL C. HARDGRAVE
EDITOR

ADVANCES IN MANAGEMENT
INFORMATION SYSTEMS
VLADIMIR ZWASS SERIES EDITOR

M.E.Sharpe
Armonk, New York
London, England

Copyright © 2011 by M.E. Sharpe, Inc.

References to the AMIS papers should be as follows:

Van Der Vyver, G.; Lane, M.; and Koronios, A. Facilitators and inhibitors for the adoption of agile methods. Keng Siau, Roger Chiang, and Bill C. Hardgrave, eds., *Systems Analysis and Design: People, Processes, and Projects*. Volume 18, *Advances in Management Information Systems* (Armonk, NY: M.E. Sharpe, 2011), 31–50.

Hardcover ISBN 978-0-7656-2353-9
Print ISSN   1554–6152
Online ISSN 1554–6160

Printed in the United States of America

The paper in this publication meets the minimum requirements of
American National Standards for Information Sciences
Permanence of Paper for Printed Library Materials,
ANSI Z 39.48–1984.

IBT (c)   10   9   8   7   6   5   4   3   2   1

ADVANCES IN MANAGEMENT INFORMATION SYSTEMS

Forthcoming volumes of this series can be found on the series homepage.
www.mesharpe.com/amis.htm

Editor-in-Chief, Vladimir Zwass (zwass@fdu.edu)

Advances in Management Information Systems

Advisory Board

CONTENTS

PART III. TECHNICAL SYSTEMS FOCUS: PROJECTS

SERIES EDITOR'S INTRODUCTION

VLADIMIR ZWASS, EDITOR-IN-CHIEF

Successful systems development is the heart of the information systems (IS) practice and, consequently, one of the key concerns of the IS discipline. In recognition of the sociotechnical, rather than purely technological, nature of the systems built around information technology (IT), this field of study devotes much attention to the social, organizational, cognitive, and behavioral aspects of systems and of their development processes. This will become readily apparent to the readers of the present volume of *Advances in Management Information Systems* (*AMIS*). The volume complements the earlier one, concerning the development methodology aspects of systems analysis and design (SA&D), is edited by the same authorities (Chiang et al., 2009), and includes contributions of well-known thinkers in the field. Taken together, the two SA&D volumes present a rich picture of the fundamental processes and methods that deliver the engines for our information society.

There are numerous, and highly interrelated, sources of complexity in SA&D. IS consist of people in many roles, systems and application software, databases and data warehouses, hardware, and telecommunications in highly dynamic interactions, with a great diversity of components and a vast number of possible states. The dynamic nature of these systems makes the task of system design that of designing a process, with many behaviors in a changing context, rather than an artifact. Moreover, IS are designed to evolve, for three principal reasons: to meet changing requirements of their owners, to adapt to technological change, and to remove defects. A truly simple mental exercise—comparing the task of implementing a supply chain management system with building a bridge—illustrates the nature of complexity in SA&D. This complexity and failures in handling it are reflected in IS project statistics. The 2009 Standish Group's CHAOS report showed that only 32 percent of IS projects fully succeed, which means they were delivered on time, within the budget, and with the required functions and features; 24 percent of the projects were failures, canceled, or delivered and not used (Standish Group, 2009). With global IT spending of about $2.7 trillion, as projected for 2009 by Gartner (Morgan, 2009), much is at stake in increasing this success rate. The potential payoff from learning how to do SA&D better is indeed high.

While some of the issues involving projects that fall short of success are certainly of a technical nature, the—by now—long experience in the field shows that most failures can be ascribed to the sources named in the subtitle of this volume: people, the social actors in their roles as users, developers, and managers; the processes deployed in systems development and the processes that IS are expected to support; and the projects that need to be organized to deliver the products expected to work across multiple organizational boundaries and over long stretches of time, as the business context and technological change shake their moorings.

Centered as the organizational IS projects are on the implementation of business-facing applications to support both the intra- and interorganizational processes, a profound and multifaceted change has taken place in the arena over recent decades (Zwass, 2009). As one facet of this change, a variety of software provisioning modes has replaced the default internal development of applications. These include the use of proprietary and open enterprise software and other packages, outsourcing and offshoring in various combinations, utility computing, service-oriented architectures, grid computing, and other emerging opportunities. The people, processes, and projects have to fit the nature of the provisioning. Successful SA&D require a rich understanding of work systems to be supported by information and IS, rather than a focus on systems and technologies; the treatment of information systems with all their components, context, and history, rather than the lens kept focused exclusively on IT; and a full understanding of social actors rather than a view of stick-figure "users." The present context for IS is the open corporation. It is open to co-creation with its customers, "co-opetition" with other firms in its space, the outsourcing of its processes, perhaps offshore, and the deployment of openly available information technologies. Multiple organizations and a great variety of individuals with different (or no) affiliations interact with a firm's IS and are at the source of the system components.

Systems development processes differ, sometimes radically. A review of the object-oriented development methodologies from the point of view of the structuring of the development process surfaces some three dozen major methodologies with their consequent processes (Ramsin and Paige, 2008). There is a tension between discipline-oriented approaches, such as predictive life-cycle development on the waterfall model, whose avowed objective is to produce systems that can be maintained in a similarly discipline-oriented manner of discrete and relatively infrequent releases, and rapid application development with one of the agile methods, privileging the working code and a change as it is asked for, aimed at the competitive advantage of the owner organization. A software application is no longer a product written in a single language. It is rather an amalgam of codes written in a variety of languages and programming idioms, such as markup, and scripting, procedural, and nonprocedural languages, built on such infrastructures as .NET or Enterprise JavaBeans (Budgen, 2003). It may also be a metered service.

SA&D research conducted in the IS space overlaps with disciplinary concerns of software engineering in computer science. The notable distinction is the consistent and integrated view of IS as sociotechnical systems, bringing together the technical subsystem of process and technology with the social one of people and organization (Bostrom et al., 2009). The richness of the field can be illustrated here with only a few examples. The cognitive fit theory is the basis for investigating the role of knowledge support in the successful tailoring of the development process to the requirements (Xu and Ramesh, 2008–9). This theory is also used to assess the fit between the actors' knowledge and the governance in systems development (Tiwana, 2009). New frameworks for the development of systems that are continually evolving in the open domain via peer production are investigated (Kazman and Chen, 2009). The formation processes of the voluntary open-source project teams are being studied (Hahn et al., 2008). Sustained participation in such teams has been found to be guided by considerations different from the initial act of volunteering (Fang and Neufeld, 2009). Component-based development of IS is being studied and implemented as an avenue to the reuse of well-tested software, fast time-to-market, and cost control (De Cesare et al., 2006). With the components evolving into services available over the Web as discoverable software resources, service-oriented architectures are being implemented by such methods as SOMA (Arsanjani et al., 2008). Web-based collaboration tools bring new organizational opportunities to development, particularly salient in the age of offshoring, such as geographically distributed design and code reviews (Meyer, 2008). Such reviews have been found effective in defect removal in the Personal Software Process approach, used to improve the performance of individual developers (Kemerer and Paulk, 2009).

Ever new application requirements challenge the existing development processes, the preparation of people, and the operation of development projects. Thus, the emerging challenge of data-intensive computing is to orchestrate widely distributed systems in order to ingest and analyze, in real or almost-real time, massive data volumes incoming via the Internet–Web compound (Kouzes et al., 2009). Robust study of the SA&D should lead to robust systems. A broad program of study of the development and implementation of successful organizational and interorganizational IS, known as design science, was initiated two decades ago (Nunamaker et al., 1990–91). A process model for conducting this research has been proposed and demonstrated in practice (Peffers et al., 2007–8). Consistent with the *AMIS* publication program, it is my hope that this volume, as well as its *AMIS* predecessor in the SA&D sequence, will enhance practice and stimulate further research.

REFERENCES

Arsanjani, A.; Ghosh, S.; Alla, A.; Abdollah, T.; Ganapthy, S.; and Holley, K. 2008. SOMA: A method for developing service-oriented solutions. *IBM Systems Journal,* 47, 3, 377–396.

Bostrom, R.P.; Gupta, S.; and Thomas, D. 2009. A meta-theory for understanding information systems within sociotechnical systems. *Journal of Management Information Systems,* 26, 1, 17–47.

Budgen, D. 2003. *Software Design,* 2d ed. New York: Addison-Wesley.

Chiang, R.H.L.; Siau, K.; and Hardgrave, B.C. (eds.). 2009. *Systems Analysis and Design: Techniques, Methodologies, Approaches, and Architectures.* Vol. 15, *Advances in Management Information Systems.* Armonk, NY: M.E. Sharpe.

De Cesare, S.; Lycett, M.; and Macredie, R.D. (eds.). 2006. *Development of Computer-Based Information Systems.* Vol. 12, *Advances in Management Information Systems.* Armonk, NY: M.E. Sharpe.

Fang, Y., and Neufeld, D. 2009. Understanding sustained participation in open source software projects. *Journal of Management Information Systems,* 25, 4, 9–50.

Hahn, J.; Moon, J.Y.; and Zhang, C. 2008. Emergence of new project teams from open source software developer networks: Impact of prior collaboration ties. *Information Systems Research,* 19, 3, 369–391.

Kazman, R., and Chen, H.-M. 2009. The Metropolis model: A new logic for development of crowdsourced systems. *Communications of the ACM,* 52, 7, 78–84.

Kemerer, C.F., and Paulk, M.C. 2009. The impact of design and code reviews on software quality: An empirical study based on PSPO data. *IEEE Transactions on Software Engineering,* 35, 4, 534–550.

Kouzes, R.T.; Anderson, G.A.; Elbert, S.T.; Gorton, I.; and Gracio, D.K. 2009. The changing paradigm of data-intensive computing. *Computer,* 42, 1, 26–34.

Meyer, B. 2008. Design and code reviews in the age of Internet. *Communications of the ACM,* 51, 9, 67–72.

Morgan, T.P. 2009. Gartner: Global IT spending will rise in 2009 (slightly). *Financial News,* February 24. Available at www.theregister.co.uk/2009/02/24/gartner_2009_it_spending/ (accessed August 7, 2009).

Nunamaker, J.F. Jr.; Chen, M.; and Purdin, T.D.M. 1990–91. Systems development in information systems research. *Journal of Management Information Systems,* 7, 3, 89–106.

Peffers, K.; Tuunanen, T.; Rothenberger, M.A.; and Chatterjee, S. 2007–8. A design science research methodology for information systems research. *Journal of Management Information Systems,* 24, 3, 45–77.

Ramsin, R., and Paige, R.F. 2008. Process-centered review of object oriented software development methodologies. *ACM Computing Surveys,* 40, 1, 3:1–3:89.

Standish Group. 2009. New CHAOS numbers show startling results. April 23. Available at www.standish-group.com/newsroom/chaos_2009.php (accessed August 12, 2009).

Tiwana, A. 2009. Governance-knowledge fit in systems development projects. *Information Systems Research,* 20, 2, 180–197.

Xu, P., and Ramesh, B. 2008–9. Impact of knowledge support on the performance of software process tailoring. *Journal of Management Information Systems,* 25, 3, 277–314.

Zwass, V. 2009. Series editor's introduction. In R.H.L. Chiang, K. Siau, and B.C. Hardgrave (eds.), *Systems Analysis and Design: Techniques, Methodologies, Approaches, and Architectures,* IX–XII. Vol. 15, *Advances in Management Information Systems.* Armonk, NY: M.E. Sharpe.

SYSTEMS ANALYSIS AND DESIGN: PEOPLE, PROCESSES, AND PROJECTS

CHAPTER 1

SOCIAL AND TECHNICAL ASPECTS OF SYSTEMS ANALYSIS AND DESIGN

JOHN ERICKSON AND KENG SIAU

Sociotechnical theory has served as an explanatory vehicle for information systems development and deployment for more than thirty years. In the competitive environment that most industries operate in, information systems are essential for solving problems, and gaining and maintaining competitive advantages. Understanding both the technical and behavioral aspects of systems is also a critical component of the systems development process. Information systems can often determine the success or failure of a business. Unfortunately, the overall success rates of systems development projects historically have been very low. The statistics cross industries, organization size, and national boundaries. Much research has been devoted to examining why systems fail so often and how they can be improved (Avison and Fitzgerald, 2003; Hardgrave et al., 2003; Schmidt et al., 2001; Smith et al., 2001; Siau et al., 1997).

A wide variety of approaches to systems development have been proposed and tried over at least the past twenty years. For example, between 1989 and 1994, the number of object-oriented development approaches grew from around ten to more than fifty (Booch et al., 2005). Recent years, between 1994 and 2008, have not seen a drop in the number of proposals regarding how best to build systems. Entirely new approaches have been designed and tried in practice. Pair programming (Williams and Kessler, 2002), extreme programming (Beck, 1999), and agile development (Erickson et al., 2005; Fowler and Highsmith, 2001) were proposed and used in the late 1990s and the early years of the next decade, while Web services, service-oriented architecture (Erickson and Siau, 2008), cloud computing, Web 2.0, and open source systems (Long and Siau, 2007) continue the trend of proliferation of system-building approaches in more recent times.

In particular, open source development can be connected to sociotechnical systems because at least one of its basic tenets—that users can meaningfully contribute to technical systems development, particularly application development—proposes that users should be more closely connected to systems building. Traditionally, applications are built so that the developing company owns the source code, and keeps it closed, for the most part, to outside programmers or users. Open source development, however, allows users from outside the developing organization to contribute to code writing, and also to programming improvement initiatives. Peer-based collaboration efforts, including open source and pair programming, that are aimed at improving applications and systems represent a fundamental divergence in thought regarding how systems should be built.

As the volume title indicates, the organizational theme is people, processes, and projects. This implies a synergy for the organization when both the human component and the technological component can be put together in attempts to gain competitive advantage. Technical approaches and practice combined with those of social and behavioral sciences have become important to ensuring business success. In addition, the sociotechnical approach can provide insight into better

Table 1.1

Cherns' Principles for Social-Technical Design

Principle 1.   Compatibility
Principle 2.   Minimal Critical Specification
Principle 3.   Variance Control
Principle 4.   Boundary Location
Principle 5.   Information Flow
Principle 6.   Power and Authority
Principle 7.   Multifunctional
Principle 8.   Support Congruence
Principle 9.   Transitional Organization
Principle 10.   Forth Bridge

organizational and process design and practice and has become a critical element that organizations must deal with effectively. The sociotechnical approach has been used as an explanatory vehicle for many years (e.g., see Ryan and Harrison, 2000; Ryan et al. 2002; Stein and Vandenbosch, 1996), with one of the early and noteworthy formulations of the theory emerging from Cherns's 1976 observations. He followed up in 1987 with a review and modifications to the 1976 work. Sociotechnical theory assumes that an organization or subcomponent can be viewed as a socio-technical system. A sociotechnical system is composed of two interindependent, closely related and interacting systems, social and technical (Bostrom and Heinen, 1977a).

CHERNS'S PRINICIPLES ON SOCIAL-TECHNICAL DESIGN

Cherns (1976, 1987) insisted that if systems builders failed to account for the social require-ments or needs of the system being constructed, those needs would be met in "some other way," and such other ways would likely impede the organization as much as help it. Cherns (1976) went on to delineate nine principles that he insisted should provide a basis for the sociotech-nical design of business or organizational systems. In his 1987 revisitation of the theory, he modified some of the existing principles and added a tenth principle. Table 1.1 summarizes Cherns's ten principles.

The first principle is compatibility. By compatibility, Cherns means that design execution should be in alignment with the design goal for the system itself. An important part of this principle is the idea that even experts (systems analysts, domain experts, etc.)—or perhaps, especially experts—must be willing to put their assumptions on the table.

Cherns's second principle, minimal critical specification, means that essential characteristics of the systems must be identified. Conversely, this principle also means that the builders should specify the minimum design necessary to meet the objectives. In other words, adherence to this principle is a way to deal with project scope creep.

Variance control represents Cherns's third principle. Underlying variance control is the basic assumption that variances should not be moved across organizational boundaries. As such, this principle is interdependent with boundary location (the fourth principle) and information flow (the fifth principle). Boundaries are often set by functional area designations and sometimes by process designations. The fourth principle states that boundaries should not be drawn in ways that impede information flow. However, given that at least some processes are transfunctional, meaning they cross functional boundaries by definition and necessity, internal boundaries can block the flow of information. This is not to say that boundaries should be eliminated, but rather that they should be carefully drawn and managed as organizational needs and boundaries change through business pressure.

The sixth principle, power and authority, states that those who need resources or inputs should have access to acquire and use them. However, this also means that with the authority comes responsibility for appropriate use. This principle can be closely associated with information flow and boundary issues (the fourth and fifth principles).

The multifunctional principle, Cherns's seventh, simply proposes that organizations must adapt to their environments. However, in the context of the fourth, fifth, and sixth principles, developers and organizations must also realize that many of the boundaries are internal and that as a result, so are some of the "environments" that they must adapt to. This is most evident when implementing an enterprise system (Doherty and King, 2005).

Support congruence represents Cherns's eighth principle. It proposes that support for human-based processes, such as human resources, marketing, and planning, should be conceived and delivered similarly to support for concrete processes typically found in a manufacturing company. Adherence to this principle can mean a significant change to policies, some of which may have been in place for a long time. Thus, resistance to change is possible or even likely.

The ninth principle is known as the transitional organization principle and presumes that transitions from legacy systems to new systems must be designed and planned. This includes training and other means of obtaining buy-in from end users and other constituents. Cherns named the final principle the Forth Bridge principle, or incompletion principle. This name refers to a famous railroad bridge in Scotland that can never be freshly painted in its entirety at one time. By the time painting is completed on both sides, the paint on the first side of the bridge has deteriorated so much that it is time to repaint it again (one could use painting and maintenance on the Golden Gate Bridge as an equally apt analogy). This principle states that systems are never really static, but rather are continually changing and dynamic, and require more or less continuous maintenance and repair. Maintenance and support continue over the life of a system, and change is continuous and/or incremental rather than all at once or not at all.

Cherns's works did not include a specific framework for examining or classifying sociotechnical systems. They were more general principles and values that others used to build upon.

OTHER SOCIAL-TECHNICAL FRAMEWORKS AND THEORIES

Once researchers had a chance to examine Cherns's ideas in detail and organizations begin to act on them, other ideas were proposed and developed to extend understanding of sociotechnical systems and their related development. Among the researchers investigating sociotechnical systems were Markus (1983), Lamb and Kling (2003), and Bostrom and Heinen (1977a, 1977b). The basic ideas driving the research are explored in the following section.

Markus examined resistance to management information systems (MIS) projects from several existing theoretical perspectives. The first theory was based on the idea that resistance to change (identified as a primary reason that systems development efforts fail) could emerge from the human or behavioral perspective. In other words, resistance to change is an internal phenomenon originating in individuals or in their groups.

The second theory presumed that resistance to change, or user nonacceptance of the system, is driven primarily by the quality and design of the system itself (Markus, 1983). Accordingly, even if a system was well constructed from a technical perspective and accomplished everything the developers wanted, but included a very poorly designed interface, then the system was still likely to fail.

The third theoretical approach was to include the human and technology-based elements as actors or components of the system. The idea was then to examine the effects of interactions between the various human and technological components of the system. Markus used a single case study to illustrate how the various elements of each of the theories could be applied as an explanatory vehicle.

Markus arrived at a number of conclusions from the case study. One conclusion was that technical systems by themselves cannot induce large changes to the organizations. The people tasked to use the systems will tend not to accept the system if it is simply imposed upon them. On the other hand, technical systems cannot operate themselves, and people must be included in the building and productions phases. Another of Markus's conclusions was that no single set of approaches would work in every situation, when speaking of information systems development projects. Markus also proposed that the specific systems designs arrived at were closely related to the interactions between users and designers. Finally, Markus claimed that the most critical implication of what she called the interaction theory was that a complete and thorough design process was essential to the success of the system. Further, she said that the design must include human elements such as social and political considerations.

Lamb and Kling (2003) conducted research developing and extending the "social actor" model. The basic idea of the model is that those that use information systems are more than " . . . a socially thin concept of users . . ." (p. 28) and should be seen from a more richly defined perspective. In particular, Lamb and Kling (2003) defined four dimensions of social actors: affiliations, environments, interactions, and identities. Each of the dimensions includes characteristics and behaviors.

Characteristics and behaviors of affiliations presume that the relationships between the actors are modified and determined to some extent by the demands of the client or other stakeholders. It is also assumed that the interactions and relationships are dynamic and vary with various resources. Relationships are assumed to cross boundaries among various interested groups. Finally, relationships change in response to the dynamics described above, moving across the organization (Lamb and Kling, 2003).

Environments are described in terms of four characteristics and behaviors. First, the environments influence the internal systems and people of the organization. Second, environments differ across industries, especially with regard to dynamics. Third, it is assumed that some technical systems are located in the environment, and fourth, other technical systems are located in the industry or in other environmental entities (Lamb and Kling, 2003).

Interactions consist of four characteristics or behaviors. The first assumes that actors communicate through standard and existing channels, while the second assumes that actors create new communication channels as necessary to ease communications. Third, the technical systems must be included as part of the interactions. Finally, the actors are assumed to perform their functions as representatives or agents of the organization (Lamb and Kling, 2003).

Identities are the " . . . avowed presentations of the self and ascribed profiles of organizational members" (Lamb and Kling, 2003). The four characteristics or behaviors include the following. First, the actors' identities are represented by a built-in part of the technical systems. Second, the technical systems and networks enhance many identities, such as gender identities, within the system. Third, the connections heightened by the technical system include more than the roles. In other words, the identities are seen and recognized across functional and other boundaries in the various components. Fourth, the actors create identities via the technical system.

Bostrom and Heinen (1977a, 1977b) concluded that many systems failures could be traced to poor designs. They expanded upon Cherns and other researchers' ideas and proposed a framework for examining and understanding the concepts of sociotechnical systems. Their idea separates a

Figure 1.1 **The Social-Technical System**

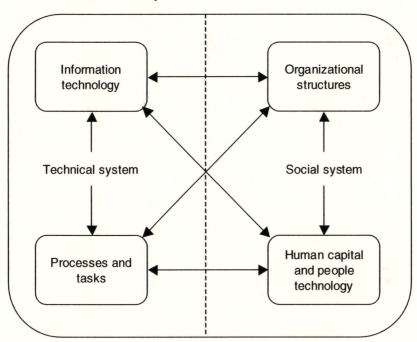

company internally into a social system and a technical system. Components (also called classes) of the social system include structure and people, while components of the technical system include technology and tasks. Each of the internal components can interact with each of the others, in what Bostrom and Heinen called secondary relationships (1977a). See Figure 1.1 for details.

CLASSIFYING CHAPTERS IN THIS VOLUME

The framework developed by Bostrom and Heinen (1977a) provides a good schema for classifying MIS research. Works can be classified as dealing with the social system comprising structure and people, or the technical system comprising technology and tasks. The necessary interactions and relationships among the components would also be an important part of the classification scheme.

The broad umbrella of social systems research chapters in this volume includes Part I, Social Systems Focus, comprising Chapters 2, 3, and 4. Part II consists of chapters exemplifying a combined perspective on systems, which we titled Sociotechnical Systems Focus, and includes Chapters 5, 6, 7, and 8. Finally, Part III, Technical Systems Focus, which includes Chapters 9, 10, and 11, contains a more technical perspective, since those chapters address issues and problems related to system modeling approaches.

In providing this classification scheme, it is not our intent to preclude other ways of classifying the chapters in this volume, nor is it our intent to say that the chapters in Part I do not include a significant technical perspective, or that the chapters in Part III do not include a significant social perspective. Instead, we intend only to provide a possible lens for readers to view the exemplar research included herein.

Part I. Social Systems Focus

Part I of the volume focuses on system development methods and the implicit effect that development methods have or can have on success or failure. In particular, the general theme revolves around agility in the systems development process. Agile systems development by its definition (Fowler and Highsmith, 2001) means that systems developers and users are more closely connected than in nonagile projects; agile projects seem to focus more on the connection and interactions between tasks and people (Bostrom and Heinen, 1977a). We classify the chapters in this section as being more related to a social systems focus than to a technical systems focus. We propose that the research described in this section studies tasks, which are by definition technical. However, the primary focus of agility is more on changing the behavior of the participants involved in the development of the systems, so we argue that the chapter should be seen as more behaviorally focused than technically focused.

In Chapter 2, Dinesh Batra applies cognitive complexity principles to justify the connections and interactions between the standard, heavy structured (object-oriented development) approaches and the more lightweight, agile development approaches. A framework is provided to guide the reader through the selection process based on various complexity factors. In Chapter 3, Glen Van Der Vyver, Michael Lane, and Andy Koronios explore the ways that adoption of agile systems development methods can be inhibited or enhanced. This exploration ultimately results in a set of factors that provides insight into the conditions necessary to drive successful projects using the proper approach (either agile or traditional). This could be classified as research involving the interactions between the social system and technology and tasks. In Chapter 4, Michael Rosemann, Jan Recker, and Christian Flender explore ways to design business processes that are "aware" of the context in which they operate. They explain how the business context can be conceptualized, classified, and integrated with existing approaches to business process modeling to make flexibility and adaptability key considerations in design.

Part II. Sociotechnical Systems Focus

Part II of the volume is themed around software projects. While software projects are often seen as heavily technical, the chapters included in this section examine how the projects are executed, thus implying a strong social content. So, we classified these chapters as exemplifying the sociotechnical approach in practice, a mix of both the technical and social. While the chapters in this section examine the technology and tasks, the interactions between the social system components and the technical system components are certainly a significant part of the projects as well. For the chapters included in this section, we strived to provide a good view of the sociotechnical approach by focusing on both technical and social components.

Chapter 5, contributed by Fred Niederman, examines the issues involving recruiting, staffing, hiring, and skills needed in a Web-enabled development environment. Chapter 6 deals with work systems and how they can be used to analyze and understand information systems. Contributed by Steven Alter, this research fits nicely within the context of Cherns (1976) and Bostrom and Heinen (1977a). A framework and guide, called the work systems method, for improving collaboration between business and information technology professionals is provided. The work system approach operates from many of the same basic assumptions as the sociotechnical approach. In Chapter 7, Paolo Salvaneschi discusses how the quality of software systems is evaluated. The author challenges readers to broaden their perspective on quality and consider it through the lens of a conceptual framework taken from the engineering discipline. This could be classified as examining interactions between information systems and processes and tasks. Chapter 8 studies the use of a cognitive mapping approach, including agent-based software, to assess and quantify the risks associated with software development projects. Cognitive mapping is useful in situations where many decision-making factors are interrelated causally and must be considered simultaneously. Written by Kun-Chang Lee and Nam-Ho Lee, the work can be seen as examining the interactions between human capital and people, and the information system.

Part III. Technical Systems Focus

Part III of the volume contains research that generally examines the importance modeling has assumed in systems development. Modeling can be used in very general ways by systems developers to provide some "as-built" drawings of the system. Alternatively, modeling can be more formally used to describe the systems in much more explicit and granular detail. Thus, for the chapters in Part III, it seems that the focus of modeling is balanced relatively equally on both the technical components and the behavioral components, especially since at least one of the chapters examines the question of how people actually use modeling as an aid to systems building.

Chapter 9, by Peter F. Green and Alastair Robb, looks at how systems development teams use modeling in practical information systems implementation projects. Although the use of models by individual developers has been explored, this study examines their use in the context of teams and finds that developers are much more likely to use combinations of models while working in a team than while working alone. This could be seen as a study involving the interactions between the organizational structures, the human capital and people, the processes and tasks, and the information system. Chapter 10 examines the Unified Modeling Language (UML) from an ontological perspective and provides a way of using ontological semantics to enable UML use for conceptual modeling. Contributed by Xueming Li and Jeffrey Parsons, the research could be seen as examining the interactions between all four of the sociotechnical components. Finally, in Chapter 11, Elvira Locuratolo studies database meta-modeling as a means of aiding the design of database structure schemas. Qualitative/conceptual measures of information implicitly specified within schemas and a qualitative/conceptual evaluation of the consistency are provided. This research also involves all four of the sociotechnical components and their interactions.

CONCLUSIONS

This volume is a valuable resource for academic scholars and practitioners alike. The chapters in this volume represent state-of-the-art and exemplary research in the field of systems analysis and design, and serve to inform readers of potential and future areas of research. Further, many of the contributing authors are internationally known and respected researchers in the area.

REFERENCES

Avison, D., and Fitzgerald, G. 2003. Where now for development methodologies? *Communications of the ACM,* 46, 1, 78–82.

Beck, K. 1999. *Extreme Programming Explained: Embrace Change.* Boston: Addison-Wesley.

Booch, G.; Rumbaugh, J.; and Jacobson, I. 2005. *The Unified Modeling Language User Guide,* 2d ed. Boston: Addison-Wesley.

Bostrom, R., and Heinen, J. 1977a. MIS problems and failures: A sociotechnical perspective; Part 1: The causes. *MIS Quarterly,* 1, 1, 17–32.

———. 1977b. MIS Problems and failures: A sociotechnical perspective; Part 2: The application of sociotechnical theory. *MIS Quarterly,* 1, 4, 11–28.

Cherns, A. 1976. The principles of sociotechnical design. *Human Relations,* 29, 8, 783–792.

———. 1987. Principles of sociotechnical design revisited. *Human Relations,* 40, 3, 153–162.

Doherty, N., and King, M. 2005. From technical to sociotechnical change: Tackling the human and organizational aspects of systems development projects. *European Journal of Information Systems,* 14, 1–5.

Erickson, J., and Siau, K. 2008. Web services, service-oriented computing, and service-oriented architecture: Separating hype from reality. *Journal of Database Management,* 19, 3, 42–54.

Erickson, J.; Lyytinen, K.; and Siau, K. 2005. Agile modeling, agile software development, and extreme programming: The state of research. *Journal of Database Management,* 16, 4, 88–100.

Fowler, M., and Highsmith, J. 2001. The Agile Manifesto. Available at http://agilemanifesto.org/ (accessed October 22, 2008).

Hardgrave, B.; Davis, F.; and Riemenschneider, C. 2003. Investigating determinants of software developers' intentions to follow methodologies. *Journal of Management Information Systems,* 20, 1, 123–151.

Lamb, R., and Kling, R. 2003. Reconceptualizing users as social actors in information systems research. *MIS Quarterly,* 27, 2, 197–235.

Long, Y., and Siau, K. 2007. Social network structures in open source software development teams. *Journal of Database Management,* 18, 2, 25–40.

Markus, L. 1983. Power, politics, and MIS implementation. *Communications of the ACM,* 26, 5, 430–444.

Ryan, S.D., and Harrison, D.A. 2000. Considering social subsystem costs and benefits in information technology investment decisions: A view from the field on anticipated payoffs. *Journal of Management Information Systems,* 16, 4, 11–40.

Ryan, S.D.; Harrison, D.A.; and Schkade, L.L. 2002. Information-technology investment decisions: When do costs and benefits in the social subsystem matter? *Journal of Management Information Systems,* 19, 2, 85–128.

Schmidt, R.; Lyytinen, K.; Keil, M.; and Cule, P. 2001. Identifying software project risks: An International Delphi study. *Journal of Management Information Systems,* 17, 4, 5–36.

Siau, K.; Wand, Y.; and Benbasat, I. 1997. The relative importance of structural constraints and surface semantics in information modeling. *Information Systems,* 22, 2/3, 155–170.

Smith, H.J.; Keil, M.; and Depledge, G. 2001. Keeping mum as the project goes under: Toward an explanatory model. *Journal of Management Information Systems,* 18, 2, 189–227.

Stein, E.W., and Vandenbosch, B. 1996. Organizational learning during advanced system development: Opportunities and obstacles. *Journal of Management Information Systems,* 13, 2, 115–136.

Williams, L., and Kessier, R. 2002. *Pair Programming Illuminated.* Boston: Addison-Wesley Longman.

PART I

SOCIAL SYSTEMS FOCUS: PEOPLE

CHAPTER 2

THE APPLICATION OF COGNITIVE COMPLEXITY PRINCIPLES FOR RECONCILING THE AGILE AND THE DISCIPLINE APPROACHES

DINESH BATRA

Abstract: *Systems development today has two major camps—agile and discipline. The agile camp subscribes to its best practices published under the Agile Manifesto, which include a focus on customer, employee, working software, and response to change. The discipline camp believes that software development processes need to be continually improved, and that planning is the key to successful development. Software experts have proposed that there is a need to balance agility and discipline; however, they have not provided precise guidelines. This chapter considers cognitive complexity factors from four theoretical sources to reconcile the debate between the agile and the discipline approaches. It identifies factors that favor agile development and those that favor discipline development. These factors are integrated and grouped according to ten systems development principles.*

Keywords: *Agile, Discipline, Cognitive Complexity, Systems Complexity, Metasocial Forces, Problem Solving, Design Complexity*

The discipline-based approaches center on process improvement and quality management (Crosby, 1979; Deming, 1986; Juran, 1988). Process capability is the inherent ability of a process to produce planned results. As the capability of a process increases, it becomes predictable and measurable, and the most significant causes of poor quality and productivity are controlled or eliminated (Curtis, Hefley, and Miller, 2002). Discipline-based approaches are planning-heavy, at times bureaucratic, and subscribe to the belief that methodical requirements, high determination, and exacting analysis documentation result in a high quality software product (Nerur and Balijepally, 2007). The approaches are best exemplified by the Capability Maturity Model (CMM) and the Capability Maturity Model Integrated (CMMI), both of which gained popularity in the 1990s (Ahern et al., 2004). Recent work by Curtis et al. (2002) extends the CMM model by addressing the critical people issues in organizations. Discipline approaches are widely used and have considerable following all over the world (Nerur, Mahapatra, and Mangalaraj, 2005). However, discipline approaches can be bureaucratic, and resource- and time-intensive, especially if the project encounters significant changes in user requirements (Vinekar, Slinkman, and Nerur, 2006).

Frustration with the bureaucratic nature of the disciplined approach led to the proposal for agile development (Boehm and Turner, 2004). The new approach is defined by its Agile Manifesto (Beck et al., 2001), which values individuals and their interactions over processes and tools, working software over comprehensive documentation, customer collaboration over contract negotiation, and responding to change over following a plan (Larman, 2003). Agile practices also include adaptive development (Highsmith, 2000), which calls for requirements, plans, estimates, and solutions to adapt in response to feedback from users, developers, and tests. Agile development is always iterative as opposed to discipline-based development, which may or may not be iterative. The degree of ceremony in agile development—the amount of documentation, and formal steps and reviews—is low. Examples include methodologies such as XP (Beck, 1999; Auer and Miller, 2002), Adaptive Software Development (Highsmith, 2000), Crystal (Cockburn, 2005), and Scrum (Schwaber and Beedle, 2002). Although the agile approach currently has only about 14 percent adoption, it is becoming popular with each passing year. However, the agile approach has its own limitations, such as limited support for large development teams, for subcontracting, and for distributed projects (Turk, France, and Rumpe, 2005).

Boehm and Turner (2004) provide an excellent comparison of the agility and discipline approaches. Based on the analysis, they reach six conclusions (Boehm and Turner, 2004, p. 148) that define the general practitioner beliefs of the systems development field:

1. Neither agile nor plan-driven methods provide a silver bullet to the problem of determining best practices in software development (or to achieving high-quality software development in a timely, efficient and cost-effective manner);
2. Agility and plan-driven methods each have areas in which they clearly dominate the other;
3. Future trends are towards application developments that need both agility and discipline;
4. Some balanced methods are emerging;
5. It is better to build your method up than to tailor it down;
6. Methods are important, but potential silver bullets are more likely to be found in areas dealing with people, values, communication, and expectations management.

While Boehm and Turner (2004) do not resolve the debate over best practices or provide specific recommendations, they mention four essential issues for comparing the discipline and agile methods: complexity, conformity, changeability, and invisibility. From a cognitive perspective, these four factors pertain to the cognitive complexity construct as detailed in Reeves (1996). For example, change and invisibility can lead to cognitive complexity, while ability to accommodate change and conformity to standard practices can ease complexity. Thus, an approach based on cognitive complexity may be considered to evaluate systems development approaches.

Systems development is a process designed to represent real-world phenomena, which are inherently complex (Niekerk and Buhl, 2003). Systems development itself is also highly complex, given that a host of methodologies and tools have not prevented widespread failure in achieving timely and in-budget completion of projects (Masticola, 2007). Languages, such as Unified Modeling Language (UML), used to help systems development are also complex (Batra and Satzinger, 2006; Siau and Loo 2006; Van der Meer and Dutta, 2009). Cognitive complexity theory is, therefore, an appropriate approach to understanding the systems development phenomenon.

The complexity construct, however, includes a large number of factors beyond the four mentioned. Accordingly, a comprehensive approach to comparing the two approaches requires examining all of the complexity factors. This chapter compares the discipline approach with the agile approach based on cognitive complexity principles derived from various reference disciplines. The scope of the chapter does not encompass very small projects (e.g., those with fewer than five developers).

EVALUATION BASED ON COGNITIVE COMPLEXITY PRINCIPLES

In examining cognitive complexity, Reeves (1999) has utilized complexity factors based on five theoretical sources. Four of the five—systems complexity, metasocial forces, problem solving, and design complexity—are directly relevant to system development complexity. For each source, Reeves (1999) presents a number of factors that are shown as complexity pairs, with the left aspect complexifying, and the right aspect simplifying. For example, the pair "dynamic-stable" indicates that dynamic behavior is complexifying, while stable behavior is simplifying. Each complexity pair can be evaluated in order to gauge which term in the pair is more closely associated with either the agile or the discipline approach.

To evaluate whether the discipline approach or the agile approach is more effective based on a given factor, we need to consider each factor and evaluate whether its complexifying aspect pertains to the software development environment and is addressed by one of the two approaches, or whether its simplifying aspect is an inherent characteristic of the approach. If complexity arises from the development environment or the application domain, then the preferred approach is the one that can best address the complexifying aspect. For example, consider the dynamic-stable pair. The dynamic (unpredictable) behavior of the development environment can lead to complexity. The agile approach can better address the complexifying behavior—dynamic—hence, it is the preferred approach for the dynamic–stable pair.

Conversely, an approach may intrinsically embrace the simplifying behavior. For example, "hurried versus thought out" presents another complexifying-simplifying pair. Since "thought out" implies planning, which is intrinsically an attribute of the discipline approach, the simplifying aspect is preferred in the discipline approach. Thus, at times, the complexifying aspect itself leads us to the better approach (i.e., the approach that can better address the complexifying aspect), while at other times, the simplifying aspect points to the better approach (the approach that may already encompass the simplifying aspect as an attribute). Generally, however, examining the complexifying aspect leads us to the preferred approach. Note that "preferred approach" means the approach that is more likely to address the complexifying aspect.

In the next four sections, complexifying-simplifying pairs from four theoretical sources—systems complexity, metasocial forces, problem solving, and design complexity—are discussed to determine which approach—agile or discipline—is preferred for a given factor. Some of the factors listed in Reeves (1999) are not relevant to systems development and are not discussed. The discussion is followed by seven recommendations that incorporate the best features of the two approaches.

SYSTEMS COMPLEXITY

Reeves (1999) lists ten factor pairs related to systems complexity, out of which two—broken symmetry–symmetry and human activity–mechanical systems—were dropped. The issue of symmetry was ignored because symmetry is not a feature of software development. The pair "human activity systems" versus "mechanical systems" was ignored because human activity systems are too similar to another factor, "soft systems." The remaining eight factors are classified in Table 2.1. These factors are based on the work of systems scientists (Banathy, 1991; Flood and Carson, 1990). Each factor in the table is presented as a complexifying-simplifying pair in the first two columns. The third column lists the favored approach—agile or discipline, or both, if they are equally favored. The fourth column lists closely linked factors from other sources included in the chapter.

Interactive Subsystems

All subsystems interact to some degree, although the degree of interaction can vary (Nickerson and Zenger, 2004). Highly interactive subsystems result in complexity (van Merriënboer and Sweller, 2005). When there are many interactions among subsystems, the behavior of a system can be

Table 2.1

Systems Complexity Factors

Complexifying	Simplifying	Favored Approach	Related Factors
Interactive subsystems (many interactions)	Singular interactions (few interactions)	Agile	Interactive subsystems (problem solving)
Many parts (unconstrained interactions)	Few parts (constrained)	Discipline	High number of variables (problem solving)
Dynamic behavior (unpredictable)	Linear behavior (predictable)	Agile	Unpredictable (problem solving) Dynamic (metasocial forces)
Open (reacts with environment)	Closed (self-contained)	Agile	
Differentiated (specialized)	Undifferentiated (unspecialized)	Discipline	
Soft systems (human)	Hard systems (mechanical)	Agile	
Anarchic (no control mechanism)	Communication/control (feedback control)	Discipline	
Embedded (hidden interactions)	Single (obvious interactions)	Agile	Hidden (problem solving) Obscure (design complexity)

emergent; that is, it cannot be predicted by merely looking at its parts. For example, if the system addresses a new domain, the interactions are not predictable. In this case, the agile approach is better because it can adapt to emerging behavior.

Many Parts

When there are many parts to a system, jumping too quickly into implementation can be risky. Discipline is critical because one needs to identify the critical parts of the system, decompose the system, determine dependencies, and devise a project plan (Project Management Institute, 2004). Thus, a discipline approach is preferred. For example, if software is to be written for an entire enterprise, the project will have many parts and will likely fail in the absence of adequate planning.

Dynamic Behavior

This factor is similar to what Boehm and Turner (2004) refer to as changeability. If a system has dynamic behavior, then the development approach needs to facilitate response to changes. For example, a rapidly expanding company will experience dynamic behavior in its business, and consequently, in its systems applications. The agile approach excels in responding to changes, and is the preferred approach.

Open

The discipline approach is suited for a stable, closed environment. If the environment is open and this openness affects the system in a significant manner, then the agile approach is preferred. For example, companies continually improve their Web sites in response to changes initiated by competing companies. The improvements impact the environment, other companies respond, and there is a continual interplay between environmental changes and company responses. The need for highly fluent responses calls for agility.

Differentiated

When a system becomes more differentiated, the domain knowledge required becomes more highly nuanced and specialized. Normally, such a system will have many parts, and each part will have to be systematically studied. A discipline approach, with its upfront planning requirements, would thus be favored.

Soft Systems

Software systems that are more likely to be problematic are those designed for, and by, humans. Human requirements, as compared to machine requirements, are inherently more complex because of the unpredictability involved. Both customer-oriented and developer-oriented thinking are desirable. The discipline approach, with its focus on processes, in particular ignores the developer. Stress among developers has been steadily increasing and is at an all-time high (Chilton, Hardgrave, and Armstrong, 2005). An agile approach, with its focus on customers and developers, is therefore preferred.

Anarchic

The agile approach features better communication only when a project is relatively small. As a project increases in size, the large number of team members required and the lack of control mechanisms can lead to anarchy. Extreme programming proponents, in particular, are hesitant about projects that require more than twenty developers (Boehm and Turner, 2004). This observation has been empirically confirmed for agile projects in general (Dyba and Dingsoyr, 2008). The discipline approach, with its formal control mechanisms, is the preferred approach in large-scale, and potentially anarchic projects.

Embedded

Hidden interactions can lead to emergence, which characterizes a system different from any of its subsystems. Hidden interactions cannot be predicted and, therefore, cannot be addressed by planning. Brooks refers to this phenomenon as invisibility (Boehm and Turner, 2004). For a hidden interaction to emerge, the software product needs to be coded and implemented. For example, user response to a new type of system is usually not known until a piece of the system is implemented. As a result, an agile approach is preferred in embedded systems because it allows for early implementation and it accepts changes more readily.

METASOCIAL FORCES

The metasocial forces of complexity (based on the work of Gergen) are: (a) dynamic rates of change and the constant introduction of novelty and (b) the sheer volume of possible interactions people have with each other, with products, and with information (Gergen, 2000). Information is the underlying force that drives these other forces because it is the source of new knowledge. Reeves (1999) lists four metasocial forces (Table 2.2) that can cause cognitive complexity.

Table 2.2

Metasocial Forces Factors

Complexifying	Simplifying	Favored approach	Related factors
Novelty (new)	Confirmation (same)	Agile	
Dynamic (constant change)	Stable (changeless)	Agile	Dynamic behavior (systems complexity) Unpredictable (problem solving)
Feature overload/variety (many choices)	Simplicity (few choices)	Agile	Unbounded (design complexity)
Hurried (unplanned)	Thought out (planned)	Discipline	

Novelty

The agile approach is better positioned to deal with the uncertainty and the unpredictability associated with novelty. A company diversifying into a new area will experience novelty in its systems as it hones its transaction, supervisory, and decision support. For novel applications, agile practices such as iteration, constant adaption, and customer participation are well suited.

Dynamic

This factor, as discussed earlier in the "Systems Complexity" section, favors the agile approach.

Feature Overload/Variety

Variety may be in the domain, or may be invented by the developer. When there are many features in a software program, careful planning is a compelling requirement. Many software projects require a large number of features. For example, tax software is full of functional features because tax rules are complex. Variety in the domain is closely related to having many parts, a factor that has already been addressed under "Systems Complexity." However, creating features that provide little value is a high-cost, low-value proposition. Agile proponents talk about the "featuritis" thinking that can creep into the discipline approach, and they recommend a philosophy based on simplicity. It is in this context that the factor "variety" is considered. The need for simplicity favors the agile approach. For clarity, this factor has been renamed to reflect choices: "feature overload" versus few choices.

Hurried

Planning reduces uncertainty in software development. Lack of planning can lead to haphazard development. Daily fifteen-minute meetings do not guarantee success, especially when the project size scales up. The philosophy that "change is welcome" can lead to a mode of thought that eschews planning and favors a frenzied race to start something and produce code. Addressing change is usually costly when coding is continually updated because adequate attention has not been paid to requirements analysis. Even in fast-paced contemporary times, the business environment does not

Table 2.3

Problem-Solving Factors

Complexifying	Simplifying	Favored approach	Related factors
High number of variables (hard to track)	Few variables (easy to track)	Discipline	Many parts (systems complexity)
Hidden (murky details)	Apparent (clarity of fact)	Agile	Embedded (systems complexity) Obscure (design complexity)
Expert (expertise required)	Novice (beginner can do)	Discipline	
Vagueness of goal (indeterminate)	Specificity of goal (singular goal)	Agile	
Ill-structured (lack of organization)	Structured (organized)	Discipline	
Interactive subsystems (hidden effects)	Singular subsystems (expected effects)	Agile	Interactive subsystems (systems complexity)
Unpredictable (cannot find cause)	Predictable (can find cause)	Agile	Dynamic behavior (systems complexity) Dynamic (metasocial forces)
Time delayed (unknown effect)	Immediate (known effect)	Agile	

completely turn upside down in a matter of a year or two, a time period that reflects the duration of the majority of projects. Hence, the discipline approach is the favorite for addressing this factor.

PROBLEM SOLVING

Software development can be considered a problem-solving process. Research in problem solving is based on work on heuristics by Polya (1985), and information processing by Newell and Simon (1972). Problem solving is defined as a process of searching through the decision space, looking for the right operator to transform the problem space into a solution. Complex problems are those that require more difficult searches through more complicated mazes of possible operators. Complexity is a matter of difficulty in finding the right operators that will eventually lead to the ultimate solution. Reeves (1999) lists eleven problem-solving factors based mainly on Funke's (1991) work on complexity. Eight relevant complexifying-simplifying pairs pertaining to problem solving are listed in Table 2.3. The remaining three factors, which seem irrelevant in the software development context, are: many solutions, nonlinear, and illogical.

High Number of Variables

This point, referred to as "many parts" under "Systems Complexity," has been covered earlier. It favors the discipline-based approach.

Hidden

This point, covered earlier as "embedded" under "Systems Complexity," favors the agile approach.

Expert

When expertise is required, a project is deemed complex. Agile methods require a critical mass of highly motivated, knowledgeable team members (Boehm and Turner, 2004). Conversely, the discipline approach attempts to standardize processes, and thus allows nonexperts to take advantage of documented experience. In fact, it can be debated that the success of the agile approach has more to do with competent developers than with its other characteristics. The discipline approach does not have this stringent requirement, and is therefore, the favored approach for this factor.

Vagueness of Goal

A discipline approach addresses vagueness through diligent research and planning. An agile approach assumes uncertainty of goals and requirements, and adapts as customer feedback based upon the delivered product brings clarity to the situation. Is one better than the other? Developing information systems is a creative process (Hevner et al., 2004), and there are limits to the amount of clarity advance planning can bring to the project's stated goal. It is common for customers to be ambiguous about the nature of a software product because they may not yet have seen one created and thus have no benchmark for comparison. An agile approach can address this issue because the development process assumes that the requirements are not entirely clear. Hence, an agile approach is preferred here.

Ill-Structured

Even if the overall goal is vague, organization is important. If the project lacks organization, then writing code for the project is futile. A lack of organization probably means that the project is too large, but the connections and dependencies among the parts are not well known. By using a discipline approach, proper structure can be imposed before embarking on software development. A company may decide to streamline its supply chain management and its customer relations management systems before commencing on a software development project. Assuming that the software project is large and ill-structured, it will require an approach that can enforce structure. The discipline-based approach, which requires analysis and imposes structure, would be preferred here.

Interactive Subsystems

This factor has been discussed under "Systems Complexity." It favors the agile approach.

Unpredictable

This factor implies that one "cannot find cause"; that is, the context involves a phenomenon whose behavior cannot be accurately forecasted. It is thus unwise to invest in extensive planning. For example, there are situations when the customer genuinely does not know what level of analysis is appropriate or what interface will better portray information. The agile approach is the preferred method here since it is likely that the software development has to proceed in an adaptive mode. This factor is similar to "vagueness of goal," discussed earlier.

Table 2.4

Design Complexity Factors

Complexifying	Simplifying	Favored approach	Related factors
Nonstandard (inconsistent)	Standard (consistent)	Discipline	
Obscure	Obvious	Agile	Embedded (systems complexity) Hidden (problem solving)
Unbounded	Constrained	Agile	Variety (metasocial)
Large/long tasks	Small/brief tasks	Discipline	
Single method	Shortcuts	Agile	

Time-delayed

This factor implies "unknown effect" and is a phenomenon common in today's environment where the effect of introducing software is usually unpredictable. For example, the effect of launching a new Web-based product or service may be unidentifiable because of the unknown responses from customers and the competition. It is risky to estimate too optimistically and invest too much when venturing into such a fuzzy zone. The agile approach, which stresses simplicity and expects dynamic behavior, presents lower risk and is the preferred approach.

DESIGN COMPLEXITY

Most of the factors listed in Reeves (1999) under design complexity, and based on the works of Norman (1988), Norman and Draper (1986), and Nielsen and Molich (1989) do not apply to systems development complexity because of their focus on devices and interfaces rather than information systems. The factor pairs "no help–help," "unnatural-natural," and "illogical-logical" are clearly not relevant. A few factor pairs such as "hidden-apparent," "inhumane-humane," and "textual-graphic" may seem applicable, but their operational definitions are different because the focus is on interfaces rather than software development. Five out of the twelve factors are relevant, however, and are shown in Table 2.4.

Nonstandard

One of the problems with the agile approach is that it does not standardize processes. The discipline-based approach results in a standardization of processes, and is, therefore, the preferred approach. Standardization leads to conformity, which is a useful characteristic when handling large projects (Boehm and Turner, 2004).

Obscure

This is similar to the factor "embedded" under "Systems Complexity," and the factor "hidden" under "Problem Solving," and it favors the agile approach.

Unbounded

This is similar to the factor "variety" under "Metasocial Forces" and favors the discipline approach.

Large/Long Tasks

If the context has large/long tasks, and if the task is indivisible, the discipline approach is preferred.

Single Method

Although standardization provides the satisfaction of falling back to a documented procedure, it can become an exercise in bureaucracy. Sometimes shortcuts provide more or less the same functionality at considerable savings of effort, time, and other resources. The agile approach focuses more on the end result and customer satisfaction, so improvisation is acceptable. For this reason, the agile approach is preferred here.

FORMULATING COMPLEXITY-REDUCING PRINCIPLES

The detailed complexity analysis in the context of systems development reveals that neither the discipline-based nor the agile approach excels in handling all facets of complexity. Some of the findings from the theoretical complexity analysis in this chapter are similar to the conclusions reported in Boehm and Turner (2004). For instance, the discipline approach is geared to handling projects that are large (i.e., "having many parts") without the use of experts, by putting structure into the project and standardizing processes, while the agile approach is geared to handling projects that are more dynamic and unpredictable. However, the complexity analysis reveals much more than the four critical factors mentioned by Boehm and Turner (2004).

There is an acute need to come up with complexity-reducing principles that can be applied to projects regardless of their size, level of uncertainty, or specialization. It is evident that there will be some tradeoff when applying such principles because of the contextual factors of the project (Lyytinen and Rose, 2006). Currently, the discipline-based and agile approaches each have their own niches (Figure 2.1). The agile approach is suitable for projects that are small and dynamic (Dyba and Dingsoyr, 2008). Conversely, the discipline-based approach is suitable for large projects that are relatively stable. The small project that is relatively static presents the trivial case for which both approaches would work. These delineations leave a critical area that is currently not addressed by the literature. What do you do when the project is not small, but the requirements are likely to be subject to a fair degree of change?

To answer this, we can take a lesson from some contemporary organizations that are large, yet agile. Consider the example of General Electric (GE), which is one of the largest old-economy companies. In the first half of the 1990s, GE used Work-Out (Ulrich et al., 2002) and other processes to build a highly flexible, boundaryless culture. In the second half of the 1990s, GE transformed itself repeatedly to keep up with the global Internet economy (Ashkenas et al., 2002). GE's success was based on a new approach that focused on flexibility across boundaries, and a new relationship with customers and employees. GE showed that being large did not imply that it could not be agile. Other companies that have shown similar change include Microsoft, Southwest Airlines, Praxair Mexico, GlaxoSmithKline, among others (Ashkenas et al., 2002). In recent times, Google and Apple, despite their size, are setting a new benchmark for agility. All of these companies

Figure 2.1   **The Suitability of Approaches by Size and Degree of Change**

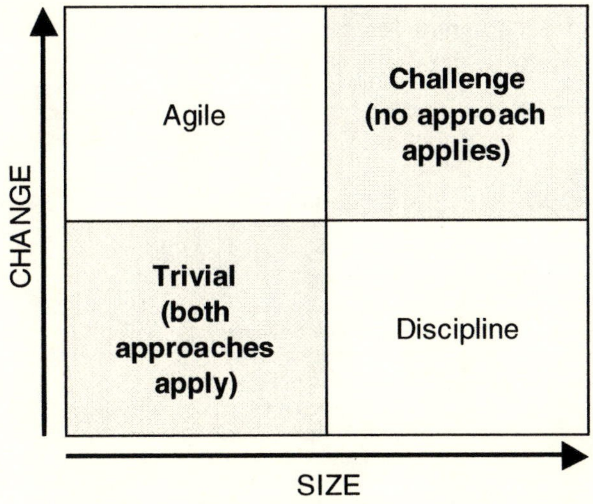

have reconsidered and redefined the vertical, horizontal, external, and geographic boundaries to eliminate inefficiencies and bureaucracies. Such companies have learned to be disciplined and agile at the same time.

The same issue can be applied to software divisions and software projects. A software for a new space mission is likely to be a sophisticated piece with very little room for defects; such a project will predominantly be discipline-based. Health information systems may witness significant innovation (agile) while maintaining the privacy and security of patients (discipline). "Green" information systems may provide sophisticated features that provide intelligent solutions for maximizing collection while minimizing wastage of energy; currently, such projects may initially be agile. However, in each such case, a thorough study of the domain and an adequate level of planning—characteristics of the discipline approach—will be required. However, the discipline approach can only go so far, and the project will need to rely on agile principles. Even though we may not know exactly how to weight and blend them, it would be useful to recommend principles that are likely to facilitate both discipline and agility. To determine these principles, we need to further integrate, cluster, and analyze the complexity factors from the four sources discussed in the previous sections.

The first step is to integrate the factors from the four sources. This is simply a union of the factors from the theoretical sources: systems complexity, metasocial forces, problem solving, and design complexity (see Table 2.5). Note that the duplicate factors have been eliminated.

The integration results in eighteen factors, each qualified by the preferred approach—discipline or agile. However, it is difficult to get the bigger picture from this table. Although duplicate factors have been removed, there are still factors that are related and suggest a common guiding principle. The factors, thus, need to be collated by category and then clustered based on close relationships to reveal guiding principles.

The factors in Table 2.5 are first collated by the preferred approach so that the two sets of factors are separated (see Table 2.6). This list can be used to further group factors based on affinity so that guiding principles can emerge.

Table 2.5

Integrating Factors from Different Sources

Complexifying	Simplifying	Favored approach
Interactive subsystems (many interactions)	Singular interactions (few interactions)	Agile
Many parts (unconstrained interactions)	Few parts (constrained)	Discipline
Dynamic behavior (unpredictable)	Linear behavior (predictable)	Agile
Open (reacts with environment)	Closed (self-contained)	Agile
Differentiated (specialized)	Undifferentiated (unspecialized)	Discipline
Soft systems (human)	Hard systems (mechanical)	Agile
Anarchic (no control mechanism)	Communication/control (feedback control)	Discipline
Novelty (new)	Confirmation (same)	Agile
Feature overload (many choices)	Simplicity (few choices)	Agile
Hurried (unplanned)	Thought out (planned)	Discipline
Hidden (murky details)	Apparent (clarity of fact)	Agile
Expert (expertise required)	Novice (beginner can do)	Discipline
Vagueness of goal (indeterminate)	Specificity of goal (singular goal)	Agile
Ill-structured (lack of organization)	Structured (organized)	Discipline
Time-delayed (unknown effect)	Immediate (known effect)	Agile
Nonstandard (inconsistent)	Standard (consistent)	Discipline
Large/long tasks	Small/brief tasks	Discipline
Single method	Shortcuts	Agile

TEN GUIDING PRINCIPLES FOR SYSTEMS DEVELOPMENT

Finally, the factors listed in Table 2.6 are rearranged so that guiding principles can emerge (Table 2.7). This is the author's interpretation based on the factors. The author is currently engaged in data collection, which may provide a more accurate insight into the factors involved. Here, the analysis and synthesis of the factors lead to ten guiding principles, which are presented. Four discipline-based and six agile-based factors are given.

1. Principle of Decomposition

Three factors—"many parts," "large/long tasks," and "differentiated"—are related, and pertain to the well-known systems concept called "decomposition." Fewer parts as well as small, brief tasks lower complexity. When knowledge becomes differentiated, decomposition can facilitate focus on smaller pieces of the system. A software project should be decomposed into fairly inde-

Table 2.6

Collating Factors by Favored Approach

Complexifying	Simplifying	Favored approach
Many parts	Few parts	Discipline
Differentiated	Undifferentiated	Discipline
Anarchic	Communication/control	Discipline
Hurried	Thought out	Discipline
Expert	Novice	Discipline
Ill-structured	Structured	Discipline
Nonstandard	Standard	Discipline
Large/long tasks	Small/brief tasks	Discipline
Interactive subsystems	Singular Interactions	Agile
Dynamic behavior	Linear behavior	Agile
Open	Closed	Agile
Soft systems	Hard systems	Agile
Novelty	Confirmation	Agile
Feature overload	Simplicity	Agile
Hidden	Apparent	Agile
Vagueness of goal	Specificity of goal	Agile
Time-delayed	Immediate	Agile
Single method	Shortcuts	Agile

Table 2.7

Formulating Complexity-Reducing Principles

Complexifying	Simplifying	Favored approach	Principle
Many parts	Few parts	Discipline	Decomposition
Large/long tasks	Small/brief tasks		
Differentiated	Undifferentiated		
Hurried	Thought out	Discipline	Planning
Ill-structured	Structured		
Nonstandard	Standard	Discipline	Standardizing processes
Expert	Novice		
Anarchic	Communication/control	Discipline	Accountability
Interactive subsystems	Singular interactions	Agile	Iterative development
Novelty	Confirmation		
Hidden	Apparent		
Vagueness of goal	Specificity of goal		
Dynamic behavior	Linear behavior	Agile	Adaptive development
Open	Closed		
Time-delayed	Immediate		
Soft systems	Hard systems	Agile	Customer focus
			Developer focus
Feature overload	Simplicity	Agile	Simplicity
Single method	Shortcuts	Agile	Heuristics

pendent, smaller parts, which in turn may be decomposed further. Agile principles can be used to develop the pieces; however, the smaller units need to be coordinated within an overarching discipline-based control mechanism. Object-oriented ideas such as encapsulation, strong cohesion, loose coupling, and interfaces can be applied at the systems level to create relatively independent subsystems that have fewer interactions.

2. Principle of Planning

Planning can address two factors—"hurried," and "ill-structured." Planning and structure can reduce uncertainty and simplify a project. If a project is large, upfront planning is essential to understand the system and to make key architectural decisions. If the project is decomposed into subsystems, which are then developed using agile approaches, a detailed coordination and control plan is required so that the project does not veer into anarchy. Excessive planning should be avoided, however. Planning can be carried so far so that it mitigates other simplifying factors. The project needs to balance planning with the need to address the dynamic behavior of a software project. Planning should be a continuous activity and should be used in agile development as is done in Scrum (Schwaber and Beedle, 2002).

3. Principle of Standardizing Processes

Standardization is a simplifying factor. As expertise is gained through repeated application, processes should be standardized, and the organization should attempt to continually improve processes. Best practices should be documented in a knowledge base. Further, baseline standards need to be defined to ensure harmony and compatibility. If a project is divided into parts, and individual parts are being developed by employing agile practices, it may lead to an anarchic environment if there are no underlying standards. There needs to be a baseline standard governing documentation. The same standard can also prevent overdocumentation as well as underdocumentation. Similarly, teams should use compatible development tools. If a "lite" version of UML is used in the software division, then all developers should be trained in the same version of UML. Processes should be evaluated and improved just as code is improved by refactoring.

4. Principle of Accountability

A project should be under control at all times and not fall into anarchy. Accountability emerges from good planning, which should ascribe responsibility to the developers and the project managers. Agile development recognizes accountability by its focus on working software, although a large project would require additional means.

5. Principle of Iterative Development

This principle can address a number of complexifying factors—"interactive subsystems," "novelty," "hidden," and "vagueness of goal." Software projects are creative endeavors (Hevner et al., 2004) and invariably face new frontiers. Novelty is common, subsystems can interact in unpredictable ways, goals can be vague despite planning, and accurate requirements sometimes emerge only if the customer can evaluate a baseline prototype. Iterative development mitigates risk. A large project can be decomposed into several relatively independent pieces. Each piece can be rated on criticality, novelty, and uncertainty to determine risk. The pieces that are considered high risk can be initiated early to provide stakeholders a glimpse of implementation. The feedback from the early development of critical pieces can lead to further enhancing iterations. Developing a complete unit at the outset is not recommended because as it interacts with other pieces, unforeseen behavior may be revealed. Continuous testing and integration can reveal hidden interactions. Discipline-based projects should always evaluate the use of iterative development to reduce risk in large projects. This manner of delivery strategy has been empirically found as a critical success factor (Chow and Cao, 2008).

6. Principle of Adaptive Development

This principle is related to the previous one, iterative development, and addresses three complexifying factors—"dynamic behavior," "open systems," and "time-delayed." In fact, Adaptive Software Development (Highsmith, 2000) is a prominent agile software development methodology. When a project is started, the stakeholders need to assume an adaptive mindset (Linder, 2004) that anticipates and accepts dynamic behavior. The agile approach is well suited to address adaptive development, but the discipline approach needs to shed its image of bureaucracy and rigidity, and accept dynamic behavior, which is plausible even in large projects.

7. Principle of Customer Focus

Software systems are generally "soft" systems, that is, they are for, and by, humans and organizations. The "customer" is a generic term for the sponsor interested in return on investment on the project, the end user who provides the requirements and will eventually use the system, or the project/functional manager at the client end interested in the timely completion of a quality project within the allocated resources. Customer focus is the primary agile development value. The discipline approach should not be tied to processes; instead it needs to explicitly recognize customer satisfaction as a primary value.

8. Principle of Developer Focus

Developers have traditionally been considered merely another cost in the system, but agile development takes a humanistic approach. Developer motivation was traditionally of a monetary nature, but agile development considers traditional rewards and punishments that the organization uses to influence job performance as only partially effective in this environment. Developers perform best when these are complemented with intangible rewards such as recognition, quality assignments, and some freedom in work hours as well as tangible rewards such as training and other benefits. This is evident by the voluntary effort contributed by developers to facilitate open-source software development. However, the contemporary developer is also under considerable stress (Chilton, Hardgrave, and Armstrong, 2005), and the field of information systems/technology will not draw the best talent unless developers are rewarded with tangible and intangible rewards while their stress and strain level is managed.

9. Principle of Simplicity

In a dynamic environment, simplicity—minimizing the number of features—is invaluable. Sometimes variety is inevitable, and adequate planning is essential; however, developers are notorious for loading software with features, even when these have not been requested. They need to seek a minimal solution, at least in the beginning stages. In a large project, this can keep the software simple, within budget, and less prone to errors. This can be achieved by following the iterative approach. For example, a developer employing a use case-based approach can develop the normal scenario in the first iteration. There is no sense in developing alternative scenarios if it turns out that the normal scenario is not acceptable to a customer. Further, there is no need to develop every conceivable deviation from the normal scenario or add features that may be scarcely used. It would be difficult to specify a hard and fast rule here, given that some situations may not lend themselves to simplicity; it is just a useful mindset in the contemporary budget- and time-conscious development environment.

10. Principle of Heuristics

Although processes need to be standardized, developers should be able to improvise and use short-cuts. Once the standards are specified and subscribed, the developers should be given sufficient leeway in finding creative and innovative solutions by using heuristics (Tversky and Kahneman, 1974) and shortcuts. Patterns (e.g., Batra, 2005) provide well-established heuristics. Subscribing to a single method is a complexifying factor. For example, novices can benefit from robustness analysis (George et al., 2007; Rosenberg, 1999), but the experts do not have to follow all of its guidelines. Similarly, practitioners may not employ all of the UML diagrams (Dobing and Parsons, 2008; Erickson and Siau, 2007; Siau et al., 2005). More proficient developers especially should be allowed to use shortcuts instead of being tethered to conventional processes.

CONCLUSION

Despite the plethora of methodologies, the field of systems development is still looking for a silver bullet to lay to rest the debate between discipline-based and agile-based approaches. In practice, both approaches—discipline and agile—with their somewhat contrasting manifestos have been reported in the literature. A systematic analysis using cognitive complexity principles indicates that a blending of discipline and the agile practices may provide a viable solution. Ten principles have been recommended in the chapter. However, cognitive complexity is just one approach to examining the issue. Future research can examine this problem in various ways. We can look at large companies that are thriving in today's dynamic environment and garner the essential principles used in the work environment. These principles may then be applied to large software projects development. We can also examine successful software companies or large projects completed on time and within budget to discover the principles used.

REFERENCES

Ahern, D.M.; Clouse, A.; and Turner, R. 2004. *CMMI Distilled: A Practical Introduction to Integrated Process Improvement.* Boston: Addison-Wesley.

Ashkenas, R.; Ulrich, D.; Jick, T.; and Kerr, S. 2002. *The Boundaryless Organization: Breaking the Chains of Organization Structure.* San Francisco: Jossey-Bass.

Auer, K., and Miller, R. 2002. *Extreme Programming Applied.* Indianapolis, IN: Pearson Education.

Banathy, B.H. 1991. *Systems Design of Education.* Englewood Cliffs, NJ: Educational Technologies.

Batra, D. 2005. Conceptual data modeling patterns. *Journal of Database Management,* 16, 2, 84–106.

Batra, D., and Satzinger, J.W. 2006. Contemporary approaches and techniques for the systems analyst. *Journal of Information Systems Education,* 17, 3, 257–266.

Beck, K. 1999. *Extreme Programming Explained.* Reading, MA: Addison-Wesley.

Beck, K. et al. 2001. Manifesto for Agile Software Development. Available at http://agilemanifesto.org/.

Boehm, B., and Turner, R. 2004. *Balancing Agility and Discipline: A Guide for the Perplexed.* Reading, MA: Addison-Wesley.

Chilton, M.A.; Hardgrave, B.C.; and Armstrong, D.J. 2005. Person-Job cognitive style fit for software developers: The effect on strain and performance. *Journal of MIS,* 22, 2, 193–226.

Chow, T., and Cao, D. B. 2008. A survey study of critical success factors in agile software projects. *Journal of Systems and Software,* 81, 6, 961–971.

Cockburn, A. 2005. *Crystal Clear: A Human-Powered Methodology for Small Teams.* Boston: Addison-Wesley.

Crosby, P.B. 1979. *Quality Is Free: The Art of Making Quality Certain.* New York: McGraw-Hill.

Curtis, B.; Hefley, W.E.; and Miller, S. 2002. *The People Capability Maturity Model: Guidelines for Improving the Workforce.* Upper Saddle River, NJ: Pearson Education.

Deming, W.E. 1986. *Out of the Crisis.* Cambridge, MA: MIT Center for Advanced Engineering.

Dobing, B., and Parsons, J. 2008. Dimensions of UML diagram use: A survey of practitioners. *Journal of Database Management,* 19, 1, 1–18.

Dyba, T., and Dingsoyr, T. 2008. Empirical studies of agile software development: A systematic review. *Information and Software Technology,* 50, 9–10, 833–859.

Erickson, J., and Siau, K. 2007. Theoretical and practical complexity of modeling methods. *Communications of the ACM,* 50, 8, 46–51.

Flood, R., and Carson, E. 1990. *Dealing with Complexity.* New York: Plenum.

Funke, J. 1991. Solving complex problems: Exploration and control of complex social problems. In R. Sternberg and P. Frensch (eds.), *Complex Problem Solving,* 185–222. Hillsdale, NJ: Lawrence Erlbaum.

George, J.F.; Batra, D.; Valacich, J.S.; and Hoffer, J.A. 2007. *Object-Oriented Systems Analysis and Design,* 2d ed. Upper Saddle River, NJ: Prentice Hall.

Gergen, K.J. 2000. *The Saturated Self: Dilemmas of Identity in Contemporary Life.* New York: Basic Books.

Hevner, A.; March, S.; Ram, S.; and Park, J. 2004. Design science research in information systems. *MIS Quarterly,* 28, 1, 75–105.

Highsmith, J. 2000. *Adaptive Software Development: A Collaborative Approach to Managing Complex Systems.* New York: Dorset House.

Juran, J.M. 1988. *Juran on Planning for Quality.* New York: Macmillan.

Larman, C. 2003. *Agile and Iterative Development: A Manager's Guide.* Boston: Pearson Education.

Linder, J.C. 2004. *Outsourcing for Radical Change: A Bold Approach to Enterprise Transformation.* New York: AMACOM.

Lyytinen, K. and Rose, G.M. 2006. Information system development agility as organizational learning, *European Journal of Information Systems,* 15, 181–199.

Masticola, S. 2007. A simple estimate of the cost of software project failures and the breakeven effectiveness of project risk management. *First International Workshop on the Economics of Software and Computation (ESC'07),* May 20–26.

Nerur, S., and Balijepally, V. G. 2007. Theoretical reflections on agile development methodologies. *Communications of the ACM,* 50, 3, 79–83.

Nerur, S.; Mahapatra, R.; and Mangalaraj, G. 2005. Challenges of migrating to agile methodologies. *Communications of the ACM,* 48, 5, 72–78.

Newell, A., and Simon, H.A. 1972. *Human Problem Solving.* Englewood Cliffs, NJ: Prentice Hall.

Nickerson, J., and Zenger, T. 2004. A knowledge-based theory of the firm—A problem solving perspective. *Organization Science,* 15, 6, 617–632.

Niekerk, K.V.K., and Buhl, H. 2003. Introduction: Comprehending complexity. In Kees van Kooten Niekerk and Hans Buhl (eds.), *The Significance of Complexity.* Hants, UK: Ashgate.

Nielsen, J., and Molich, R. 1989. Teaching user interface design based on usability engineering. *SIGCHI Bulletin,* 21, 1, 45–48.

Norman, D. 1988. *The Psychology of Everyday Things.* New York: Basic Books.

Norman, D., and Draper, S. (eds.). 1986. *User Centered System Design.* Hillsdale, NJ: Lawrence Erlbaum.

Polya, G. 1985. *How to Solve It.* Princeton, NJ: Princeton University Press.

Project Management Institute. 2004. *A Guide to the Project Management Body of Knowledge:* Project Management Institute.

Reeves W.W. 1996. *Cognition and Complexity: The Cognitive Science of Managing Complexity.* London: Scarecrow Press.

———. 1999. *Learner-Centered Design: A Cognitive View of Managing Complexity in Product, Information, and Environmental Design.* Thousand Oaks, CA: Sage.

Rosenberg, D. 1999. *Use Case Driven Object Modeling.* Reading, MA: Addison-Wesley.

Schwaber, K., and Beedle, M. 2002. *Agile Software Development with Scrum.* Upper Saddle River, NJ: Prentice Hall.

Siau, K., and Loo, P.P. 2006. Identifying difficulties in learning UML. *Information Systems Management,* 32, 3, 43–51.

Siau, K., and Erickson, J., and Lee, L.Y. 2005. Theoretical vs. practical complexity: The case of UML. *Journal of Database Management,* 16, 3, 40–57.

Turk, D., France, R., and Rumpe, B. 2005. Assumptions underlying agile software-development processes. *Journal of Database Management,* 16, 4, 62–87.

Tversky, A., and Kahneman D. 1974. Judgment under uncertainty: Heuristics and biases. *Science,* 185, 1124–1131.

Ulrich, D.; Kerr, S.; and Ashkenas, R. 2002. *The GE Work-Out: How to Implement GE's Revolutionary Method for Busting Bureaucracy and Attacking Organizational Problems—Fast!* New York: McGraw-Hill.

Van der Meer, D., and Dutta, K. 2009. Applying learner-centered design principles to UML sequence diagrams. *Journal of Database Management,* 20, 1, 25–47.

van Merriënboer, J.J.G., and Sweller, J. 2005. Cognitive load theory and complex learning: Recent developments and future directions. *Educational Psychology Review,* 17, 2, 147–177.

Vinekar, V.; Slinkman, C.W.; and Nerur, S. 2006. Can agile and traditional systems development approaches coexist? An ambidextrous view. *Information Systems Management,* 23, 3, 31–42.

CHAPTER 3

FACILITATORS AND INHIBITORS FOR THE ADOPTION OF AGILE METHODS

GLEN VAN DER VYVER, MICHAEL LANE, AND ANDY KORONIOS

Abstract: This chapter examines factors that facilitate or inhibit the adoption of agile methods in an organization. The chapter presents an overview of agile methodologies and a critical analysis of their core values, and seeks to find the middle ground between the perhaps exaggerated claims of agile enthusiasts and those who claim that agile methods are nothing but Rapid Application Development in another guise. The limits of agility are explored from a theoretical and empirical perspective, the latter via a qualitative study conducted using senior managers and information technology practitioners. The chapter concludes that agile methods do appear to offer promising productivity gains in particular situations and organizational contexts but are not a panacea for the ills of software development in general. A significant amount of further empirical research is required to establish the viability of agile methods and identify those contexts where they offer optimal value.

Keywords: Agile Methods, Agile Corporation, Extreme Programming, XP, Organizational Culture, Outsourcing, Offshoring

There is an ever-burgeoning array of software development methodologies and techniques. These techniques range from "traditional" approaches, such as structured systems development, to Rapid Application Development (RAD) approaches where speed of delivery and flexibility are the focus. Although there are those within the information technology (IT) profession who swear by one particular approach or another, many organizations have adopted a 'horses for courses' approach. This approach ideally attempts to match the development methodology to the demands and requirements of the business in general and the system under development in particular. So, for example, a project initiated to deliver a general ledger system for a major banking group is likely to make use of a structured, highly formalized approach. On the other hand, a project initiated at the same bank to deliver as quickly as possible a small system that will take advantage of a short-term market opportunity is probably best suited to a RAD approach.

Although choosing the most appropriate methodology or suite of methodologies for a particular project may be highly desirable, many factors militate against this occurring. These factors may include the personal preferences of key players, political maneuvering, conflict within the organization, constraints emanating from established policies and procedures, factors related to organizational culture, and the peculiarities of the project itself.

We focus on a particular methodological approach referred to as agile, which is touted by many as the emerging force in the applications development methodology arena. Agile methodologies have emerged in recent years and appear well placed to help address some of the major problems

31

that have beset software development for years. In the brutally competitive and inexorably fast-paced environment that characterizes business today, corporations can no longer afford projects that come in hopelessly late or over budget. Agile methods promise to deliver a better product rapidly at a lower cost, embedded within a process that is always focused on the client.

There is substantive evidence that agile methodologies have made inroads into the corporate world, although it will take some time to evaluate the extent of these gains or indeed the extent to which agile methods are able to deliver productivity improvements. There is now a significant volume of literature dealing with agile methods, but only a limited proportion of that comes in the form of unbiased, objective analysis. Unfortunately, much of what is written about the methodologies seems to emanate from people with vested financial interests, agile evangelists, and agile enthusiasts. As is often the case with apparently revolutionary innovations, much hyperbole surrounds agile methods and what they can and cannot deliver. We believe that while these methodologies have significant potential, much impartial research is required to establish how well they work and what circumstances best suit them.

We use a qualitative study to investigate the factors that facilitate and inhibit the adoption of agile methodologies in the organization. We believe that exploratory studies of this nature that seek to uncover rich and detailed insights are highly appropriate for the study of methodologies that are in the process of gaining a foothold.

AGILE METHODOLOGIES

Agile methodologies are arguably among the most client-focused of all in the panoply of techniques used in creating software. Perhaps this is because they emerged not from the deep recesses of some laboratory or abstract theoretical framework but from practitioners attempting to solve difficult business problems. Many of these practitioners were in the vanguard of those that faced the harsh realities of the post–dot-com world, and their experiences taught them that a new approach to information and communication technologies (ICT) was necessary.

There is some debate about the extent to which agile methods are revolutionary or even truly innovative. Much of the literature we will discuss below presents agile methods as highly innovative, but some practitioners and scholars dispute this position, and a balanced analysis cannot discount these opinions. Shaw (2004), for example, views agile methods as a fashion that has replaced RAD and maintains that there is little difference between the methods. He argues that some of the better-known agile methodologies such Crystal and Scrum bear a striking resemblance to Dynamic Systems Development Method (DSDM), a well-known RAD approach. This opinion stands at the opposite extreme of those who view agile methods as revolutionary. In this chapter we adopt the middle path. Our point of departure is that agile methods do appear to offer something fresh and innovative, but they have a history and are part of the process of evolution and adaptation of software development methodologies. Indeed, agility as a key determinant of adaptation and survival in the brutally competitive information age has become a common theme in many areas of business research, ranging from corporate agility (Amos, 1998) to agility in the workforce (Bridger, 2002).

Core Values

Agile methodologies place an emphasis on adaptation rather than the optimization of processes (Highsmith, 1998). In the networked, knowledge-based economy, adaptation is significantly more important than optimization. Highsmith points out that achieving results in such a business context requires an adaptive approach that works within constraints, development approaches that facilitate self-organization and flexibility, and a culture of collaboration. Agile methods are focused on short development phases, each with clearly defined outputs, and only as much documentation as is required (Shaw, 2004). Although some agile methods use prototyping techniques, the norm is the delivery of a functional product in the minimum possible time (Coram and Bohner, 2005).

The Agile Alliance Group (Beck et al., 2001) identifies four core values that reveal the essence of agility:

- Individuals and interactions are valued above processes and tools.
- Working software is valued above comprehensive documentation.
- Customer collaboration is valued above contract negotiation.
- Responding to change is valued above following a plan.

The values of the Agile Alliance Group are open to critique on a number of fronts. Although there is much to be said for better communication in software development projects, it would be dangerous to ignore processes and tools, particularly when the project is highly complex. The fallibility of human rationality and judgment in highly complex situations is well documented, and this is exacerbated when the situation is uncertain (Simon, 1976; Webber, 1997). In situations of complexity and uncertainty, formal procedures and processes can help alleviate some of the problems associated with poor decision making (Simon, 1976; Van Der Vyver, 2004).

Cockburn and Highsmith (2001) argue that the constant change (or uncertainty) in software development projects is not well suited to the use of formal processes and procedures because people are required for creative solutions, and processes cannot compensate for poor team members. Their argument is not convincing, and we argue that projects with any degree of complexity require a solid procedural and strategic firmament. That is not to say we discount the possibility that agile methods could be used in such projects, a topic to which we shall return when we discuss agile methods in large projects.

Coram and Bohner (2005) correctly point out that documentation can be very time consuming, and whatever value it has is inevitably less than the working software. It is true that many projects have delivered far too much documentation. Indeed, it is also true that some projects require little or no documentation. On the other hand, there are some projects where a significant amount of documentation is not only unavoidable but mandatory. The financial services industry, for example, is governed by extremely complex legislation, policies, and procedures. It would be potentially disastrous if a project team working on even a small component of a system where issues of compliance are critical relied on one or a few clients for requirements specification and produced little or no documentation at the end of the process. The team would need to examine applicable documents in detail and provide substantive documentation detailing how the software complied with all requirements.

Agile methods are extremely client-centered. A member of the client organization is placed at the core of the team. This representative of the client must be a person who is committed, eager to collaborate with the development team, highly knowledgeable about requirements, and empowered to act on behalf of the client (Boehm, 2002; Coram and Bohner, 2005). The client knows exactly what is happening and is able to test the software on a regular basis. Agile theorists emphasize the fact that projects change as they progress and point out that perhaps the greatest advantage of agile methods is their ability to readily accommodate change (Boehm, 2002). The client representatives on agile projects clearly need to be special people, but very little research has been conducted into the selection of the right people. Clearly, it cannot be easy to find the right client representative, and a poor choice would potentially destroy the project. Furthermore, it is not always easy for the project team to identify when the client representative is a poor choice or is struggling to cope.

Given that agile theorists are absolutely committed to flexibility, highly detailed plans are obviously anathema. Coram and Bohner (2005) point out that this does not imply that agile developers are hackers, but the plans they use are lightweight and easy to modify. The problem of large-scale systems is once again relevant here, as is the problem of complexity. Even some small systems can be so complex and need to meet so many external requirements that highly detailed plans are a matter of necessity.

Agile methods are ideal for small teams working on projects of limited scope that can be completed in a relatively short time (Coram and Bohner, 2005; Filey, 2006). Filey (2006) argues that they are ideal for start-up companies with limited resources that are involved in Web development. With the obvious exception of Web development, these arguments are highly reminiscent of those put forward for the use of RAD techniques.

Extreme Programming (XP)

There are a number of agile methodologies, but extreme programming (XP) is the best known and most widely adopted (Fowler, 2005). Indeed, in some ways the agile movement is synonymous with XP. In XP, there is a strong emphasis on collaborative development where knowledge transfer between the customer and developers operates very much as it would in the RAD approach. XP goes much further, however, and adopts a collaborative approach within the development team by using the "whole team" approach and "paired programming" (Beck, 1999). This approach seeks at all costs to avoid the compartmentalization of effort. To the extent that it is possible, all team members participate in every facet of the development process. Team meetings occur regularly, usually several times a day. The customer is likely to be present at a significant proportion of these meetings as XP does not favor offsite, remote customers (Beck, 1999). These meetings serve as pauses in a development process that proceeds in short, intense spurts of activity. In this way, various members of the team work independently for a few hours and then meet to demonstrate what has been achieved. These sessions provide team members with rapid feedback, and problems have little time to escalate before they are revealed. Often, all work is open to scrutiny even as it happens (Beck, 1999; Cockburn and Highsmith, 2001). So, for example, a project leader could watch the activities of team members as they work and offer advice on the fly.

The philosophy of XP extends even beyond this intense level of collaboration. When applied to its full extent, the XP philosophy is intolerant of any individual effort. The creation of software is achieved by pairs of programmers working on the same machine (Abrahamsson et al., 2002). Every line of code is therefore reviewed by at least one other person, and this ensures a better product. Typically, one person writes code while the other observes and attempts to identify errors and potential problems. Periodically, roles are reversed. Teams attempt to identify problems even before programming starts, almost attempting to test the program before it is created (Beck, 1999). Williams et al. (2000) take issue with those who argue that the approach is inefficient. They argue that the approach involves a trade-off of high quality code with few bugs for fewer lines of code.

The XP methodology has twelve core practices (Beck, 1999):

1. Satisfy the customer—create software that adds value, on time and on budget.
2. Embrace change—be prepared to make changes at all times, even when the project is nearly complete. The project exists solely to make a contribution to the competitive advantage of the customer.

3. Deliver—speed and frequency of delivery are critical.
4. Collaborate intensely—isolation is the enemy of agility. The agile team should work with business people on a daily basis.
5. Be committed—the best projects are populated by motivated and committed people who take pride in what they produce.
6. Interact and communicate—agile methodologies stress the importance of face-to-face communication. This applies to within-team communication as well as communication with people outside the team boundary.
7. Produce tangible outcomes on a regular basis—in the agile arena, the measure of progress is software that actually works. This should be delivered on an ongoing basis, preferably daily. Working software is therefore delivered incrementally.
8. Foster sustainable development practices—adopt agile practices across the board allowing sponsors, developers, and users to maintain a constant pace indefinitely.
9. Attend to the details, focus on quality—always strive to achieve excellence and focus on high quality design and programming.
10. Aim for simplicity—in agile terms, aim to maximize the amount of work that can be avoided.
11. Self-organize—teams that are self-organized are the most efficient and produce the best solutions.
12. Promote reflection—foster regular self-examination encouraging teams to reinvent themselves and adapt to change.

In Figure 3.1, the XP life cycle is matched with the traditional system development life cycle. In XP everything happens much more quickly, and there is an emphasis on the priority of client stories, which represent the business requirements for each system release. The XP approach involves many small releases of system features, with developers writing the tests before actually writing the specific code. The involvement of the customer from the inception of a project through to acceptance testing ensures strong buy-in on the part of clients.

THE LIMITS OF AGILITY

The key points of critique we raised in our discussion on agile methods in general are equally applicable to XP. Turk et al. (2005) point out that much of what we know about agile methods in practice is anecdotal, and that little empirical research has been done to validate the efficacy of the methods. Indeed, their review is perhaps the most comprehensive critique of agile methods that has been produced, although they focus on extreme programming. They examine the unstated assumptions underlying XP and argue that the method is best suited to situations where the core assumptions hold. They list (pp. 77–82) a number of situations where the core assumptions do not hold at all or are of limited utility:

- Distributed development environments
- Subcontracting, outsourcing, and offshoring
- Developing reusable software
- Developing safety-critical software
- Large and/or complex projects

We argue that the situations set out above constitute some of the key facilitators and inhibitors of the adoption of agile methods in an organization and would serve well as a point of departure

36

Figure 3.1 **Different Activities of XP Associated with the Phases of the System Development Lifecycle**

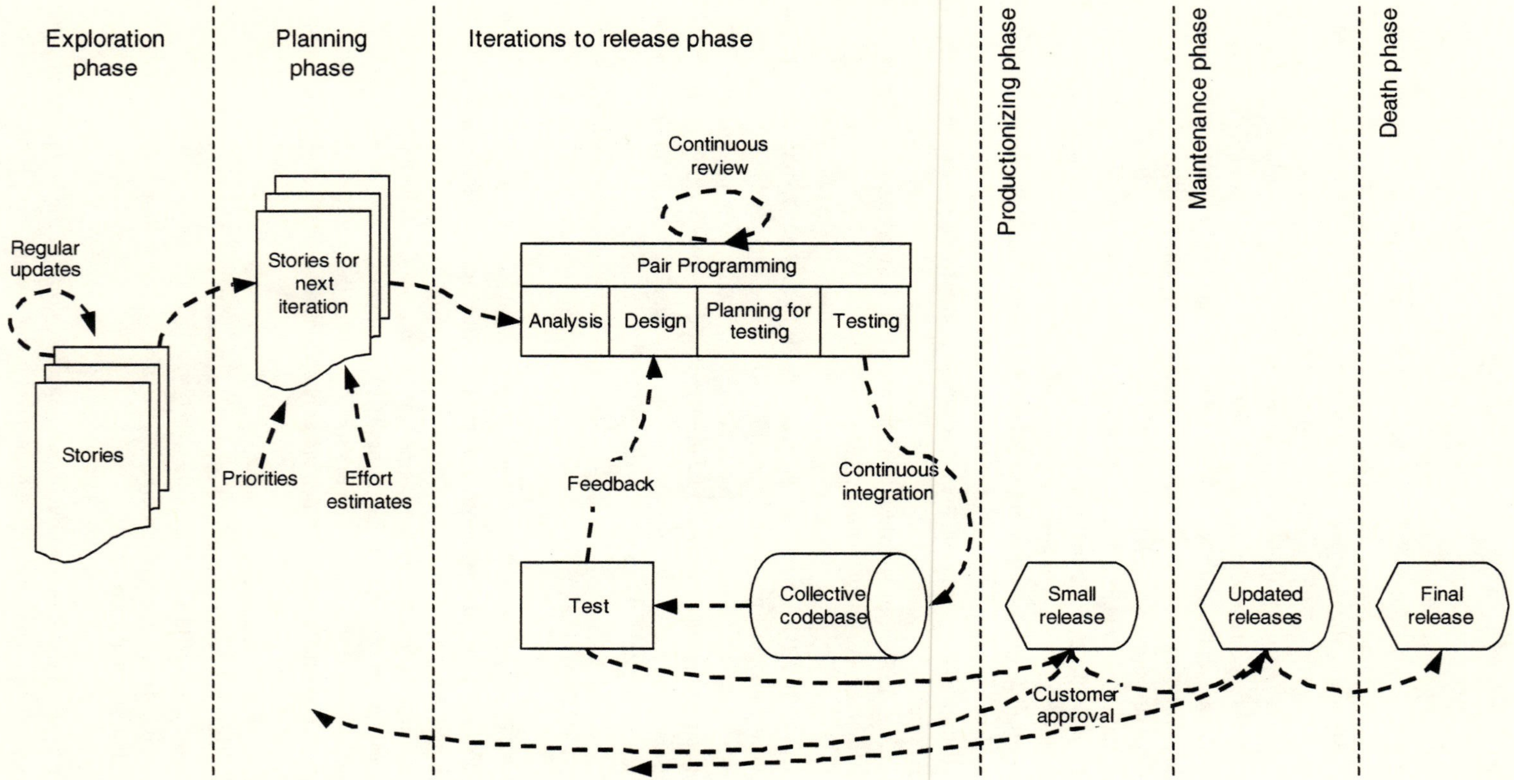

Source: Adapted from Abrahamsson et al. (2002, p. 19), and reproduced with permission.

for systematic empirical study. The limits of agile methods with regard to outsourcing and large/complex projects are of particular interest, not least because some agile practitioners argue that agile methods are applicable in these situations.

Project Size

Agile methods are ideally suited to the needs of small-sized teams developing software with vague or rapidly changing requirements where speed of delivery is critical (Cockburn and Highsmith, 2001; Rumpe and Scholz, 2003).

Large and complex organizations are likely to use a wide range of software, ranging from software that is relatively simple and runs into only a few hundred lines of code to extremely complex systems running into millions of lines of code. The systems that drive the business tend to mirror the business—they are large and complex.

Turk et al. (2005, pp. 81–82) argue that large, complex systems are not amenable to agile methods because they require much higher levels of control, integration, and documentation. These systems require regular management intervention and widespread use of formal procedures. They are not amenable to ad hoc testing or incremental change. Indeed, the systems are often so complex that even small changes need to be carefully analyzed due to the unforeseen impacts they might have. Agile methods are best employed when the requirements are not well defined, change does not have a significant impact, the system is not safety or mission critical, and extensive analysis and testing are not required (Coram and Bohner, 2005).

This position is challenged by some. It is now not uncommon to see the argument that agile methods can be used in large-scale, enterprise-level projects, as long as the method is adapted (Cao et al., 2004; Simons, 2002b; Sutherland, 2001). These adaptations include a sound architecture, a focus on up-front design, short release cycles, flexible pair programming, surrogate customer engagement, regular builds, well-developed communication networks, and a variety of other techniques that add structure to the project (Cao et al., 2004; Murthi, 2002; Spayd, 2003).

Kähkönen (2004) believes that agile methods can be adapted to large organizations or projects by adopting a community of practice approach. Communities of practice comprise people who are bound by informal relationships and share a common practice. (Kähkönen, 2004, p. 2). These communities or informal networks that may even extend beyond the organizational boundary are based on shared interests and values (Kähkönen, 2004). Communities of practice overlap each other and cut across team boundaries and, argues Kähkönen, can be leveraged in order to facilitate the use of agile methods in the corporation as a whole and in larger projects.

Despite doubts in some quarters, adherents of agile methodologies view the methodologies as disciplined and potentially able to align with the requirements of rigorous software process improvement models such as the Capability Maturity Model (CMM; Paulk, 2001, 2002). Paulk argues that agile methodologies are capable, to an extent, of coexisting with CMM, but much depends upon the degree to which the methodologies are not corrupted and there is a technology-environment fit. Agile methodologies are compatible with CMM, especially at the lower levels, but aligning the two in all environments may prove a major challenge. Furthermore, agile methods are not highly compatible with levels 4 and 5 of CMM (Paulk, 2001).

The fact that most of the research has relied upon relatively narrow case studies, often written by people who are clearly agile converts, makes us somewhat skeptical about the applicability of agile methods to large projects. Those who argue that agile methods are applicable rely upon the imposition of structure or a combination of agile and more traditional methods. We argue that the adaptations required challenge and eventually hopelessly compromise the assumptions of agility. Indeed, some of the proposed adaptations are so complex that they would impose upon the organization structures that rival the most structured of traditional methods.

Outsourcing

Very little empirical work has been done on the efficacy of agile methods when outsourcing is involved, perhaps because the two practices appear to be inherently contradictory. One of the key objectives of this study is to learn more about this relationship. This is necessary at a time when some argue that agile methods might be adapted to suit outsourcing projects (Hayes, 2003; Nisar and Hameed, 2004; Rees, 2004; Simons, 2002a, 2000b).

Turk et al. (2005, pp. 78–79) argue that agile methods offer limited support at best for subcontracting. Most subcontracting relationships are driven by a contract that specifies deliverables, deadlines, and milestones up front, particularly when the contract has been won via a bidding process. Ambler (2003) points out that, even when the outsourcer is asked to produce a bespoke solution from the ground up, highly detailed contracts are required to manage the outsourcing relationship. Contractual arrangements are also associated with significant amounts of documentation, in part motivated by a desire to improve communication (Ambler, 2003). Arrangements of this nature seem wholly unsuited to an approach that seeks to minimize documentation while emphasizing flexibility and the ability to change rapidly.

Communication is the force that drives agile projects (Ambler, 2003). The core values of the agile movement call for intense collaboration on a daily basis and place great value on face-to-face communication. Communication should be wide-ranging and not only restricted to the team, because communication is the source of organizational learning. It is inconceivable that any outsourced project would allow for even the minimum levels of communication required, let alone optimal levels. The distance factor combined with issues related to language and culture makes the situation even more challenging when it comes to offshoring.

Given the major issues outlined above, it is surprising to find a paper claiming that agile methods are better aligned with offshoring than are traditionally structured (plan-based) methods (Nisar and Hameed, 2004). The paper is a case study based on an outsourcing vendor. Nisar and Hameed (2004) argue that even the most intractable problems associated with aligning agile methods with offshoring can be overcome. They suggest, for example, that the communication problems can be overcome via weekly online video chats, daily progress reports via Instant Messenger, just right documentation, delivering "almost-daily" builds, and increasing the amount of time spent onshore by analysts and ambassadors.

The fundamental question is whether the authors are describing an agile method, once all the adaptations have been applied. As is commonly the case, attempting to adapt the agile method has increased the complexity level of the process many times and has increased the cost of the project. We are left with a technique that might be agile in name but hardly conforms to the assumptions of the Agile Alliance.

Ambler (2003) takes a somewhat ironic but nevertheless thought-provoking position on the alignment between outsourcing and agile methods. He believes that agile methods are the answer to outsourcing rather than tools that companies might want to use in collaboration with outsourcing. Using agile methods with in-house teams delivers most of the benefits of outsourcing with none of the risks.

Individual and Organizational Personality

Geniuses like Isaac Newton would not have thrived in an agile environment (Skowronski, 2004). Problem solvers need time and solitude to reflect. Consultation with outside sources is also vital, and this time is not devoted to actual production. The constant frenetic group interaction of agile methods provides no time for reflection and creates noise that inhibits creativity and problem solving (Skowronski, 2004).

A small number of interesting articles have appeared addressing the role of personality and cognitive characteristics in the information technology (IT) profession (Rosenbloom and Ash, 2005; Van Der Vyver, 2004) and XP programming in particular (Chao and Atli, 2006). These studies suggest that successful IT professionals have distinctive personality traits and cognitive dispositions. For example, there may be some truth in the well-known dictum that talented programmers tend to be introverted. The software development methodology employed in an organization should accommodate the organization's best programmers (Skowronski, 2004). Relatively simple systems may be well suited to agile methods, but complex systems pose serious risks.

Perhaps the same applies to the structure and culture of the organization as a whole. Organizations with relatively simple structures and homogeneous cultures seem better candidates for the introduction of agile methods than, for example, large bureaucracies. Very little applicable research has been conducted, but Steindl (2006) argues that agile methods can transform the organization and make it market- and value-driven. The explosion of agility can begin at the project level and then gradually expand to encompass portfolios of projects and finally the enterprise as a whole.

Alternatively, the process can be driven top-down, beginning with a vision of an agile corporation. Steindl believes that agility will be the key determinant of corporate survival and believes that most corporations have the ability to reinvent themselves if they establish the appropriate procedures and practices. We are somewhat skeptical about these arguments and, given the lack of empirical work, an important objective of this chapter is the further exploration of this theme.

RESEARCH METHOD

A qualitative approach was deemed appropriate to guide the focus of the first phase of the study, given the limited amount of existing empirical research (Miles and Huberman, 1994; Yin, 1994). We wished to capture rich domain knowledge from experienced executives, managers, and practitioners in order to identify the key issues in relation to the research questions, and eventually develop an appropriate conceptual model that reflects the reality of current practice.

The first round of interviews involved fifteen executives and senior managers working at organizations in the Australian financial services sector. A second round of interviews involved eight project managers and team leaders. The interviews contained a number of questions relating to ICT issues within the organization and agile methods in particular.

The interviewees came from a variety of backgrounds, including:

- Large national financial institutions.
- Medium-sized national financial institutions.
- Companies producing software for the financial services industry ranging from large to relatively small in size.

We posed the following two questions:

1. What organizational factors inhibit or facilitate the adoption of agile methods, in particular XP (extreme programming)?
2. Are agile methods compatible with highly structured organizations?

An opinion survey was also conducted via an online XP discussion group to solicit the opinions of practitioners with a professional interest (or involvement) in agile methods. The objective of the opinion survey was to encourage a relatively free format discussion about which environments and system types are most suited to agile methods. Twenty practitioners responded to this qualitative opinion survey.

The interviews were transcribed and imported into an appropriate analytical tool (NVivo). The responses to the online survey were also imported into NVivo. Given that only a limited amount of research has been done in this area and because of the importance of uncovering relevant information, we adopted a liberal approach when searching for relevant facilitators and inhibitors. Our quantitative criterion was simple: All facilitators and inhibitors included were mentioned at least once by two or more interviewees.

Although we interviewed a significant number of relatively senior ICT practitioners, we used a sample of convenience. The respondents were also not particularly diverse in that they were not drawn from a large variety of business backgrounds. Furthermore, the online survey was interesting and reached the intended target group, but data collected in this manner must be treated with circumspection. It is also important to note the potential influence of organizational context, which could act as a biasing factor. The majority of interviewees (80 percent) came from larger organizations, and their responses dominate our analyses. In the majority of these organizations, in-house development continues to dominate (alongside enterprise resource planning), and large volumes of legacy code remain.

FINDINGS

It appears that companies in Australia are adopting agile methods in significant numbers. Approximately 70 percent of those interviewed indicated that agile methods were used at least to some extent in their organizations. It should be noted, however, that agile methods did not mean the same thing to all organizations. In some cases, the term "agile method" refers to a blend between RAD approaches and an approach that subscribes to the values of the Agile Alliance.

The interviewees were positive on the whole but reported a significant number of potential problems. Data analysis revealed a number of issues that facilitated or inhibited the successful adoption of agile methodologies. A number of these issues are related to previous findings, but a number of new issues also emerged. The main issues that emerged were categorized as facilitators and inhibitors to the adoption of agile methodologies. Key facilitators aiding the adoption of agile methodologies in organizations are listed in Table 3.1. Key inhibitors to the adoption of agile methodologies in organizations are listed in Table 3.2.

Agile Practitioners

The practitioners who responded to the online survey were enthusiasts to the core. The capability of agile methodologies such as XP to adapt quickly to the changing requirements of a customer and business environment was considered a very important factor by practitioners. As is suggested

Table 3.1

Key Organizational Facilitators in the Adoption of Agile Methodologies

	Facilitator	Comments
1.	The correct mix of people within a supportive culture	Agile methods thrive in decentralized cultures where teams are empowered and work close to the client. The right mix of people is also critical, especially the right client and a good mix of strong analysis and technical skills.
2.	An agile champion	Agile methods stand a better change of acceptance when a senior figure in the business champions them. The chief information officer is useful, but a senior figure from outside IT (e.g., the chief executive officer) is much better.
3.	Organization is relatively small	In this study, the most enthusiastic adopters were small organizations.
4.	Organization already uses R&D for specific projects	A number of large organizations have used R&D for specific systems for a long time. This is fertile ground for agile methods.
5.	Projects are not too big	There seems to be a point at which agile is no longer deemed suitable. This varies by organization.
6.	Market pressures demand short time frames for releases	A number of large organizations identified this as a key driver for using agile methods. Some projects simply cannot wait for the waterfall approach.
7.	Customer pressure for feedback/prototyping approaches	Short time frames between releases of working software allow developers to gather quick feedback from the customers and users.
8.	Customer involvement and commitment	Customers are the key drivers—not the IT people. Agile thrives where there is a culture of close cooperation between IT and customer units.
9.	Relatively small teams that work together closely.	Team size ideally ten or less. Most people emphasize closeness. This means physical proximity, identification with team, commitment, ability to get along with team.
10.	Organization accepts need for horses for courses approach	Applies particularly to large organizations. This type of organization accepts that some projects require a highly formalized approach while other are amenable to agile.
11.	Development for the Web	Across the board, agile methods were seen as the most suitable, but organizational constraints still get in the way—for example, offshoring of Web development.
12.	Requirements change regularly and cannot be specified in advance	Agile methodologies avoid overspecification upfront.

in previous theory (e.g., Paulk, 2001, 2002), Web-based information systems of limited scope emerged as the pervasive "system of choice" for agile developers. A few words of caution are appropriate. It is possible that the people who participated in the online survey had little experience working on any other type of system.

Web-based information systems are evolutionary in nature and experience many micro and macro changes. XP accommodates and acknowledges that there will be frequent changes in an

Table 3.2

Key Organizational Inhibitors to the Adoption of Agile Methodologies

	Inhibitors	Comments
1.	Traditional waterfall development mindset	Organizations steeped in waterfall mindset with regard to information systems development are reluctant to adopt agile methodologies such as XP.
2.	Highly formalized organization	Bureaucratic organizations that rely heavily on formal processes/procedures and documentation.
3.	Outsourcing and offshoring, particularly where the relationship is contractually based	Many issues: communication, control, distance, assumptions of agility cannot be truly met.
4.	Large projects	Not one person from a large organization viewed agile methods as suitable for large projects.
5.	The wrong people	People who are not suited to working in agile teams. A client who is not committed and/or does not have the knowledge. A team that does not have the required skills. A team where there are a number of passengers.
6.	The wrong project	Some projects require a highly formalized approach, for example, where a system is being developed that must conform to complex legislation.
7.	The wrong team culture, environment, and atmosphere	Team-building critical to agile—often ignored.
8.	Time commitment from end users	Organizations cannot afford the time commitments required from key personnel.
9.	More extreme methods preferred	XP enforces a disciplined approach to information systems development.
10.	Unrealistic expectations concerning pace of development	Agile organizations may have unrealistic expectations.
11.	Negative perceptions of R&D teams	Some view agile with suspicion and attempt to mobilize political forces against agile method.
12.	Risk	High-risk projects or projects where it is essential to understand and measure risks involved.
13.	Time	The organization cannot afford to lose key staff for long periods.

information system. The following comments by a practitioner emphasize the ability of XP to adapt to change in a business environment:

> I worked on a few large web dynamic web sites for about a year—content management, shopping-cart-style ordering, user registration, mass email based on searches, that kind of thing. Features tended to get added to the live site every 1–3 weeks. We always had some version of each site that we could quickly push to the live site if we needed to (e.g. to fix a bug or rush a feature).

The capability of XP to facilitate frequent releases of working software underpins the capability of agile methodologies to adapt to change by allowing the developers to release high quality working software in short time frames:

I would not be qualified to say agile methods are the best approach for web development, but I have been pretty successful using XP for my web development projects. I find the frequent releases to be a good fit for web development since it keeps the feedback cycle short and get the product in front of your customer quickly. Once the customer sees it, then you can get the real feedback on how you are doing.

Furthermore, frequent releases of working software have the added advantage of keeping the feedback loop between the developer and customer short. Frequent releases allow the customer to provide real feedback to the developer almost instantaneously and keep the project on the right path:

Feedback is important. Because new releases are adopted immediately, feedback comes quickly. This makes steering the project easier. The emphasis on short releases ensures you do not get off target for too long, and I find this to be an advantage since the web projects I have worked on are often ill-defined.

The continuous testing and integration regime of an agile methodology such as XP enforces the delivery of high quality working software while still addressing the issue of needing to deliver working software in short time frames:

I have found that XP helps to maintain very high levels of quality through unit tests, simple design and test driven design. The high quality gives you a lot of confidence in your website which is an advantage since a lot of websites are flaky.

Another practitioner comment emphasizes the overall advantages of agile methodologies such as XP, which were highlighted in Table 3.1 and discussed subsequently:

Speaking broadly, I think XP's advantages for fast-paced web projects are even stronger than for other types of project:

- Having all the running copies of the program under your direct control makes frequent releases much easier.
- Because your competitors are just one bookmark away, it's much harder to insulate yourself from competitive pressure. That makes the ability to adapt quickly much more important. It also gives you a bigger advantage if you can keep ahead of your competitors.
- Because new releases are adopted immediately, feedback comes quickly. This makes steering the project easier.
- Since bugs can be very, very public, XP's ability to drastically reduce bug counts and bug severity are a big win.
- In fast-paced environments, priorities often change rapidly. Releasing frequently means that when a project suddenly gets shelved, relatively little work sits around unreleased.

One practitioner worked for an organization where the manager was talked into adopting a waterfall approach for a large Web project. This resulted in very poor outcomes in terms of the finished product. Interestingly, management was in favor of adopting an agile methodology such as XP, but corporate politics dictated a waterfall approach for the project:

Right now, I'm doing some consulting for an organization that had someone else develop their web site (mostly intranet and extranet). They did it waterfall: big contract, big requirements doc, possibly big design doc, big price tag. The project is very late, parts don't function, other parts function very differently than what the organization needs, and still other parts are almost physically painful to use. The customers have literally never seen the people who are actually creating the system. The saddest part is that the customers' manager, while not at all experienced in software development, is a big fan of approaches like XP: incremental progress, iterative steering, and no solo work. The developers had to argue him into the waterfall, big-bang approach. Not all of the problems with the latter project are due to using a non-agile method, but most of them are. And an agile method would have ameliorated most of those problems: e.g. the customer could have had half of the features a year ago, which would have given them a lot of value (I explicitly asked them this).

Another issue that emerged from the responses of the practitioners was that in some organizations there was significant pressure to relax or abandon the disciplined approach of an agile methodology such as XP. This is due to the intense pressure to deliver products and services in the marketplace given the short windows of opportunity that are now commonplace. XP is a disciplined approach, and management needs to be aware that the core practices of XP, while flexible, cannot be compromised because of market pressures to deliver in incredibly short time frames:

Oh, wait, there's one other limitation, and this one is a real one: XP demands doing things right from the beginning. This pays off in the long run, but initial progress on an XP project feels slower than just jumping in and hacking stuff out. On fast-paced projects, this initial feeling of slowness makes XP adoption much harder than in environments where people are accustomed to taking a longer view of things. XP requires some discipline. It also requires managers and customers to support that discipline, instead of undermining it with pressure, fits of anxiety or cajoling to "skip testing, just this once." But doing anything right requires some discipline, and more pressure seems to require more discipline in just about any endeavor. At least with XP, there's a small, clearly stated set of practices to be disciplined about, and all of them are pretty obviously related to quality and speed.

Interestingly, one practitioner noted that one of his customers wanted to release new features immediately despite the significant risk involved in releasing software that has not been rigorously tested. The practitioner also noted that the client in question was no longer a customer because of his unrealistic expectations in terms of delivery time frames for new features and enhancements.

Believe it or not, one of our customers balked at one-week iterations because they were too far apart! We'd been becoming progressively more XP from the ad-hoc side, and he'd become accustomed to having features released the minute we were confident in them (sometimes declining to look at them first).

Perhaps the most interesting paradox to emerge from this study was that agile methods do not always fit very well with agile organizations. In some organizations, agile methods are too slow.

Executives and Managers

These interviewees took a broader view. At the one extreme, a few were highly enthusiastic, and typically work in organizations that use agile methods extensively. At the other extreme, a few were hostile to agile methods or knew nothing about them. The majority were prepared to examine agile methods critically and use them in applicable situations.

Perhaps the most consistent predictor of enthusiasm for agile methods turned out to be the size of the organization. All the "software houses" were enthusiastic about the approach and used it to some degree, one using it extensively. The largest organizations were more guarded, and agile methods were not extensively used. A variety of cultural and structural factors, some of them unexpected, contribute to this state of affairs.

A senior manager in a medium-sized organization that retains most of its IT in-house offered the following comments:

> We don't use agile methods . . . don't really know much about them . . . maybe we are out of touch . . . but, from what you've said, I would be open to them. Most of our work is maintenance of big systems—lots of legacy stuff. All of this is formalized and centralized in the IT department. We do have a couple of small teams doing ad hoc work . . . you know RAD using SQLServer rather than the Oracle product. They talk with people then return and churn out prototypes. They've done some good work on small projects where speed was critical, but I wouldn't use these people on a large project. They've developed reputations, you know . . .

It is likely that such an organization would benefit from using agile methods instead of the undisciplined RAD methods currently in use. While the teams involved have delivered, it seems likely that their ad hoc approach and (probably) excessive independence have caused "reputation" problems. An executive in a larger organization focused on structural impediments to agile methods:

> Despite all the hype we are still relatively hierarchical and compartmentalized. We do things by the book using techniques which are proven. It may be that agile methods would be great for Web development, but that is only a small part of our work. We need precision, things must be properly analyzed! We favor specialist business analysts who speak the language of the customer. Customers don't have time to hang around working on agile projects. Anyway, who would we get? Do you really think the sharpest people out there would want to spend days away from their job doing systems tests?

This respondent comes from a traditional organization with a long history and, by all accounts, a relatively stable and reliable customer base. The organization is relatively structured and bureaucratic, and it is clear that cultural and structural factors militate against change. It should be said that this might not apply to agile methods alone. This organization is likely to resist any change in the approach to applications development.

A couple of the themes discussed by the previous respondent were common to a significant number of respondents. In particular, there was concern that experienced staff would be required to spend large amounts of time working on IT projects when they were required at the coalface. The alternative would be seconding less valuable staff, but there would be a potential trade-off in terms of system quality. Many respondents favored using seasoned business analysts with domain knowledge as intermediaries.

The smallest organization we interviewed employs about thirty people. This company produces specialist software for sale. The organization is highly enthusiastic about agile methods and uses them extensively but within limits:

> Here we do more with less. We work 40–45 hours per week and hire extra resources when needed—the result is low turnover, employees who are not overstretched and no burnout. We use agile methods extensively . . . pair programming, code open to view, small prototyping iterations . . . but we need to choose employees carefully. We employ people who are "different"—we like fun people with personality. We use agile across the board—using .Net, PHP and Perl, but we don't have the ideal amount of access to our outsourcing partners. In these cases, we do need a reasonable amount of documentation.

The comments regarding the type of people employed by the company are interesting as they seem to suggest that certain types of people are better suited to working in an agile environment—although this may be related to the culture and structure of the organization, which is very flat and informal.

We found that outsourcing can have a potentially devastating impact on the adoption of agile methods. Even the organization mentioned in the previous set of comments found that agile methods required massive adaptation when it came to dealing with outsourcing clients. The comments of an executive from another small-medium software house bring the problem into focus:

> There is a tidal wave of offshoring to come. Even if I have a small job, say $100, I send it off to India late afternoon, and the code is waiting for me in the morning. Sure, standards can be variable, but the key is specification.

These thoughts are mirrored by a senior manager at a large organization that outsources/offshores a significant component of its IT:

> Outsourcing seems to be saving us money, but many of us continue to have our doubts. We are highly cautious about offshoring . . . our relationships are highly formal and driven by contract. Our partners have formal structures and procedures—after all, and one of their key selling points is CMM level 5. When we send work over, we need to devote a lot of time to preparation. The specs must be spot on—detailed. They seem to be using traditional development methods as might be expected with the CMM/everything documented approach.

These comments regarding the amount of specification required for outsourcing in general and offshoring in particular were echoed virtually across the board. The growing importance of the Capability Maturity Model was also mentioned by a number of other respondents. The consensus opinion is that many vendors, especially in India, are now aiming for levels 4 and 5, and this in turn makes relationships more formal. It is interesting to juxtapose the comments of the previous respondent with those of a senior manager at a large outsourcing vendor (which in turn offshores some of the work):

> When we were awarded the contract we had no idea of the complexity or the silos of IT. The relationship is highly formal—trust does not come into it. We are involved in constant negotiations and re-negotiations. We need to constantly re-bid for the work . . . win some, lose some. A significant amount of the work we once had has passed back in house. Even small change requests require pages of documentation and specification—20 pages would not be uncommon. We offshore the less complicated stuff . . . extremely well-defined applications.

Clearly, outsourcing relationships are highly complex and formal at the top end. Although it is possible that different types of relationships exist, this type of relationship does appear to be typical of large, complex agreements. There is little doubt that agile methods would not thrive in this type of environment.

A senior manager from a large financial institution provided us with some insights into her conceptualization of the place of agile methods in organizations of this nature:

> We have an eclectic mix of systems here . . . and a lot of them. ERP's, major legacy systems, small specialized systems. . . . For major projects, we use highly formalized methodologies and have done so for a long time. We wouldn't consider agile methods for large projects or those where there is a significant amount or risk. We have used RAD approaches for smaller projects for a long time, and these have mutated into agile projects because we've been burned by a few projects where there was no discipline. We use these approaches when there is pressure to deliver quickly and the development will take a month or two at the most. The teams are small, five or six, and the intensity is high.

A project manager from the same institution who has a wealth of experience managing traditional and agile approaches emphasized the fact that agile projects need the right people:

> You can't put just anybody into an agile team. Some people, especially some of our best techies, just don't work well in this type of setup. They feel surrounded. You also must make sure that team gels, and this is doubly true when you use pair programming. You need people who are technically good but open to criticism—it's not easy getting them. And, you need to train them to do agile right.

Finally, a significant number of people mentioned an issue that has received little attention in previous research, namely, the client who works with the team:

> How many agile projects have delivered the wrong product cheaply and on time because they listened to a client who had little idea of what was going on? Do you really think companies can afford to let the people who really know the score hang out with agile teams for weeks on end—no way! If you're lucky, you get someone who is competent . . . if you're not, you get someone the rest are happy to see the back of . . .

CONCLUSION

Agile methodologies are gaining widespread acceptance, but they are often adapted to meet organizational circumstances. Furthermore, they are perceived as inapplicable in certain situations, for example, large projects and projects involving outsourcing. This research supports the previous work suggesting that agile methods such as XP are highly favored by practitioners involved in developing systems for the Web. Furthermore, agile methods are ideal for smaller projects where speed is important but a disciplined approach is required.

Based on the responses of the executives, managers, and practitioners involved in this study, we come to the following conclusions:

1. Outsourcing and offshoring, particularly when large-scale contractual agreements are involved, do not offer fertile ground for agile methods. This type of agreement usually involves highly formalized procedures, voluminous documentation, and high levels of specification.

Most of this is done via intermediaries, and there is often little contact between developer and client.

2. The Capability Maturity Model is growing in importance with regard to outsourcing. This makes relationships more formal, and agile methods are not well attuned to the higher levels of the model.

3. Large, complex projects are not well aligned with agile methods. When agile methods are used in such projects, the degree of adaptation required strips them of their inherent agility.

4. Particular organizational structures and cultures are more conducive to the adoption of agile methods than others.

5. Agile methods require the right people, the right project, and the right team environment.

6. Agile does not just happen. Teams require training in the method, mentoring, and an environment that is supportive.

7. Agile methods are perceived as more disciplined and structured than RAD approaches in general, but some people continue to view agile methods as just another RAD approach. There is some justification for this argument. The evolutionary trajectory of development methodologies encompasses both approaches, and agile methods are inevitably close relatives of RAD approaches. They are not the same, however. Extreme programming, in particular, is not typical of RAD approaches and is one of the characteristics of the overall methodology that is truly innovative, if contentious.

8. Some managers consider that particular personality types are better suited to working in agile teams than others.

9. The practitioners involved in this study identified four factors that facilitate the adoption of agile methods within organizations: ability to adapt quickly to change, short time frames for releases, instant feedback from customers, and high-quality, bug-free software. The first three factors are significant in that they are commonly found in an agile corporation. This type of corporation thrives on rapid adaptation, and corporate clients are in all likelihood intimately involved in systems development. Feedback from customers is therefore immediate. Agile corporations also are competing in environments where systems are mutating continuously to meet the challenges of new competitors, new markets, and new opportunities. Agile methods can deliver the systems to meet these demands. An interesting point that emerged from the findings is the indication that high-quality, bug-free software is now demanded by clients, regardless of the fact that development teams are working at "lightning" speed. In iterative approaches such as RAD, it was often accepted that a trade-off for speed was the presence of some errors. These errors were resolved during late iterations of the system construction or even post-implementation. This is probably acceptable for systems that will be used by internal users, but the reality of systems developed in the agile corporation is that they are placed on the Web, in the sight of customers and competitors. Upon implementation, they can be immediate sources of profit (or loss), and they must work.

10. Agile methods are clearly well aligned with the agile corporation in general, but there are points of potential tension. Perhaps paradoxically, the practitioners involved in this study highlighted the fact that agile methods require a disciplined approach. These are not ad hoc methodologies that can be adapted to every organizational contingency. They are able to deliver good systems relatively quickly, but they have a cycle of their own. Because these methods are associated with speed, corporations tend to take them for granted and push the limits. When the speed at which agile methods are able to deliver quality product becomes too slow and corporations push for product releases at very short intervals, the methodology is compromised. Although these problems are a potential source of concern, most practitioners in this survey identify corporations who are committed to the waterfall model as the biggest problem. Many agile practitioners are working in environments that are ambivalent to their approach at best and openly hostile at worst.

Agile methods are clearly impacting applications development, but more empirical research is required to determine whether they are suited to a variety of organizational forms and project types. These findings support previous research and theoretical formulations and provide some new insights, particularly with regard to agile methods and organizational culture. As is the case with the majority of the limited number of previous empirical studies, this study is of limited scope, and a larger-scale study might challenge some of our conclusions.

ACKNOWLEDGMENTS

We would like to acknowledge the members of the Agile Research Group, School of Information Systems, University of Southern Queensland—Mark Toleman, Fiona Darroch, and Mustafa Ally—whose enthusiasm for agility is infectious and who introduced us to the methods and their potential.

REFERENCES

Abrahamsson, P.; Salo, O.; Ronkainen, J.; and Warsta, J. 2002. *Agile Software Development Methods.* Espoo, Finland: VTT.

Ambler, S. 2003. Outsourcing examined. Dr. Dobb's, April 1. Available at www.ddj.com/dept/architect/18 4414972?cid=Ambysoft (accessed July 17, 2007).

Amos, J. 1998. *Transformation to Agility: Manufacturing in the Marketplace of Unanticipated Change.* New York: Garland.

Beck, K. 1999. *Extreme Programming Explained: Embrace Change.* Reading, MA: Addison-Wesley.

Beck, K. et al. 2001. Manifesto for Agile Software Development. Available at http://agilemanifesto.org/ (accessed July 17, 2007).

Boehm, B. 2002. Get ready for agile methods, with care. *Computer,* 35, 1, 64–69.

Bridger, D.J. 2002. Workforce agility: The new employee strategy for the knowledge economy. *Journal of Information Technology,* 17, 1, 21–32.

Cao, C.G.L., et al. 2004. Evaluation of physical versus virtual surgical simulators. In *Proceedings of the 48th Annual Meeting of the Human Factors of Ergonomics Society, 1675–1679.*

Chao, J., and Atli, G. 2006. Critical personality traits in successful pair programming. AGILE, 89–93

Cockburn, A., and Highsmith, J. 2001. Agile software development: The business of innovation. *Computer,* 34, 9, 120–122.

Coram, M., and Bohner, S. 2005. The impact of agile methods on software project management. In *Proceedings of the Twelfth IEEE International Conference and Workshops on the Engineering of Computer-Based Systems.* Greenbelt, MD: IEEE Computer Society Press, 363–370.

Filey, A. 2006. Adopt and benefit from agile proceeses in offshore software development. *Architecture Journal,* 8. Available at http://msdn2.microsoft.com/en us/library/bb245671.aspx/ (accessed July 17, 2007).

Fowler, M. 2005. The new methodology. Available at www.martinfowler.com/articles/newMethodology. html (accessed July 17, 2007).

Hayes, G. 2003. Everything you know about offshore outsourcing is wrong. *Datamation.* Available at http://itmanagement.earthweb.com/columns/article.php/1856621 (accessed July 17, 2007).

Highsmith, J. 1998. *Adaptive Software Development: An Evolutionary Approach to Managing Complex Systems.* New York: Dorset House.

Kähkönen, T. 2004. Agile methods for large organizations: Building communities of practice. In *Proceedings of the Agile Development Conference,* February 11, Salt Lake City: IEEE Computer Society Press.

Miles, M., and Huberman, M. 1994. *Qualitative Data Analysis: An Expanded Sourcebook,* 2d ed. Thousand Oaks, CA: Sage.

Murthi, S. 2002. Can eXtreme programming work for large projects? *New Architect,* 7, 10, 14–15.

Nisar, M., and Hameed, T. 2004. Agile methods handling offshore software development issues. In *Proceedings of INMIC.* IEEE Computer Society Press, 417–422.

Paulk, M.C. 2001. Extreme programming from a CMM perspective. *IEEE Software,* 18, 6 (November/ December), 19–26.

———. 2002. Agile methodologies and process discipline. *Cross Talk,* October, 15–18.

Rees, D. 2004. Distributed Agile Development. Available at http://www.itwales.com/998851.htm (accessed July 17, 2007).

Rosenbloom, J.L., and Ash, R. 2005. *Big Five Personality Characteristics of Established Information Technology Professionals.* Lawrence: University of Kansas Press.

Rumpe, B., and Scholz, P. 2003. Scaling the management of extreme programming projects. *Project and Profits: Special Issue on Management of Extreme Programming Projects,* 3, 8, 11–18.

Shaw, B. 2004. Agile evolution. *Computer Bulletin,* November, 18–19.

Simon, H.A. 1976. *Administrative Behavior.* Macmillan: New York.

Simons, M. 2002a. Internationally Agile, Informit.com. Available at www.informit.com/articles/article. asp?p=25929&rl=1 (accessed July 17, 2007).

Simons, M. 2002b. Big and agile? *Cutter IT Journal,* 15, 34–38.

Skowronski, V. 2004. Do agile methods marginalize problem solvers? *Computer,* 37, 10 (October), 118–130.

Spayd, M. 2003. Evolving agile in the enterprise: Implementing XP on a grand scale. In *Proceedings of the Agile Development Conference,* 60. Salt Lake City: IEEE Computer Society Press.

Steindl, C. 2006. From agile software development to agile businesses. In *Proceedings of the Thirty-First EUROMICRO Conference on Software Engineering and Advanced Applications.* IEEE Computer Society Press.

Sutherland, J. 2001. Agile can scale: Inventing and reinventing SCRUM in five companies. *Cutter IT Journal,* 14, 5–11.

Turk, D.; France, R.; and Rumpe, B. 2005. Assumptions underlying agile software development processes. *Journal of Database Management,* 16, 4, 62–87.

Van Der Vyver, G. 2004. The overconfidence effect and IT professionals. In *Proceedings of the Thirteenth European Conference on Information Systems.* Turku, Finland.

Webber, R. 1997. Modern imperatives. In G. Bickerstaffe (ed.), *Mastering Management.* London: Pitman.

Williams, L.; Kessler, R.R.; Cunningham, W.; and Jeffries, R. 2000. Strengthening the case for pair programming. *IEEE Software,* 17, 4 (July–August), 18–25.

Yin, R.K. 1994. *Case Study Research: Design and Methods.* Thousand Oaks, CA: Sage.

CHAPTER 4

DESIGNING CONTEXT-AWARE BUSINESS PROCESSES

MICHAEL ROSEMANN, JAN RECKER, AND CHRISTIAN FLENDER

Abstract: Flexibility has emerged as an important requirement in the design of business processes. Research on process flexibility, however, has traditionally been focused on the intrinsic capability of a process to adapt to a new environment (e.g., workflow escalation, ad hoc modeling). This chapter proposes to extend the existing body of research by studying the extrinsic drivers for process flexibility, that is, the root causes that actually drive the demand for flexible business processes. The drivers for flexibility can be found in the context of a process and may include time, location, weather, legislation, or performance requirements. We argue for a stronger and more explicit consideration of these contextual factors in the design of business processes in order to make processes more adaptive. The chapter discusses why context matters and how context can be conceptualized, classified, and integrated with existing approaches to business process modeling. We use a goal-oriented process-modeling approach to be able to identify relevant context elements and propose a framework and a meta model for classifying relevant context. These extensions are an essential foundation for the definition and implementation of truly agile processes, and, as such, of high practical and theoretical value.

Keywords: Business Process Flexibility, Business Process Modeling, Context Awareness.

Business process management (BPM) continues to receive significant attention as a top priority, and building business process improvement capabilities is seen as a major challenge by senior executives (Gartner, Inc., 2010). In line with the rising popularity of BPM, over the past decade scholarly work has tried to address some of the challenges related to process modeling and management. One of the most prevalent and dominating research foci that has emerged is the notion of agile, or flexible, business processes (Balabko et al., 2005).

The need for increased attention to flexibility stems from two main drivers. First, the trend toward decreasing time-to-market and time-to-customer demands and an increasing frequency of product innovations combined with market changes such as globalization and new levels of compliance require adaptive business processes. The observation that organizations often face continuous and unprecedented changes in their respective business environments can be seen as an emerging *demand for process flexibility* (Pine, 1999; Quinn, 1992). Such disturbances and perturbations of business routines need to be reflected within the business processes, in the sense that processes need to be able to react to perturbations, namely, they need to be flexible with regard to the mutual specification of processes and environment (Knoll and Jarvenpaa, 1994; Soffer, 2005). Second, there is a technology-driven *opportunity for process flexibility* in the form of service-oriented architecture and advanced workflow technology. While the general idea of encapsulating functionality and applications related to object orientation and component technologies has been discussed in research for many years, only the breakthrough in widely accepted XML (Extensible Markup Language)—and related standards—made the implementation of this concept feasible. Web services now provide unseen flexibility in the internal orchestration and overall choreography of business processes and trigger the design of entire new business models (Mulholland et al., 2006). In many cases, however, it is not known what processes within the organization's process landscape would actually benefit from such flexibility.

In simple terms, flexibility is the capability to change without loss of identity (Regev et al., 2007). Business process flexibility can be seen as the capability of a process to yield to externally triggered change by modifying only those aspects of a process that need to be changed and keeping other parts stable, i.e., the ability to change the process without completely replacing it (Bider, 2005; Regev et al., 2007). Thus, process flexibility consists of an extrinsic trigger for change and intrinsic change mechanisms toward self-organization. However, not every change necessarily requires process changes. Instead, necessary and sufficient prerequisites have to be fulfilled before it becomes relevant and feasible to change the process.

Yet, existing related research that deals with change management and evolution management typically addresses issues of change only *after* requirements have already been identified and evaluated (Arnold and Bohner, 1996). The focus has traditionally been on requirements traceability and impact analysis when a change has already occurred (Ramesh and Jarke, 2001). The same holds for research related to process flexibility. Most of the existing approaches have concentrated on intrinsic ways of adopting or modifying business processes *after* a need for process change has arisen. The actual drivers for flexibility have not yet been discussed thoroughly. As a consequence, current process modeling techniques only capture the reactive part of process flexibility, but lack contextualization, that is, the stimulus for change.

We argue that it is exactly this stimulus for change that needs to be taken into consideration. The motivation for an increased consideration of context in a process model is that it provides a stronger cause-effect relationship between the demands for process flexibility and their impact on processes and vice versa. Relevant changes in the business environment can be anticipated and subsequently trigger the timely adaptation of business procedures. Hence, explicit context awareness encourages monitoring of the relevant process context (e.g., weather, competitors' price changes, etc.). The early identification of context changes together with knowledge about what type of process changes are required lead to increased process flexibility, decreased reaction time, and improved risk management.

This chapter discusses the challenge of process contextualization and summarizes our research on context awareness in process design (Ploesser et al., 2009, 2010). We proceed as follows. First, we provide a motivating example to clearly position what drives our research and to outline research objectives addressed in the chapter. Second, we discuss related work on context awareness in other research disciplines in order to introduce a useful definition and understanding of context in the environment of business process management. We use a meta model to formalize the identified relationships. Third, current process modeling techniques are briefly evaluated, and an extension of these techniques with an explicit consideration of context is proposed. We introduce an "onion model" as a first framework for classifying relevant context. Fourth, we present a procedure for applying the onion model to identify and type-relevant context. A case study provides empirical evidence to support this procedure. Fifth and finally, we briefly summarize the chapter and outline fruitful research directions.

A MOTIVATING EXAMPLE

In the following we provide brief insights into an example that we encountered during our research project on deadline-based escalations (van der Aalst et al., 2007), which motivates dealing with context-aware business processes. Our case describes a scenario in which the demand to include an environmental element such as *weather* as a contextual variable in a process model is prevalent in order to call the correct process.

In most cases, process models are disconnected from the relevant context in which they are valid, and there is often no traceability to the situation in which the process should take place. A workaround that can be observed in modeling practice is that relevant contextual variables become an explicit part of the control flow, leading to a decision point such as "Check, if process occurs within storm season." Yet, such a workaround leads to unnecessary model extensions, mixes individual runtime with build-time decisions, and tends to reduce the acceptance of the process models by end users who would not be exposed to this decision in the daily execution of the process. A second commonly employed workaround, which is discussed in our example, is to design multiple process models for different scenarios (e.g., for different countries) and to highlight process deviations within these models (e.g., by color coding). The shortcoming of this approach is the high degree of redundancy among the models. Figure 4.1 shows how such a workaround has been employed in one of Australia's largest insurance companies that faces a need for swift and rapid process changes in certain weather conditions, for example, during storm season (October-March). The considered process is designed to handle inbound phone calls from customers who have a range of different insurance claims including household, car, and so on. The process is supported by a call center operating in Brisbane.

While this process runs smoothly for most of the year, the organization faces a dramatically increased number of incoming phone calls (from 9,000 to more than 20,000) during the Australian storm season. In order to cope with this increased call traffic, the insurance company operates an event-based response system that differentiates calls into a number of categories of situations based on how severe the storms are. Individual response strategies have been defined for each of these categories, utilizing additional external resources together with changes in the procedure by which claims are lodged. First, additional resources are utilized through redeployment of employees from other departments and hiring of casual staff, denoted in Figure 4.1 as *Call center agent* (novice). While most of these people are trained, their performance in terms of average call handling time is lower than the performance of the professional call center agents. Second, a streamlined way of lodging the claims is applied in order to reduce the average call handling time and to reduce the waiting time in the queue. In this "rapid lodgment of claim" process (see Figure 4.1) only a reduced amount of information is collected from the claimant. This leads to an average call handling time of 380 seconds for experienced call center agents and 450 seconds for additionally employed agents, down from the usual average of 550 seconds. One mechanism to deal with the different performance of these two types of agents is call routing, which directs new and straightforward cases to the casual additional workforce, while more complicated follow-up calls are directed to the experienced workforce.

Two managers in charge of claim services and the related back-office processes evaluate the severity of the weather conditions; that is, they monitor the relevant environmental setting of this business process, and trigger the different escalation categories leading to different variations of the process.

This example shows how a change in the environment requires flexible process adaptation. A process model should be linked to its relevant context in order to be able to select the applicable

54

Figure 4.1 An Example for Weather as a Contextual Variable That Impacts Control Flow and the Involved Organizational Resources

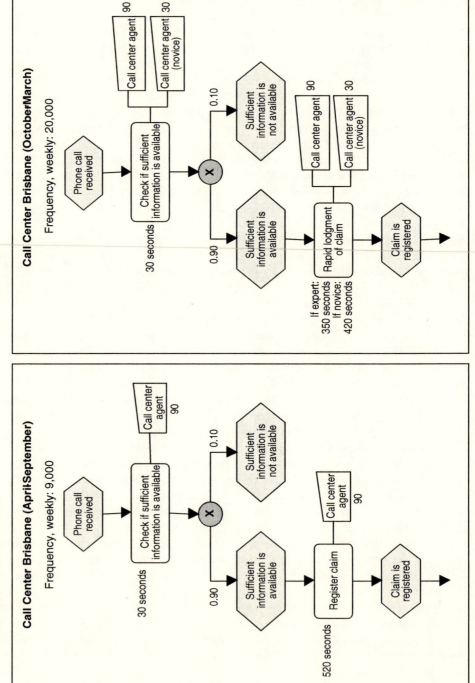

model so that there is a direct relationship between context and the way the process is executed and the selection of the organizational resources. This change can then be anticipated and triggered when the relevant change occurs (e.g., a change in weather). The knowledge of the cause-effect chain (storm season → more damages → increased volume of claims → increase call pickup time → decreased customer satisfaction), the capability to effectively monitor the contextual variable, and the demands in terms of speed of change will determine what context factor will be monitored (e.g., weather changes or call pickup time). Current process modeling techniques, however, provide only little support for modeling the relevant stimuli for change.

We conclude that challenges exist to identify, document, and analyze the requirements for flexibility, namely, factors that drive change *explicitly* within a process model rather than implicitly or outside of it. This will help to better understand the interrelationships between changes in the relevant environmental setting of an organization and the imposed process changes. Overall, such contextualized process landscapes can provide an efficient source for impact analyses. The potential benefits are improved process modifications (as described in our example), better risk assessments, and more agile process executions. The combination of all implicit and explicit circumstantial requirements that impact the situation of a process can be termed the *context* in which a business process is embedded (Schmidt, 2000).

But what exactly constitutes the context of a business process? This question can be broken down into two research questions:

1. What contextual variables have impact on process design and/or execution (e.g., location but not legislation)?
2. How do different values for these variables actually impact process design and subsequent changes (e.g., processes in France require additional quality assurance, but the same processes in Italy do not)?

This in turn leads to the question of how the context of a business process can be conceptualized. We subsume these and related questions under the notion of *contextualized (or context-aware) business processes.*

The objective of our research is to take current process modeling research out of its narrow focus on the control flow and its immediate constructs and to put it into the wider scope of the organizational environment by studying the mutual specification of processes and context. This has been motivated by repeated calls for a research agenda on process modeling that provides a holistic view on problems, issues, and phenomena associated with process modeling (Dalal et al., 2004). The aim of this chapter is to make a first step toward a conceptualization of the context of business processes that may be used as a reference frame for the development of improved and extended, theoretically sound, and practically applicable process modeling techniques. As a second objective, we propose a conceptual integration of context with process models by means of a meta model so as to derive a procedure for identifying context relevant to a given process. This information would then allow us to leverage the formalized notion of context awareness in support of process flexibility, for example, by means of context monitoring or context mining approaches.

BACKGROUND AND RELATED WORK

Our research can be broadly subsumed under the two research streams of process flexibility and context awareness, both of which denote established research areas. We do not claim to be the first to discuss the notion of context. Contextualization has, for instance, been suggested as an abstraction mechanism for conceptual modeling (Analyti et al., 2007). As this and other examples show, we see potential and first evidence that our research can leverage and integrate existing approaches while facilitating a new and extended, and overall more comprehensive, perspective to the field of process modeling. In the following we briefly recapitulate theories and approaches that we deem suitable as a starting point for our investigation.

Process Flexibility

A reasonable argument for the increased consideration of context in the area of business process management is the relationship of an organization to its changing environment. The continuously, and often unprecedentedly appearing turbulences of the situation (e.g., and in addition to the previous examples, changes of national policies, new taxes, terror attacks) in which business processes are embedded and enacted creates a demand for flexibility in the processes themselves in order to be able to cope with such dynamics. At the same time, as already outlined, emerging technologies such as service-oriented architecture or adaptive workflow technology provide increased opportunities for flexible business processes.

In essence, a business process connects different views upon an organization (e.g., data, organizational resources, and information technology). A business process model is typically a graphical depiction of at least the activities and control-flow logic that constitute a business process (Curtis et al., 1992). Additionally, many process models also include information regarding the involved data, actors (either human resources or machines), and potentially other artifacts such as external stakeholders or performance metrics (Recker et al., 2009). Goals that define the purpose of a process may also be included in a business process model (Soffer and Wand, 2005). Usually, hard goals (i.e., functional goals such as purchasing goods in a timely manner) and soft goals (i.e., nonfunctional goals such as minimizing purchase costs) are differentiated.

Recently, a number of research efforts have extended this traditional notion of business process modeling toward agility on the one hand and the integration of some contextual elements on the other. Regarding the former, several approaches have emerged for "adaptive" or "flexible" process designs that are able to cope with changes that may occur during the lifetime of a business process. Rosemann and van der Aalst (2007), for instance, developed a process-reference modeling technique that supports adaptability by extending traditional techniques with variation points. Schmidt (2005) suggested an approach to support process flexibility through the use of Web services, and Narendra (2004) introduced a method to provide support and management for adaptive workflows. Other research has proposed the extension of traditional process modeling approaches with some contextual information. Rosemann and zur Muehlen (2005), for instance, showed how risk modeling can be integrated with event-driven process chains, and Regev et al. (2005) extended the scope of process models to include regulatory perspectives by means of use and misuse cases.

Context Awareness and Understanding

The basic idea of context awareness is not new. However, a commonly accepted comprehensive understanding of this idea is still outstanding. In order to progress the state of research, we adopted the idea of context awareness from related disciplines such as Web systems engineering (Kaltz et al., 2005), mobile applications research (Mikalsen and Kofod-Petersen, 2004), and conceptual modeling (Analyti et al., 2007). In the information systems (IS) discipline, the term "context aware" was coined by Schilit and Theimer (1994). A very generic definition of context is provided by Dey (2001, p. 5), who defines context as "any information that can be used to characterize the situation of an entity." Typically, approaches to incorporating contextual factors into information systems, such as approaches in the mobile applications area, focus around users and their interaction with the systems (Dey, 2001; Schilit and Theimer, 1994). Context in this area of research is often reduced to the notion of locality (e.g., What is the closest restaurant? How do I make a booking? How do I disable incoming phone calls if I am in a meeting room?), and user characteristics (e.g., What type of food does the user of the mobile application like?). Existing frameworks such as the ECOIN framework (Firat et al., 2005) attempt to represent context as properties that can be interpreted based on either the inbuilt framework structures or on very generic ontologies that have no structure prior to design time. However, attempting to introduce these interaction-focused approaches to the area of process flexibility requires that the process is aware of its surroundings *irrespective* of user interactions. In order to facilitate this general awareness in a structured manner, categories and layers could be used to develop a sound understanding of the relevant context.

Regarding approaches for structuring and describing context, we found that in the area of context modeling a substantial amount of research has already been conducted, for example, in the form of context ontologies (Chen et al., 2003). For instance, the Context Ontology Language (Strang et al., 2003) is designed to accommodate selected aspects of context such as temperature, scales, the relative strengths of aspects, and further metadata. It is designed to relate measurements back to the semantics expressed in a system. In terms of limitations for the process flexibility discussion, however, it lacks linkages to causes, both in terms of guiding goals and environmental stimuli.

Another fruitful area for investigating the notion of context awareness in process modeling can be found in the requirements engineering discipline. A number of authors have investigated contextual factors in the engineering, elicitation, documentation, and use of requirements for systems development. A common feature of this work is that goals are often used as a basic concept to distinguish between intrinsic factors (i.e., system or system description–inherent) and extrinsic factors (i.e., those that have an influence but are traditionally not explicitly included). Rolland et al. (1998), for instance, suggest a context-oriented procedure based on objectives to identify requirements chunks in goal-based modeling. The basic idea for determining goals and relevant context in a model is centered around the notion of a requirement chunk, which is a pair <Goal, Scenario> and denotes a potential way of achieving a goal in a given scenario (i.e., one instantiation of the process). As a second example, Yu and Mylopoulos (1994) use the i* framework to capture rationales behind processes relating to goals, tasks, resources, and actors. Their framework allows for the explicit articulation of the interdependencies between a process and (some parts) of its environments, mainly, the stakeholders and related environmental resources.

INTEGRATING CONTEXT WITH PROCESS MODELS

We conclude from our research review that a number of authors have already recognized the need for contextualizing processes, that is, to provide more explicit consideration of the environmental setting of a process. Several researchers have attempted to provide solutions to some of the related challenges, for example, by using goals to identify environmental requirements or by explicitly linking location with user information. While these approaches are stimulating and seem promising, a general and generic understanding of the contextualization of process models is still missing. Next, we approach this challenge and discuss how context information, on a generic level, can be integrated with current approaches to process modeling.

The scope of a business process model, which incorporates external context factors into its design, must be large enough to include factors that may implicitly be recognized by the designer but may not necessarily be constant across the life cycle of the process. For example, the national interest rate has an impact on inventory management strategies, and varies, of course, over time. Relevant context is characterized by the fact that it impacts the structure of the process model (e.g., the control flow, the involved organizational resources, the required data, etc.). Contextual changes that have an impact on the detailed execution of a step in a process (e.g., the sequence in which a number of purchase requests are approved) will not be considered. This also means, of course, that the granularity and scope of the process model influence the relevant context.

The granularity and scope of a business process model are closely linked to the goals of the depicted process. It would appear then that goals could also be used to answer the questions "Is a certain context variable relevant?" and "What potential values of context should be considered?" These goals, when applied to process modeling, determine relationships between process steps in terms of their strategic, operational, or otherwise regulatory steps (Regev et al., 2007). Attempts to incorporate goals into process models have already been made in the past. For example, Kueng and Kawalek (1997) suggest an approach in which goals provide the basis of process definition. Their suggestion combines the identification of goals and corresponding constraints, the definition of measurement criteria, and the decomposition of goals so that they can be transformed into activities. Khomyakov and Bider (2001) suggest a state-oriented view of processes that focuses the changes that each activity introduces to the given process. They also propose that each change brings the process closer to its goal, that is, its final state. They represent a process model as a trajectory in the space of all possible states.

It thus follows, as in related approaches in the requirements engineering discipline, that the use of the notion of process goals is promising for identifying and integrating context in a process model. By examining why a process exists and what the objectives and goals of the process are, the context factors that are relevant to the process can be predetermined and modeled at a formal level over and above the typical description levels of organization, data, resource, and information technologies (IT) (Jablonski and Bussler, 1996; Scheer, 2000). By integrating contextual aspects with goal-oriented business process modeling, the flexibility required to handle changing environmental circumstances can be modeled to provide for the determined set of soft goals in relation to the desired hard goals. As an example of incorporating goals into processes with reference to contextual factors, consider the following banking industry example. A bank's overall goal is to provide banking services. In fulfilling this goal, the bank's major objective is to provide shareholders with maximum profit. Many contextual factors must be taken into account in achieving this goal. Arguably, a factor with great impact in this case is the savings/investment (supply and demand) curve. In a situation where more money is being saved in the bank versus money being lent out, the bank would have a short-term soft goal of increasing loans to profit from its cash supplies. This short-term soft goal is linked to both context, that is, time frame or interest rate of the national bank, and the overall strategic goal, that is, maximizing profit. The chain of events needed to increase loans may be modeled formally by a business process model, which relates the current context (demand-supply relationship) to the identified soft goals and proposes required process changes, if necessary.

In order to introduce and better understand the notion of context in process modeling, we refer back to the understanding of a "business process" as a structured flow of activities that supports business goals and is facilitated by data, supported by applications, and enacted by organizational resources (Harmon, 2003; Sharp and McDermott, 2001). It requires business objects as input (e.g., raw material, an incoming invoice) and transforms them within the process to outputs (e.g., a final product, a paid invoice). The core of a process is its control flow, that is, the temporal and semantic relationships between the activities of a process. Various transition conditions can be used to specify this control flow.

The business process meta-model (Figure 4.2) captures these elements and their relationships in detail. This meta-model is based on the model developed by zur Muehlen (2004). The separation of the "core" process model elements into control flow, data, application, and resource is inspired

Figure 4.2   **Extended Business Process Meta Model**

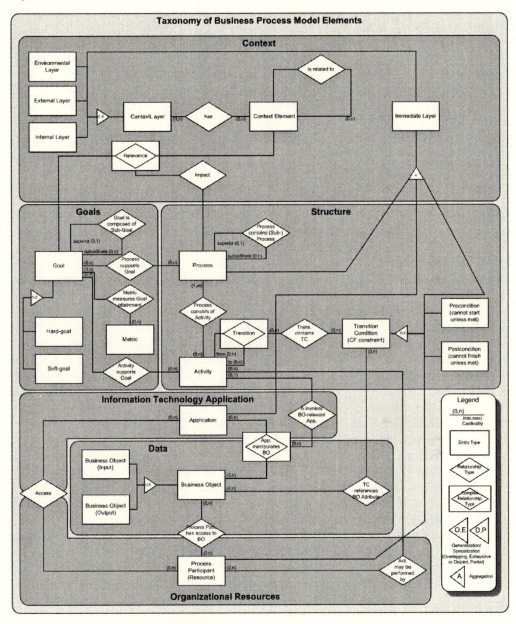

Source: Based on zur Muehlen, 2004.

by the perspectives originally proposed by Jablonski and Bussler (1996) in the mobile framework, which has emerged as the standard reference for distinguishing core elements in process modeling (see, e.g., Russell et al., 2005; Russell, ter Hofstede et al., 2006; Scheer, 2000; van der Aalst et al., 2003). This meta model has also been used in prior research to suggest the incorporation of process-related risk symbols into process models (Rosemann and zur Muehlen, 2005). Our dis-

Table 4.1

Popular Process Modeling Techniques and Supported Perspectives

Technique	Control flow	Data	Application	Resource
Extended Event-driven Process Chains (eEPC)	+	+	+	+
Business Process Modeling Notation (BPMN)	+	+/–	+/–	+
Petri Nets	+	–	–	–
IDEF3	+	+/–	–	–
Yet Another Workflow Language (YAWL)	+	+	+/–	+
Unified Modeling Language Activity Diagrams (UML AD)	+	+	–	+/–

cussion of the relevance of goals to process modeling (Khomyakov and Bider, 2001; Kueng and Kawalek, 1997; Soffer and Wand, 2005) further includes hard and soft goals as relevant elements and shows how context is related to the goals of a process.

Our meta model in Figure 4.2 describes how the notion of context can be integrated with traditional perspectives and elements in process models. It shows how goals determine which of the (potentially unlimited) sets of contextual elements in the environment of a process is *relevant* in the sense of being a factor in how well a process achieves a determined set of goals. The next section of this chapter discusses in more detail the elements in the "context" part of the meta model.

As the discussion above indicates, context is a very comprehensive concept. A large variety of elements and variables can be imagined to influence the way a process achieves its goals. The range of context elements and variables can hence potentially be unlimited. Accordingly, we suggest an approach to structure the range of context elements into disjoint categories (i.e., context subtypes). This will allow conceptualizing and operationalizing different types of context. As the meta model shows, we propose a taxonomy that divides the different facets of context into four layers.

We call all elements that are directly related to the traditional focus on control flow information (e.g., control flow, data, application, resources) the *immediate context* of a business process. As previously indicated, existing process modeling researchers (e.g., in the workflow area) typically consider exactly these elements as a standard process description in their studies (Jablonski and Bussler, 1996), for instance, in the definition of exception-handling procedures in workflow models (Russell, van der Aalst et al., 2006). In order to determine how current process modeling techniques support capturing context, they can be differentiated by the degrees to which they are able to capture information that goes beyond this traditional description of control flow, that is, the sequence of activities and events/states, including required transition conditions, the related data, resource, and application. Table 4.1 provides an overview of the components of this immediate context that are supported in popular process modeling techniques. In this table, a "+" indicates direct support for a context element, a "+/–" indicates partial support, and a "–" indicates a lack of support. Extended Event-driven Process Chains (eEPCs), for instance, provide a means of integrating data models with process models (Scheer, 2000) and as such provide explicit and comprehensive support for the data perspective in process models. BPMN, on the other hand, restricts its support for the articulation of process-related data to the modeling of "data objects" with which function may be annotated. Yet, no information about data structure, data types, or data relationships can be articulated. Thus, BPMN's support for this perspective is only partial.

From Table 4.1 we conclude that existing techniques focus on different aspects of business processes and their immediate context. Hence, they only suit selected perspectives and objectives. In particular, we observe a missing consideration of contextual aspects that transcend the traditional close proximity to regular control flow. As a counterexample, eEPCs, for instance, can be extended to support the explicit representation of business-related risks in process models (Rosemann and zur Muehlen, 2005). Across all process modeling techniques, however, we observe a lack of consideration for further contextual elements beyond the traditional immediate context in a structured way. This in turn hinders the development of advanced process models that provide an enhanced ability to conceptualize, communicate, and understand business processes and their context of operation.

A FRAMEWORK FOR UNDERSTANDING CONTEXT IN PROCESS MODELING

In order to provide a structure for research on context-aware process models that extends the focus beyond elements within the immediate context, we propose a stratified layer framework that extends the scope of process modeling by incorporating and differentiating four types of context—immediate, internal, external, and environmental—into the concentric layers of an *onion model*.

This onion model can be interpreted as an intuitive graphical description of a concept derived from cybernetics and systems theory. It depicts embedded layers surrounding organizational processes as dynamic systems (Wiener, 1948). We have turned to cybernetics as a theoretical foundation for our onion model for four main reasons. First, cybernetics essentially is a model to describe the formal structure of regulatory systems (von Bertalanffy, 1968), such as organizations. Second, it has been suggested that processes themselves are regulatory systems (Regev et al., 2005). Third, cybernetics as an approach to understanding organizations stresses the importance of uncertainty, organizational complexity, and dynamics. Fourth, some of the well-established process modeling techniques (e.g., eEPCs) were originally based on principles of cybernetics and systems theory (Scheer, 2000). It thus appears reasonable that an onion model drawing on similar principles can be useful for understanding the interrelationships between an organizational system and its environment, and how these interrelationships affect complexity and dynamics, in short, the flexibility of processes within the system. Such models are widespread in related disciplines such as management science (Rüegg-Stürm, 2005), and in fact, a similar onion model has previously been used in the process modeling area to identify and display the relationships between different types of stakeholder roles relevant to business process fit (Alexander, 2004).

The core of our onion model comprises the processes and its immediate contextual variables. While such a process could be seen as a well-defined and executable sequence of steps and involved resources, it is heavily impacted by its context. The further we move out of this core of the onion model, the more broadly we consider relevant context and elements that potentially impact this process. A second layer comprises the system organization and all of the elements that facilitate the execution of a process. Again, the organization as such can be seen as an open and self-regulating system. However, it will be impacted by its relationships with elements external to this system (layer 3) and the overall environment in which the organization is embedded (layer 4).

Figure 4.3 shows a populated onion model, which serves as a taxonomy and can be used to identify, classify, understand, and integrate relevant context with business process models. Our onion model is populated in each layer with *exemplary* contextual factors. We have identified these factors in our exploration of current process modeling projects in large Australian organizations (Raduescu et al., 2006), most notably in case studies of the coffee and airline industries (e.g., Rosemann et al., 2006). As a first attempt, the taxonomy provides an initial reference on which

Figure 4.3 **Onion Model for Context Classification and Typing**

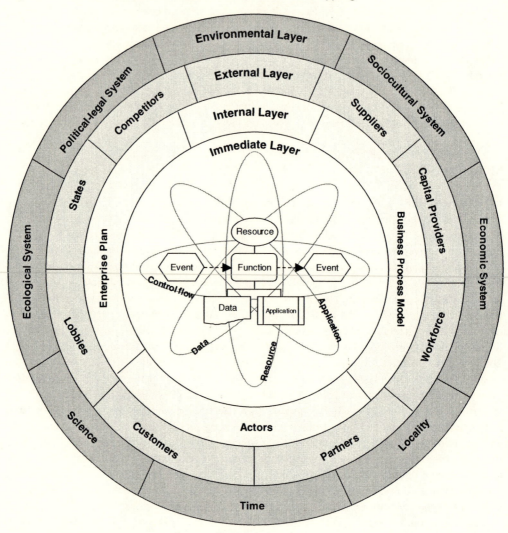

Source: Rosemann et al., 2006.

future research in the area of process contextualization can be based. As described above, we differentiate four types of context, based on their proximity to the "core" business process (i.e., the traditional perspectives in a process model that we have labeled immediate context). Below, we introduce and discuss these different types, starting with the immediate context that, as noted above, is the traditional core of business process models.

Immediate Context

The immediate context of a business process includes those elements that go beyond the constructs that constitute pure control flow, and covers those elements that directly facilitate the execution of a process. Due to this central role, elements tend to be well considered in existing business process modeling techniques (see Table 4.1). These elements are typically essential to the understanding and execution of a business process (e.g., What *data* do I require? Which organizational *resource* is in charge of the next activity? What *application* supports this process step?). Following existing classifications (Jablonski and Bussler, 1996; Scheer, 2000), the immediate context includes data (input, output), organizational resources (e.g., organizational unit, group, position, person), and IT and related applications (e.g., middleware, Web server, database system). Without any contextual changes, the elements that constitute the immediate system would be sufficient for the execution of a business process. This conception remains the prevalent approach to process modeling to date; however, we suggest extending this view toward a wider perspective on the environment of a business process.

Internal Context

The immediate system (the process) is embedded in the wider system of an organization. Various elements of an organization have indirect influence on a business process, and we call this second layer the internal context. The internal context covers information on the internal environment of an organization that impacts the process. Following the stratified layer model of an organizational system and its environment as used in Rüegg-Stürm (2005), the internal system of an organization incorporates elements such as resources, norms and values, concerns and interests, strategy, structure, and culture. These categories cover, for example, the corporate strategy (enterprise plan) and related process objectives. A change from a quality-focused strategy to a cost-cutting strategy, for instance, will have an impact on a broad range of business processes (e.g., elimination of quality control activities, scaling down of special resources). Policies are another important internal context variable as they are the main constraining factor on business process design activities. An explicit understanding of the effect of a policy on a process provides not only guiding information for a process improvement discussion, but can be equally important information for an intended change of a (counterproductive) policy. As can be seen, the internal context captures all elements that are part of the organizational system in which a process is embedded. Consequently, typical further examples for internal context variables are the main internal stakeholders in an organization and their risk perceptions, communication, and logistical infrastructures (e.g., regional distribution of factories) and financial and other resources (legal experts, R&D). Especially financial and human resources can form an important enabling or constraining factor in the capability to change. Moving from the immediate context of a process to the next layer of a surrounding system can lead, of course, to a system different from the typical boundaries of an organization. For collaborative business processes that span multiple organizations, for example, the internal context would be the sum of the involved organizations.

External Context

The external context captures elements that are part of an even wider system whose design and behavior is beyond the control sphere of an organization. Yet, these elements still reside within the business network in which an organization operates. Although this context is not in immediate proximity to the day-to-day business operations of the organization, it still has a relatively high impact on the way the organization designs and executes its business processes. Drawing again on the view of an organization as a system within external and environmental systems (Rüegg-Stürm, 2005), the external context comprises, among others, categories of context elements related to suppliers, competitors, investors, and customers. External context variables can further be identified from frameworks such as the "Five Forces" model (Porter, 1979) and may include the abovementioned stakeholders (e.g., suppliers, customers, financial and logistical service providers) as well as their strategies, demands, resources, and failures. Furthermore, it includes factors specific to the industry (e.g., overall demand for the services of an industry, technological innovations) and regulations such as industry-specific practices (e.g., supply chain management practices). In general, external context often demands the compliance of internal business processes and as such provides a set of constraints that have to be considered and continuously observed in order to achieve conformance objectives in addition, or as a substitution, to performance objectives (Parkinson and Baker, 2005).

Environmental Context

The environmental context, as the outermost layer, resides beyond the business network in which the organization is embedded but nevertheless poses a contingency effect on the business processes. It captures the overall environment as a system with comprehensive boundaries. In management science, an organizational system's environment is often characterized by the categories society, nature, technology, and economy, in each of which contextual variables of relevance may reside (Rüegg-Stürm, 2005). These environmental variables include factors such as weather (e.g., increasing call volume during storm season), time (e.g., different business operating models on Sundays or before Christmas), and workforce-related factors (e.g., overall shortage or strike). A well-known example is the U.S. Homeland Security Advisory System with its alert levels green (low), blue (guarded), yellow (elevated), orange (high), and red (extreme). Each of these levels is clearly associated with a comprehensive set of process changes within the relevant departments and armed forces. While some of these environmental variables may change regularly and can have a very strong impact on a business process (consider our motivating example and the impact of weather conditions), many of these variables and especially their current values can have a very long life span (e.g., availability of natural resources in a country, currency, political system, preferred business language). Other factors can be attributed to the macroeconomic setting in which an organization operates. Examples include legislative regulations such as national policies (e.g., workplace regulations) and other requirements (e.g., Sarbanes Oxley, Basel 2).

Having introduced four different layers of contextual categories and examples of elements within these categories, it is necessary to note that interrelationships may occur between the elements in the various layers. This means in turn that a context element does not necessarily have a direct impact on a process. Instead, the impact may be of an indirect nature due to existing interrelationships with other elements in the same or more inward layer. At least three different forms of links can be observed.

1. An element in the same or a more inward context layer can mediate the impact of a context element.
2. An element in the same or a more inward context layer can moderate the impact of a context element.
3. An element in the same or a more inward context layer can mitigate the impact of a context element.

As our following case study illustrates, examples for these indirect effects and links between contextual elements may take many forms and, while outside the scope of this chapter, it would be a stimulating research challenge to explore these relationships further.

Figure 4.4   **Procedure for Context Identification**

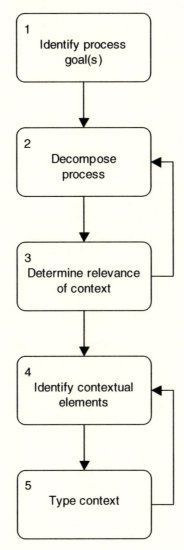

APPLYING THE FRAMEWORK

Procedure

Above we have described an onion model that can be used to classify different types of context that are relevant to business processes. The question that arises next is how to use this framework in order to identify which of the potentially unlimited types of contextual elements is relevant and should be considered and monitored so as to anticipate the necessary process changes.

Following the meta model shown in Figure 4.2, we suggest that the notion of process goals allows us to reason about potential contextual elements that are relevant to the process and should thus be included in the process model. Understanding a process as a set of states with the ultimate aim of reaching a final state (Khomyakov and Bider, 2001), we can use the notion of hard goals and soft goals as proposed by Soffer (2005) to distinguish between the set of information relevant to achieving a process goal that is contained in the traditional description of a process (i.e., in the immediate context) and the set of information relevant to achieving the goal but not explicitly captured in the description (and thus contextual). Having identified these contextual elements, our onion model shown in Figure 4.3 can then be used to type these elements based on their proximity to day-to-day business process operations.

In a basic format, a procedure for deriving relevant context information to be included in a process model should consist of the following steps. Figure 4.4 gives the overall procedure.

1. Identify the hard goals and soft goals related to a given process and their appropriate measures.
2. Decompose a given process according to the goals in a set of goal-relevant information that is either immediate (i.e., information that is contained in the traditional process specification) or a set of goal-relevant information that is not contained in the traditional process definition, that is, extrinsic (internal, external, or environmental).
3. Determine the impact of goal-relevant, extrinsic information on the achievement of the goal to determine the relevance of the contextual element. Repeat this step for each set of goal-relevant information that is extrinsic to the traditional process description.
4. Identify contextual elements and explore potential interrelationships with other contextual elements that may mediate, moderate, or mitigate the impact of the identified contextual elements.
5. Type contextual elements with the help of the onion model and identify relevant value ranges. If required, repeat steps four and five until all contextual elements have been identified and typed.

We use a case study to show how this procedure can be applied.

Case Study

In our study of current process modeling projects in large Australian organizations (Raduescu et al., 2006), we explored the ticket reservation and check-in process of a major Australian airline. This process, while seemingly stable, is exposed to a large number of contextual impacts and is thus regularly required to change "on the fly."

Usually, the process is triggered when a customer selects a destination, along with departure and return dates and times. An online form can be used to draft an itinerary based on certain preferences such as departure times, type of plane, overall costs, and so on. After confirmation and electronic payment an eTicket is issued, which is an electronic version of a traditional paper ticket. It allows travelers to check in at the airport using photo identification and, where applicable, to check in and select available seats over the Internet from home or at dedicated "quick check-in" terminals at the airport. Normally, traditional counters are also available for check-in. Independent of the check-in option selected, at some stage a traveler is required to undergo safety checks, such as passport controls for international flights and baggage checks before boarding the aircraft. Figure 4.5 gives the corresponding process model. In this model, parts of the process that are subject to change due to variations in the context are highlighted gray.

The process typically runs smoothly in regular business environments. However, certain environmental situations may occur that require the process to change. For instance, staffing levels for

Figure 4.5   **Airline Process Model with Context Consideration**

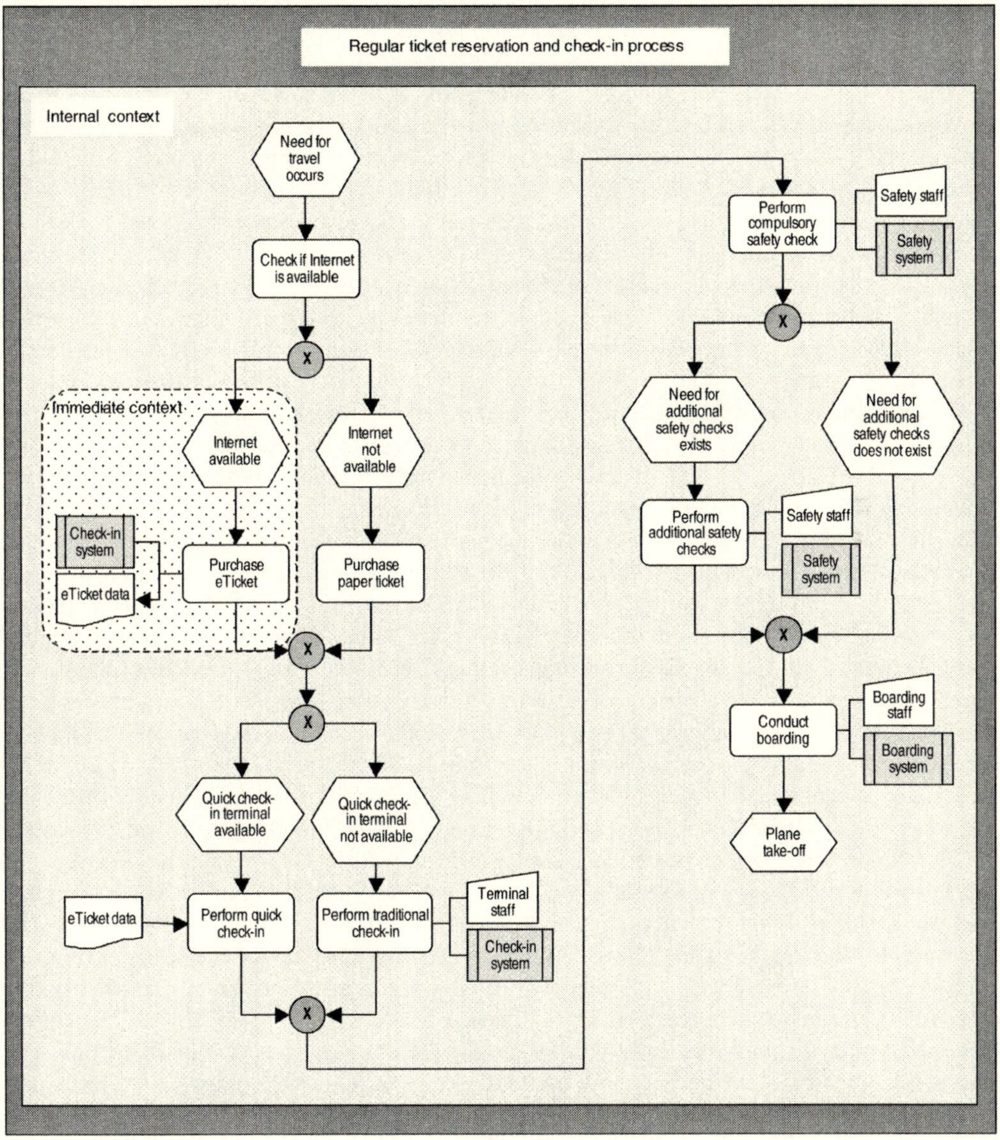

traditional check-in counters are estimated based on an average "eTicket to paper ticket" ratio or the availability of quick check-in terminals. Weather conditions, server breakdown, holiday season, system failures, and other circumstances may lead to more traditional check-ins than expected and/or serviced. Consequently, several mitigation strategies need to be executed in order to avoid having customers miss deadlines due to large check-in queues. First, more check-in counters need to be staffed. Second, business and first class check-in counters should be used to process economy passenger check-ins as well. Third, the lodgment time of check-ins has to be reduced. Usually, this is achieved by disallowing seating modifications or special seating requests.

Referring back to the procedure for identifying contextual impacts, we can investigate the above-described process as follows. First, we start by identifying the process goal (minimize overall time for ticket reservation and check-in). Therefore, we assume a main objective, namely, "Minimize throughput time" (Step 1: identify process goals). According to Rolland et al. (1998), we consider the relationship between a goal and a corresponding process as a requirement chunk in order to decompose and analyze (Step 2: decompose process) both goal and process simultaneously until we are eventually able to derive contextual elements having an impact on the subprocess with respect to its subgoal. The identified chunk may look like <"Minimize throughput time," "Airline ticket reservation and check-in process">. In order to compare the deviation between goal and process, we consider a goal as well as the immediate context of the process as states. Both notions are necessarily comparable since the states a process attains during its execution necessarily affect the states of a goal definition (Soffer and Wand, 2005). For example, the time as part of a goal definition (e.g., within an operationalized goal "online ticket reservation must not take more than ten minutes") is necessarily affected by the path of state changes the reservation process takes for its accomplishment.

The decomposition of the airline ticket reservation and check-in process and the goal of minimizing throughput time reveal more detailed subprocesses and subgoals, so that eventually the immediate context of single functions facilitates the determination of contextual elements potentially occurring within the outer layers of our onion model (Step 3: determine relevance of context). In Figure 4.5, the eEPC shows the highlighted immediate context of the function "purchase eTicket" in sufficient level of detail. From there, contextual elements can be identified by posing the following question: Which elements distinct from the information contained in the immediate context of the function "purchase eTicket" have an impact on the goal "minimize throughput time" (Step 4: identify contextual events). Contextual variables include, for instance, elements affecting the availability of an Internet connection, a properly operating mode of the check-in system as well as the compulsory type and amount of data necessary for a ticket purchase. By applying the categorization and classification of context layers and categories for the typing of contextual elements, the environment in which a process is embedded becomes increasingly tangible and enables the anticipation of potential external triggers and their causal relationships (Step 5: type context). Consider again the immediate context of "purchase eTicket." An internal server crash, for example, would affect the availability of an Internet connection and would occur within the internal context, since it is related to the application system and networking infrastructure of the airline company. A negative effect on the check-in system could be caused by the appearance of a system overload due to too many customers using the system concurrently, which would conceptually be located in a category "customer" in the external layer. According to this procedure the context of a decomposed function or subprocess will successively lead to a clearer and more transparent idea of potential drivers having an impact on the ticket reservation.

By using the procedure, we derived another example of a contextual "impact" on the airline ticket reservation and check-in process that relates to increased safety considerations. An alert system, similar to that used by the U.S. Department of Homeland Security, is installed to distinguish three levels of awareness. Several scenarios (e.g., certain VIPs arrive or depart, major public events, terrorism, etc.) lead to different safety levels that in turn require safety procedures to change. For instance, tests for explosive goods that are usually conducted on a random basis become mandatory, or a second hand-luggage safety check immediately prior to boarding is performed. Furthermore, some flights require additional identification procedures (e.g., biometric data verification for flights to/from the United States). One impact of these procedures is that different staffing levels are required for each case.

This case description raises the question of how the adaptation of the process to changing contexts can be supported and the relevant details explicitly captured and used. The related challenge is to identify different types of contextual influences and determine their consequences for each part of the traditional business process. This in turn allows for comprehensive context monitoring, which enables the early anticipation and execution of required process changes. By examining the chain of events that necessitates changes in the process, reactions can be anticipated based on observations in the early stages of the chain, that is, at best in the environmental context. This demonstrates the importance of understanding relationships between contextual variables. For example, a change in weather conditions (e.g., storm, tsunami, tornado) may lead to an increased number of travelers who wish to reroute their flights on the departure date. The related process changes can be anticipated simply by regularly observing the weather forecast, which in turn enables, for instance, the predetermination of required staffing levels. The same principle holds for later stages of the chain, even if the time frame for process adaptation is shorter. For example, waiting queue dynamics (internal context) can be observed at the terminals in order to establish a potential need for additionally staffed terminals or the opening of business and first class counters to economy class travelers.

In conclusion, based on the reference procedure described in Figure 4.4, we were able to identify, capture, and classify relevant context, in particular, changes within and interrelationships between contexts, and their impact on the business process. In short, studying the goals of a process contributes to determining relevant context layers outside of an organization (i.e., external and environmental). With the knowledge of goals as well as the semantics of the different context layers (that is, the scope of the business process), types of context with a direct impact on the business process *outside* of an organization can be identified by asking questions relevant to given goals (e.g., are weather conditions relevant to achieving the process objective?). In order to establish relevant context *inside* an organization (i.e., in an internal and immediate layer), the direct effects of the context on the immediate layers are determined as well as the effects of external and environmental context upon internal context (e.g., the establishment of new national legislative requirements leading to the modification of organizational policies). Referring to our case of the Australian airline company, Table 4.2 gives some examples of identified context variables that pose an effect, direct or indirect (i.e., mediated, moderated, or mitigated), on the ticket reservation and check-in process. In this table various instances of context are given and described in plain English. Also, the ultimate consequences to the immediate core of a process and related perspectives are enumerated.

Table 4.2 shows the application of the procedure described above to identifying and typing context relevant to the airline process. It further shows how to investigate relationships between the context elements of the different context layers. That is, after establishing relevant contextual elements, the potential relationships between these elements are investigated. For instance, the terror attack on London Heathrow, which in itself appears to bear only small significance to Brisbane airline procedures, has led to the passing of the Patriot Act on a nationwide (namely, environmental) level. The Patriot Act requires organizations in certain industry sectors to revise and extend safety regulations. Hence, the external (i.e., industry sector–specific) contextual system in which an organizational system is embedded, mediates the impact of the environmental contextual variable "passing of the Patriot Act." For the Brisbane-based airline organization, the industry safety regulations have been implemented by internal policies regarding airline safety. This internal contextual information then directly impacts the process-related control flow, data, resources, and applications (see Table 4.2).

Table 4.2

Examples of Context Relevant to the Ticket Reservation and Check-in Process

	Immediate context			Internal context	External context	Environmental context
Control flow	Data	Organization	IT			
	Flight rerouting information	Increased terminal staffing levels				Storm
Additional security checks, repeated execution of safety checks	Increased customer data requirements	Increased security staffing levels	Biometric identification system	Establishment of airline safety policies	Passing of industry safety regulations	Passing of Patriot Act
Focus on eTicket processes, increased customer self-service	Electronic customer and flight data	Increased terminal staffing levels	Web-based reservation and check-in system		Market price changes	
Manual check-in, seat reservation, and safety check processes	Paper-based customer, flight and seating information	Increased terminal and safety staffing levels	Web-based reservation and check-in system not available	System failure		

CONCLUSION

This chapter was motivated by various observations of current challenges in process modeling. While popular process modeling techniques are typically able to adequately handle the core constructs of a process and its immediate context in the form of data, applications, and resources, a wider consideration of contextual information still has only limited support. The present approach to process modeling may be a reason for some of the observable suboptimal designs of business processes in different contexts (e.g., different times of the year, different customers, locations) with a high level of redundancy (e.g., due to multiple process models for different scenarios), significant maintenance efforts (e.g., changing processes at the beginning of each season), low scalability in the case of multiple contextual variables, and in general a poor understanding of the context-process relationship. In order to advance this area of research, we investigated the current body of knowledge and suggested an approach for integrating context into process models. We used a meta model to formalize our idea of how processes and their goals can be used to identify context that is relevant to the process. We also proposed a framework that helps in gaining a better understanding of different types of context and their impact on business processes. We provided a basic procedure model on how to apply the framework for the identification and classification of context. We provided evidence for the applicability of the framework using an airline case study.

A noted limitation of the research described in this chapter stems from the fact that in terms of research, the area of process flexibility and process contextualization is still in the explorative stages. The conceptual integration of our context reference framework with existing process modeling techniques and the development of a corresponding and appropriate notation are currently under way. Furthermore, it remains for our findings to be comprehensively tested with respect to the impact that explicit context consideration in process models has on further dependant variables of interest, such as the perceived understandability of the model, the agility of the described process to react to externally triggered changes, and so forth. However, our case study demonstrates initial evidence for the general applicability of our approach.

Future research will derive extensions of selected popular process modeling techniques (e.g., EPC, BPMN) in order to explicitly integrate the different types of context that have been identified into existing business process modeling techniques. Such enhanced models have the potential to provide the conceptual foundation for truly agile processes, in which, for example, process mining techniques could play an important role in monitoring and evaluating relevant contextual variables and events (e.g., weather) and triggering the requisite process changes. Our work provides a theoretical reference cornerstone upon which different relevant types of context can be captured and monitored so that a stronger, potentially automated, link can be established between the stimuli for change and the reaction to the change within a business process model.

REFERENCES

Alexander, I.F. 2004. A better fit—Characterising the stakeholders. In J. Grundspenkis and M. Kirikova (eds.), *CaiSE'04 Workshops,* Vol. 2, 215–223. Proceedings of the Sixteenth Conference on Advanced Information Systems Engineering, Riga Technical University, Riga, Latvia, June 7–11.

Analyti, A.; Theodorakis, M.; Spyratos, N.; and Constantopoulos, P. 2007. Contextualization as an independent abstraction mechanism for conceptual modeling. *Information Systems,* 32, 1 (March), 24–60.

Arnold, R., and Bohner, S. 1996. *Software Change Impact Analysis.* Los Alamitos, CA: IEEE Computer Society Press.

Balabko, P.; Wegmann, A.; Ruppen, A.; and Clément, N. 2005. Capturing design rationale with functional decomposition of roles in business processes modeling. *Software Process: Improvement and Practice,* 10, 4, 379–392.

Bider, I. 2005. Masking flexibility behind rigidity: Notes on how much flexibility people are willing to cope with. In J. Castro and E. Teniente (eds.), *Proceedings of the CAiSE'05 Workshops,* Vol. 1, 7–18. FEUP, Porto, Portugal.

Chen, H.; Finin, T.; and Joshi, A. 2003. An ontology for context-aware pervasive computing environments. *Knowledge Engineering Review,* 18, 3, 197–207.

Curtis, B.; Kellner, M.I.; and Over, J. 1992. Process modeling. *Communications of the ACM,* 35, 9, 75–90.

Dalal, N.P.; Kamath, M.; Kolarik, W.J.; and Sivaraman, E. 2004. Toward an integrated framework for modeling enterprise processes. *Communications of the ACM,* 47, 3, 83–87.

Dey, A.K. 2001. Understanding and using context. *Personal and Ubiquitous Computing,* 5, 1, 4–7.

Firat, A., Madnick, S., and Manola, F. 2005. Multi-dimensional ontology views via contexts in the ECOIN semantic interoperability framework. In P. Shvaiko, J. Euzenat, A. Leger, D.L. McGuinness, and H. Wache (eds.), *Contexts and Ontologies: Theory, Practice, and Applications. Papers from the 2005 AAAI Workshop,* 1–8. Menlo Park, CA: AAAI Press.

Gartner, Inc. 2010. *Leading in Times of Transition: The 2010 CIO Agenda.* EXP Premier Report, January 2010. Stamford, CT: Gartner, Inc. Press.

Harmon, P. 2003. *Business Process Change: A Manager's Guide to Improving, Redesigning, and Automating Processes.* Boston: Morgan Kaufmann.

Jablonski, S., and Bussler, C. 1996. *Workflow Management. Modeling Concepts, Architecture, and Implementation.* London: Thomson Computer Press.

Kaltz, J.W.; Ziegler, J.; and Lohmann, S. 2005. Context-aware web engineering: Modeling and applications. *Revue d'Intelligence Artificielle,* 19, 3, 439–458.

Khomyakov, M., and Bider, I. 2001. Achieving workflow flexibility through taming the chaos. *Journal of Conceptual Modeling,* 21 (August), 1–14.

Knoll, K., and Jarvenpaa, S.L. 1994. Information technology alignment or fit in highly turbulent environments: The concept of flexibility. In J.W. Ross (ed.), *Proceedings of the 1994 Computer Personnel Research Conference on Reinventing IS,* 1–14. Alexandria, VA: ACM Press.

Kueng, P., and Kawalek, P. 1997. Goal-based business process models: Creation and evaluation. *Business Process Management Journal,* 3, 1, 17–38.

Mikalsen, M., and Kofod-Petersen, A. 2004. Representing and reasoning about context in a mobile environment. In S. Schulz and T. Roth-Berghofer (eds.), *First International Workshop on Modeling and Retrieval of Context* (MRC'04), 25–35. University of Ulm, Germany, September.

Mulholland, A.; Thomas, C.S.; and Kurchina, P. 2006. *Mashup Corporations: The End of Business as Usual.* New York: Evolved Technologist Press.

Narendra, N.C. 2004. Flexible support and management of adaptive workflow processes. *Information Systems Frontiers,* 6, 3, 247–262.

Parkinson, M.J.A., and Baker, N.J. 2005. IT and enterprise governance. *Information Systems Control Journal,* 3, 17–21.

Ploesser, K.; Janiesch, C.; Recker, J.; and Rosemann, M. 2009. Context change archetypes: Understanding the impact of context change on business processes. Paper presented at the 20th Australasian Conference on Information Systems, Melbourne, Australia.

Ploesser, K.; Recker, J.; and Rosemann, M. 2010. Building a methodology for context-aware business processes: Insights from an exploratory case study. Paper presented at the 18th European Conference on Information Systems, Pretoria, South Africa.

Pine, B.J. 1999. *Mass Customization: The New Frontier in Business Competition.* Boston: Harvard Business School Press.

Porter, M.E. 1979. How competitive forces shape strategy. *Harvard Business Review,* 57, 2, 137–145.

Quinn, J.B. 1992. *Intelligent Enterprise: A Knowledge and Service Based Paradigm for Industry.* New York: Free Press.

Raduescu, C.; Tan, H.M.; Jayaganesh, M.; Bandara, W.; zur Muehlen, M.; and Lippe, S. 2006. A framework of issues in large process modeling projects. In J. Ljungberg and M. Andersson (eds.), *Proceedings of the Fourteenth European Conference on Information Systems,* 1594–1605. Göteborg: Association for Information Systems.

Ramesh, B., and Jarke, M. 2001. Toward reference models for requirements traceability. *IEEE Transactions on Software Engineering,* 27, 1, 58–93.

Recker, J.; Rosemann, M.; Indulska, M.; and Green, P. (2009). Business process modeling: A comparative analysis. *Journal of the Association for Information Systems,* 10, 333-363.

Regev, G.; Alexander, I.F.; and Wegmann, A. 2005. Modelling the regulative role of business processes with use and misuse cases. *Business Process Management Journal,* 11, 6, 695–708.

Regev, G.; Bider, I.; and Wegmann, A. 2007. Defining business process flexibility with the help of invariants. *Software Process: Improvement and Practice,* 12, 1, 65–79.

Rolland, C.; Souveyet, C.; and Ben Achour, C. 1998. Guiding goal modeling using scenarios. *IEEE Transactions on Software Engineering,* 24, 12, 1055–1071.

Rosemann, M., and van der Aalst, W.M.P. 2007. A configurable reference modelling language. *Information Systems,* 32, 1, 1–23.

Rosemann, M., and zur Muehlen, M. 2005. Integrating risks in business process models. In B. Campbell, J. Underwood, and D. Bunker (eds.), *Proceedings of the Sixteenth Australasian Conference on Information Systems.* Sydney: Australasian Association for Information Systems.

Rosemann, M.; Recker, J.; Flender, C.; and Ansell, P. 2006. Context-awareness in business process design. In S. Spencer and A. Jenkins (eds.), *Proceedings of the Seventeenth Australasian Conference on Information Systems.* Adelaide: Australasian Association for Information Systems.

Rüegg-Stürm, J. 2005. *The New St. Gallen Management Model: Basic Categories of an Integrated Management.* Hampshire, UK: Palgrave Macmillan.

Russell, N.; van der Aalst, W.M.P.; ter Hofstede, A.H.M.; and Edmond, D. 2005. Workflow resource patterns: Identification, representation, and tool support. In Ó. Pastor and J. Falcão e Cunha (eds.), *Proceedings of the Seventeenth International Conference on Advanced Information Systems Engineering* (CaiSE'05), *Lecture Notes in Computer Science,* Vol. 3520, 216–232. Porto, Portugal: Springer.

Russell, N.; van der Aalst, W.M.P.; and ter Hofstede, A.H.M. 2006. Workflow exception patterns. In E. Dubois and K. Pohl (eds.), *Proceedings of the Eighteenth International Conference on Advanced Information Systems Engineering* (CaiSE'06), *Lecture Notes in Computer Science,* Vol. 4001, 288–302. Klagenfurt, Austria: Springer.

Russell, N.; ter Hofstede, A.H.M.; van der Aalst, W.M.P.; and Mulyar, N.A. 2006. Workflow control-flow patterns: A revised view. *BPM Center Report,* No. BPM-06–22. BPMcenter.org.

Scheer, A.-W. 2000. *ARIS—Business Process Modeling,* 3d ed. Berlin: Springer Berlin.

Schilit, B.N., and Theimer, M.M. 1994. Disseminating active map information to mobile hosts. *IEEE Network,* 8, 5, 22–32.

Schmidt, A. 2000. Implicit human computer interaction through context. *Personal Technologies,* 4, 2–3, 191–199.

Schmidt, R. 2005. Flexible support of inter-organizational business processes using web services. In J. Castro and E. Teniente (eds.), *Proceedings of the CAiSE'05 Workshops,* Vol. 1, 51–58. FEUP, Porto, Portugal.

Sharp, A., and McDermott, P. 2001. *Workflow Modeling: Tools for Process Improvement and Application Development.* Boston: Artech House.

Soffer, P. 2005. Scope analysis: Identifying the impact of changes in business process models. *Software Process: Improvement and Practice,* 10, 4, 393–402.

Soffer, P. and Wand, Y. 2005. On the notion of soft-goals in business process modeling. *Business Process Management Journal,* 11, 6, 663–679.

Strang, T.; Linnhoff-Popien, C.; and Frank, K. 2003. CoOL: A context ontology language to enable contextual interoperability. In J.-B. Stefani, I. Demeure, and D. Hagimont (eds.), *Distributed Applications and Interoperable Systems, Lecture Notes in Computer Science,* Vol. 2893, 236–247. Heidelberg: Springer Berlin.

van der Aalst, W.M.P., Rosemann, M. and Dumas, M. 2007. Deadline-based escalation in process-aware information systems. *Decision Support Systems,* 43, 2, 492–511.

van der Aalst, W.M.P.; ter Hofstede, A.H.M.; Kiepuszewski, B.; and Barros, A.P. 2003. Workflow patterns. *Distributed and Parallel Databases,* 14, 3, 5–51.

von Bertalanffy, L. 1968. *General System Theory: Foundations, Development, Applications.* New York: George Braziller.

Wiener, N. 1948. *Cybernetics or Control and Communication in the Animal and the Machine.* Cambridge, MA: MIT Press.

Yu, E.S.K., and Mylopoulos, J. 1994. Using goals, rules, and methods to support reasoning in business process re-engineering. In *Proceedings of the Twenty-Seventh Hawaii International Conference on System Sciences* (HICSS'94–4), Vol. IV: *Information Systems: Collaboration Technology, Organizational Systems and Technology,* 234–243. Maui, Hawaii, January 4–7.

zur Muehlen, M. 2004. *Workflow-Based Process Controlling: Foundation, Design, and Application of Workflow-driven Process Information Systems.* Berlin: Logos.

PART II

SOCIOTECHNICAL SYSTEMS FOCUS: PROCESSES

CHAPTER 5

STAFFING WEB-ENABLED E-COMMERCE PROJECTS AND PROGRAMS

FRED NIEDERMAN

Abstract: Electronic commerce has continued steady growth since the beginning of the new century. While the methods for providing e-commerce products and services are largely invisible to consumers, behind-the-scenes technologies and staff are needed to build and maintain the systems upon which they are based. This chapter examines aspects of the work performed to support e-commerce. It examines how organizations structure the projects and teams within which e-commerce work is performed and the skill sets of e-commerce employees. The chapter concludes that no one method of organizing the processing of work, or the portfolio of staff skills has yet come to be dominant.

Keywords: MIS Personnel, E-Commerce Personnel, Teams, Skills, Qualitative Methods

BACKGROUND

The Internet, since its launch in the late 1960s, has significantly changed the world. It connects hundreds of thousands of different networks from over 200 countries. Millions of people working in science, education, government, and business professions utilize the Internet to exchange information or perform business transactions. According to Internet World Stats (2009), the number of Internet users around the world tops 1.1 billion. More than 211 million of these are in the United States and 130 million in China. The Internet has penetrated people's everyday life, altered the way companies do business, created new services and jobs, and changed the way people work.

E-commerce is a major and growing portion of the U.S. retail economy. This has led to penetration of the Internet by "clicks and mortar" companies with both Web and traditional presence. The Census Bureau of the U.S. Department of Commerce announced recently that, "the estimate of U.S. retail e-commerce sales for the second quarter of 2004, not adjusted for seasonal, holiday, and trading-day differences, was $15.7 billion, an increase of 23.1 percent (±3.5 percent) from the second quarter of 2003" (U.S. Department of Commerce, 2004). Using Internet technology, companies often find new outlets for their products and services abroad (Quelch and Klein, 1996) by linking directly to suppliers, business partners, and customers.

We frequently observe e-commerce programs and projects gone awry.[1] Burke and Morrison (2001) have documented the mechanics of how this happens. Organizations have a tendency to vastly underestimate the difficulty in shifting from a static Web page that serves basically as an automated brochure to a dynamic Web program that provides online information exchange and facilitates real-time transactions. Perhaps they also underestimate the difference between Web-enabled projects and those involving "traditional" management information systems (MIS) development—aimed at centralized mainframe or personal computer utilization or at decentralized client-server applications on proprietary and limited networked systems. Producing Web-enabled software requires the convergence of a number of components including existing organizational infrastructure, new and enhanced hardware and software designed for use with the Web, sensitivity to the needs and preferences of external users and customers, and skills and methods for producing and maintaining these organizational assets.

This chapter focuses on staffing issues regarding Web-enabled e-commerce projects. We expect that the creation of Web-enabled services would add complexity to the task faced by information technology (IT) workers (Niederman and Hu, 2003). This complexity would come from inter-actions with external users/customers as well as interaction between a larger array of technical components than that found in traditional mainframe and even client-server architectures. In the Web-enabled domain, users are largely external to the firm; thus, the organization has less leverage for recovering from poor design with training and "workarounds." Users in some types of Web-enabled programs are unknown to the organization (e.g., Amazon does not know individual users or their profiles prior to their commencing interactions) and, thus, have more variety of potential usage patterns and needs. The sheer number of users in this sort of Web-enabled program may preclude even the possibility of examining the whole range of potential needs and patterns across all user types. Web-enabled programs are likely to cut across internal departments within a firm as users expect seamless response to their transactions and are not usually inclined to navigate through an organizational bureaucracy to achieve their purposes. In addition, in order to invoke Web-enabled projects, organizations may not choose to retrofit existing information systems for up-to-date Web capabilities. Thus the IT workers will have the additional challenge of coordinat-ing both Web-based interfaces and source information coming from a wide range of "legacy" systems. In research based on job advertisements, Gallivan et al. (2004) found some shifting in the desired skill set of MIS job applicants as a whole; however, no analysis was performed to indicate whether this was due to the growth of a new category of e-commerce workers or a broader shift in MIS work and tasks overall.

The purpose of this study is to specifically investigate staffing roles and skills in moving to the Web-enabled domain as well as to investigate contextual issues regarding the work environment for e-commerce staff. Before addressing these issues, however, we begin by defining more care-fully what we mean by Web-enabled programs.

Defining Web-Enabled Programs and Projects

In this study, "Web-enabled" refers to three distinct but related types of programs. These are first organizational programs that use information technology to link their operations with suppli-ers or other business customers, which are frequently referred to as B2B (business-to-business e-commerce). The second type of organizational programs links the organization directly to end customers. These are frequently referred to as B2C (business-to-consumer e-commerce). Note that where the "customer" is another company, such as a distributor or retail outlet, the applica-tions are likely to have more commonality with the business to supplier than with the business to end customer in terms of the nature of the users. The third type of organizational program is the "intranet," which uses the tools of the Web, browsers, servers, home pages, and the like, but is typically used within a firm and restricted to organizational employees. It thus resembles the other Web-enabled programs on the "back end" in terms of technical structure and programming tools and techniques, but focuses on a more limited range of end users who may share lexicon, culture, goals, and other attributes that may be heterogeneous when dealing with individuals outside of one's own boundaries. Though conceivably a fourth type of Web-enabled business, the virtual community could also be considered a Web-enabled enterprise; many of these institutions intermix professional project activity with user-developed content. Although these continue to evolve and some increasingly resemble B2C sites, we viewed these as outside the scope of this particular investigation.

We expect generally that e-commerce work within organizations will be organized into a set of interconnected projects. The notion of an e-commerce project here is intended to be broad and inclusive. Some project theorists, notably Evaristo and van Fenema (1999), distinguish between programs (consisting of sets of related projects) and individual projects. However, in practice, large projects may have many interrelated aspects or "subprojects" and, for our purposes, the specific distinction is not crucial. The discussion of e-commerce projects here is not intended toward the most micro-level project that may use only one of many skills without regard to others, nor to describing a permanent departmental structure. Rather, this chapter considers e-commerce projects as activities large and small toward the creation and maintenance of organizational e-commerce capabilities.

Focus on Web-Enabled Programs and Projects

This chapter aims to describe staffing in the Web-enabled environment rather than to directly address the question "to what degree do Web-enabled e-commerce projects differ from traditional MIS projects?" We did, however, ask respondents how management differed between traditional and Web-enabled projects. Though we did not define "traditional" IT, the respondents seemed to interpret this as anything MIS related that did not fit in the e-commerce realm. There was an almost equal split between those who felt there was no difference and those who noted differences generally deriving from more interaction with business and a broader array of users (see Table 5.1). This is very consistent with the author's experience in discussing with project managers whether IT projects or product development efforts differ from those used on other projects. There appears to be some sense that all projects have some common core issues and concerns, but that projects within a particular domain have their own particular characteristics and, in their most sensitive details, each project is ultimately unique. In this context, the chapter addresses the particular characteristics of staffing in the Web-enabled/e-commerce domain. Findings are intended to supplement rather than supplant what is known about staffing and project management in general across domains.

LITERATURE REVIEW

Fit Theories

Management and industrial psychology researchers for generations have been studying issues of employee outcomes, including "performance, motivation, extra-role behaviors, work attitudes, retention, group cooperation and group performance" (Werbel and Gilliland, 1999, p. 209). One major direction of that research holds that the fit between the work environment (in a variety of aspects) and the attributes of the individual should predict various work-related and individual outcomes (Kristof, 1996; Livingstone et al., 1997). Where the match is close, outcomes should be better than where there is a significant gap between individual and organization. For example, an element of the "taxi driver" job is the ability to drive efficiently from place to place. Individuals with a high-level skill at "finding shortcuts" should be more productive than those who

Table 5.1

Comparison of E-Commerce and "Traditional" IT Projects

Respondent number	Does ecommerce management different from other projects?
001	Not different
004	Not different
006	Not different
007	Testing and availability difference
011	Different skills sets; transitioned 3 years ago to browser-based systems, now these are almost only ones developed
012	Broader scope if project has marketing component
014	More user interaction; more executive sponsorship because it affects customers directly
015	Having to work with customer priorities; More communication and knowledge sharing required
016	More emphasis on usability, look and feel; managing external expectations
017	E-commerce more difficult
018	Business involvement
019	Time urgency

have a hard time finding shortcuts. However, as the nature of work has been changing largely in response to the growing prevalence of information technology that helps organizations reorganize, replace, and invent new work, the simple match between job requirements and individual skills has explained less of the variance in outcomes. A number of additional matches have been proposed to supplement the job environment–individual attribute match. For example, one study focusing on the employee selection process proposes three fits that are important in influencing outcomes. Werbel and Gilliland (1999) propose that the person-job, person-organization, and person-workgroup fits are each critical in different situations. In this formulation, person-job fit is the congruence between the "demands of the job and the needed skills, knowledge, and abilities of a job candidate" (Werbel and Gilliland, 1999, p. 211, referencing Edwards, 1991). The idea of person-organization fit would add to "technical job performance" factors such as prosocial behavior, organizational citizenship, and organizational commitment. Person-workgroup fit "refers to the match between the new hire and the immediate workgroup (i.e., coworkers and supervisor)" (Werbel and Gilliland, 1999, p. 217).

The strengths of one individual may be complemented by the strengths of another individual to provide stronger overall team outcomes. Although the discussion of these types of fit are presented by Werbel and Gilliland within the context of employment selection, it stands to reason that similar issues can be addressed, though perhaps on a smaller scale, with respect to the selection of individuals within a firm for work on a specific project or in a particular work role. In addition, we propose a new match dimension. The new match addresses the issues of job strain and retention as the "compensation" needs of an individual and the benefits provided by the job. Together with the job need–individual skill match, these theories comprise a job demand/job supply theory.

Table 5.2

High-Level Skills Needed by Developers of eCommerce Systems

Knowledge area	High-level skill
Technical	1. Web programming
	2. Web networking
	3. Web databases
	4. Web security
	5. Web management
	6. Web site design
Human	7. Interpersonal communication
	8. Problem solving
	9. Conflict resolution
	10 Collaboration
	11. Dealing with change
Organizational	12. Organizational goals and objectives
	13. Organizational policies and procedures
	14. Organizational functions and processes
	15. Organizational culture
	16. Organizational constraints

Source: Table 1 replicates Aladwani, 2002. Reproduced with permission of AIS SIGED IAIM.

E-Commerce–Specific Employee Research

Human resources in many organizations account for the lion's share of budget. Planning for the right staffing and skills for provision of future services is an important and difficult task (Schwarzkopf et al., 2004). Effective utilization of human resources is a key component of managing in the MIS and e-commerce arenas. As technologies support increasingly more sophisticated Web activities, the demand for knowledge and skills of e-commerce personnel expands correspondingly. It is logical to assume that the key success factor for the development and implementation of e-commerce applications is the technical and organizational competence of the e-commerce personnel. It is therefore of significant importance for managers of e-commerce projects to bring the greatest possible understanding of the dynamics leading to heightened or diminished productivity to their personnel decisions.

There has not yet been much discussion on the topic of e-commerce knowledge, skills, and abilities in the MIS literature. Aladwani (2002), following frameworks of other research identifying IT personnel skill needs (Lee et al., 1995; Nelson 1991; Trauth et al., 1993; Rada, 1999), has identified sixteen distinct skills (see Table 5.2). In the paper the ranks by practitioners and academics are contrasted in terms of both usefulness and competence of new IT graduates. This valuable study should be extended by (1) including background from the substantial knowledge developed by human resource and industrial psychologies regarding predictors of work outcomes, and (2) considering a more detailed level of skill requirements recognizing the differences between traditional IT and emerging e-commerce projects.

One recent study has contrasted the perceived usefulness of job skills and the responding Webmasters' perceptions of their competencies for each skill (Wade and Parent, 2001–2). Overall this study suggests that technical skill deficiencies lead to lower productivity, with organizational skill deficiencies also, and in a more pronounced manner, leading to lower productivity. However, this study, springing from an IT employee model, contrasts technical and organizational skills rather than IT and Web-production skills.

Although the development of e-commerce Web sites has a strong technical component, Holzschlag (2000) has proposed viewing the development of a Web site as more of an artistic production. By interacting in a constant feedback loop with customer/users, the development process has some analogy to the development of films and other creative products. The term "Web publication specialist" is used to emphasize the many nontechnical elements necessary for successful e-commerce development, which include interface and functionality design involving artistic, usability, policy, and functionality issues. Specialists in this area would not necessarily have or need technical IT skills. The category of Web publication specialist refers to those individuals with marketing, communications, and other backgrounds that are necessary to develop successful Web projects. Skills in this area, as applied to IS projects, have not been fully studied. Moreover, these skills may be difficult to specify since elements of innovativeness, creativity, and the ability to generate excitement are difficult to quantify.

McKee (2001) and Wenn and Sellitto (2001) considered necessary e-commerce skills by examining the requirements for successful e-commerce projects and the specific skills needed to accomplish these tasks. McKee (2001) presents a detailed diagram, derived from practice, of elements needed to build a successful e-commerce site. His work highlights the variety of skills ranging from the most technical infrastructure manipulation to sensitivity regarding business needs and marketing processes. Wenn and Sellitto (2001) focus on some of the tools, languages, and standards that are either required or recommended for more robust performance on e-commerce sites. Both sets of research suggest that the full range of skills need not be present in every team member.

This leads to the overall research question of this study: How are Web-enabled programs and projects staffed in terms of required individual skills, blending of individual skills into team capabilities, and assignment of individuals to tasks?

METHOD

Because the domain of Web-enabled/e-commerce staffing has not been extensively explored, it is appropriate to use a qualitative method appropriate for developing rich descriptions and understandings in an exploratory research framework. Prior to extensive and precise measurement, the range of potential states to be measured needs to be determined. The goal of this research is to present a portrait of the varied approaches organizations are taking to staffing e-commerce projects and programs.

Interview Protocol Development

The investigator and a colleague drafted an interview protocol for a broader study of which this chapter represents a discrete segment. The overall interview protocol content was formulated in six topical areas:

1. Individual characteristics (including demographics, norms, competencies, and preferences);
2. The nature of e-commerce work in that particular organization;
3. How the work is structured;
4. How project teams are selected and composed for membership in the projects;
5. The outcomes and results of the particular approaches observed; and
6. Expectations regarding the continued evolution of e-commerce personnel and tasks.

This protocol was pilot tested with two respondents. No problematic segments were revealed, and the same protocol was used with the rest of the study participants.

Sample

The intention of this research has been to develop a multifaceted picture of Web-enabled/e-commerce staffing. As a result, data were gathered by conducting interviews with individuals involved with e-commerce. Twenty individuals with a wide range of viewpoints were interviewed. The strategy for selecting participants involved seeking a broad range of e-commerce workers engaged in development or ongoing support of e-commerce projects. The selection of individuals playing a wide range of roles is based on the primary goal of developing a range of possible states or values for various aspects of the individuals' roles in the development process. Organizations likely to have individuals meeting the qualifications below were also asked to participate by inviting volunteers to participate in structured interviews. Participants were recruited from personal contacts through organizations such as local chapters of the Society for Information Management (SIM) and Project Management Institute (PMI) as well as from contacts arranged by academic colleagues and by former students with Web-enabled/e-commerce workers in their organization.

To qualify as a research participant, the studied participant needed to be involved at present or in the past with the technical or content aspects of at least one e-commerce project. All of the interviewees met these criteria. Their areas of responsibility ranged from project management on a limited number of e-commerce projects to responsibility for the organization's entire e-commerce program. Respondents included a number of individuals primarily assigned to IT departments and others resident in non-IT business units. Respondents included two self-employed consultants with experience involving e-commerce projects across a range of organizations (see Table 5.3 for a list of respondent job titles). Respondents worked for a wide range of companies that varied by industry and size (see Table 5.4 for basic organization data). In most cases, only one respondent was interviewed from a given organization. However, four individuals, including both IT specialists and individuals from the business-user community in one manufacturing company, were also included in the sample.

Interview Procedure

Respondents participated in a structured interview (see Appendix 5.1 for a listing of the interview questions analyzed for this research). These interviews were tape-recorded and transcribed. References to particular organizations, projects, or individuals were omitted and/or reformulated. The first sixteen interviews were carried out between May and August 2004 in person in St. Louis or by telephone. Another four interviews were added in Atlanta between September and November 2005. The purpose of the additional interviews was to broaden the range of respondents' experience, particularly in the area of direct business-to-customer e-commerce. No systemic difference in interview responses was noted as a result of either time or location. Much variance, however, was observed in terms of different organizational cultures and different scope of e-commerce activity. E-commerce activity ranged from one organization based entirely online to another that was slowly transitioning from a sophisticated electronic data interchange (EDI) to a Web-based supply chain presence with key distributors.

All interviews were conducted by the chief investigator/author, although research colleagues and graduate students participated in four of the interviews. Each interview lasted approximately one hour. Although a semistructured interview protocol format was used to guide the interviews, specific questions varied among respondents. In the interview situation, respondents sometimes

Table 5.3

Respondents' Job Titles

Title	Number of observations
Director of E-Business	3
Chief Information Officer	1
Consultant	1
Contractor Consultant—Comparable to Senior Analyst Role	1
Director Academic IT Services	1
Director of Information Technology	1
Director of IS, (particular product area)*	1
Director of Venture Relations	1
Electronic Commerce IT Team Lead	1
IT Project Manager	1
Manager of E-Business	1
Manager of the Customer Interface Group	1
Manager, Special Projects	1
Product Manager**	1
Senior Business Analyst	1
Technical Project Manager	1
Technology Officer	1
Web Developer, Level-2 Team Lead	1
Total	20

*Specific product area name removed for confidentiality of respondent.
**Responsible for specific e-commerce/IT products.

Table 5.4

Company Information

Industry	Annual sales (mil)	# Employees	# Respondents
Agriculture1	12,000	28,000	1
Agriculture2	3,373	13,200	1
Consultant1	—	1	1
Consultant2	—	1	1
Consultant3	—	1	1
Education*	452	4,416	2
Finance1*	315	1,300	2
Finance2	223	1,000	2
IT Service Provider1	n/a	n/a	1
IT Service Provider2	1,382	2,067	1
Manufacturing1	13,958	106,700	4
Manufacturing2	50,485	157,000	1
Manufacturing3	5,880	34,300	1
Marketing Services	1,440	5,700	1
Total			20

Source: Hoovers and organizational Web sites; note specific Web sites not listed to preserve anonymity of the organizations.
*Firm data from 2002; all other data collected from 2003.

elaborate on early questions in ways that answer later questions or render them irrelevant. For the purpose of eliciting the maximum content from the interviewee, the researcher pursued questions with additional follow-up for clarification or extension and revised the wording of specific questions to place them in the relevant context for the particular interviewee. While this limits the comparability of the responses, for the purpose of creating an understanding of concepts and values, it permits maximum opportunity for the discovery of unexpected responses.

Analysis

Data were analyzed in three major steps. First, following transcription, responses to discrete questions were grouped in a single file. Second, the author and a colleague individually reduced each response to key phrases that indicated the essential response to that question. These were discussed to consensus by the researchers. Responses that contained nuances beyond simplification through reduction to key phrases were retained for possible use in the text as illustrations. Third, the key phrases were examined for development of discrete categories of response, which are presented in the following discussion.

RESULTS

> I think probably the one key that surprises . . . people who don't work in IT [more] than anything else is that they go after people who are very good at both written and verbal communication because so much [is] requirements gather[ing] and just the relationship building. I think people still have this vision of IT as, you know, being guys with long beards and thick glasses who sit in a room with no lights and type all day. And so much more of it, even . . . the full-time employees that are there are much more like IT consultants out to their business community within the same organization much as we are to them too. And I think that's probably the one skill set across the board no matter which of those groups you're looking for. You're really looking for somebody with integrity and good communication skills.

Overall, determining staffing for e-commerce projects is made complex by the fluid nature of the task. Much staffing is determined in initial hiring (or otherwise acquiring human resources—for example, through contracting or outsourcing). A first line of staffing for e-commerce projects appears to be the shifting of personnel already within an organization to assignment for these tasks. The range of individuals and skills to be drawn upon is then fixed aside from the ability to transfer existing skills to new tasks and to invent and discover new techniques in the process of working. Moreover, not all individuals working on e-commerce projects are assigned to them full time. Non-IT department personnel might be assigned to customer relations, where making sure that electronic ordering and other supply chain tasks runs smoothly is part of a larger function. Some IT specialists in particular programming languages, telecommunications, or database may move through particular e-commerce projects while retaining a portfolio of non–e-commerce responsibilities in the firm. These conditions made it difficult for respondents to generalize about skills within their project teams. As one respondent commented,

> Typically when you're talking about these kind of [projects] particular personnel have particular skill sets so someone may know JAVA and not know XML. Someone may know HTML and Sequel and may not know Oracle.

While some respondents did provide a listing of some specific skills, comments provided a richer examination of particular skills or approaches that the respondents deemed important (see Table 5.5).

Although the comments offered by the respondents were diverse and reflected varied aspects of skill requirements in practice, some themes emerged. A strong emphasis was placed on various types of communication and interpersonal skills. But, at least in some cases, these go beyond simply being able to write and speak clearly. These include the ability to penetrate to the significance and underlying purpose of IT and business activities. On the other hand, not all team members need to have all of the interpersonal skills.

> [I] would have somebody who's an expert communicator communicating with the subject expert, somebody who had excellent written communication skills to be able to coherently write down something . . . to effectively act as a translator between those of the tech world and those of the business world.

Explicitly or implicitly each of the respondents reinforced the need for appropriate technical skills in addition to communication, business, and related skills. However, the specific skills needed varied by organization and, sometimes, from project to project.

Respondents were also asked how they formulate teams for particular projects, and a second question was aimed at how individuals were assigned to particular teams/projects. In practice the answers to these questions overlapped significantly and will be discussed together (see Tables 5.6 and 5.7). Responses varied in level of abstraction, including those describing how individuals are assigned to particular projects and those describing approaches to such assignments. For example, two methods of assignment to projects emerged: assigning whoever might be available and starting with task "demand" for particular skills and assigning individuals who "supply" those skills. One respondent indicated that his organization used both of these methods, with the "who's available" method taking precedence when staffing was urgent. At a higher level of abstraction, respondents noted that employees may be assigned to particular technologies or platforms; assignment to particular projects then becomes automatic relative to the technology or platform required for the project. Another approach included rotation of team members. This respondent was primarily oriented to the implementation of packages for supporting business processes, and the rotation was focused on business employees rotating into the implementation process. Part of the thinking behind this approach was that these employees would return to their normal posts able to diffuse knowledge regarding the new application.

The e-commerce work demands for skills, abilities, and knowledge can be defined variously at different levels. One would expect that in the staffing process, assignment to a department or program would require establishing a pool of individuals with a broad set of skills who could respond to a wide range of project demands—including unanticipated and emergent opportunities that may create unexpected skill demands on relatively short notice. One would also expect that assignment to particular projects would be constrained by the set of skills available within the already established pool, further constrained by the limits of individuals to operate on multiple projects (as well as costs associated with trying to move between projects), and also feeding constraints back into the selection of projects to undertake.

In summary, staffing and skills should be considered from multiple perspectives. In each of these work environments, there appears to be an inner pool of staff assigned to many projects (occasionally with a small group to all projects). As a result, the development of that pool through hiring and training is critical. There also appears to be an "outer pool" of staff made up of either technical specialists who are loaned from IT departments or business process specialists loaned from user groups who are brought into projects for specific purposes. One respondent alluded to rotating the business process specialists as part of an overall strategy for diffusing the new technology throughout the organization. Technical skills appear to be overridingly important, though

Table 5.5

Key Skills for E-Commerce Project Staff

Respondent number	Web-enabled e-commerce project skills
001	Graphic design, programming, middleware, sometimes DBA, oracle developer
002	Combination of perfectionist and ability to see ahead to avoid disasters (with reference to project managers most particularly)
003	Marketing people pick up the IT skills. I'm the only one who can't program although I have programmed in Basic when I was in college; more interested in usability than graphics
004	Use tools that are already familiar (implied is the idea that having to learn new skills during a project is minimal)
005	Lots of teamwork
006	Depends on the project. User business process knowledge, some technical skills to map back to legacy systems
007	Business knowledge; senior person to mentor junior staff members; designers strong in databases, Java architecture, DB architecture, mainframe architecture, "team lead"—making sure code is clean coming out of testing
008	Individuals with wide range of skills; but we are looking to migrate everything to a UNIX platform so we're trying to get people up to speed with UNIX skills; analysis skills, logic and programming, testing, multitasking, and keeping track of projects/ deadlines; we should include some marketing skills, but haven't yet
009	Willingness to look at things differently be open to alternative approaches
010	Technical skills, graphics (two people)
011	Communication skills, Technical lead should know about business processes; work with creative agency outside of team
012	Experience in Microsoft products, Sequel, and Visual Studio; strong skills to stay focused and work independently
013	Core business logic of a program; user interface design
014	Business knowledge ("the accounting side, the inventory side, the sales side, or the marketing side")
015	Programming, database, EDI translator skills, XML, communication to SAP; one specialist in graphics and user interface; interpersonal skills
016	Communication and problem solving; business process experience; experience with the tool development set; component interface and application messaging skills
017	Analytical thinking; communicate well; good at working with other people; hard worker. A strong visual sense for taking ideas and concepts and putting them into a clear visual representation. Domain knowledge is important, but depends on the team
018	They have to be understanding of e-commerce; experience with large and small customers; not just programming; analytically solve problems; ability to "ask stupid questions"; communicate well with the customer; work a lot of hours, be proactive; database, skills at user interface
019	Graphics, Java, integrating to other systems (sometimes skills provided by partner or software vendor), database, some DBAs; adaptability; having initiative; better awareness of business-related issues
020	Technical skills sufficient for running the systems that vary by project; understanding the overall goals of the company

Table 5.6

Team Creation and Project Staffing Approaches

	How do you create teams to work on these projects?
001	Match requirements of client to team skills; Working to develop crossover skills
002	Blending tech and functional area staffs; informal discussion; skill set plus work load, interest, history of working with other team members
003	Find individuals with project-needed skills; business-knowledge fit
004	Urgent—whoever's available; Not urgent—match individual skills to project needs
005	Repeatable projects, relationships with business people; teams include business people; availability
006	Rotational program for business people to interact in development projects and return to teach others; IT people manage legacy systems to which e-commerce packages provide access; open staffing within firm; float a requisition
007	Start with core design group, consider needs and bring in additional staff
008	Defining the work leads to understanding the skill needs
009	People pulled in as we need them; projects in addition to "standard work"
010	Team oriented projects including business users; projects specific to technology manager
011	Try to keep people who work well together on different projects
012	Employees sorted by technology group; respond to projects regarding their technology
013	Employees added to team when "gap" is recognized; project demand, match skill set; develop specializations and standing project teams
015	Who is available from particular technology group
016	Blend of specialists and generalists
017	Because we support production issues, if there is a production problem it goes to her team. Staff has to know how integrations work together, and we need people that can see how things link and work together. If something is not a strength, say user interface, then that work is deferred to another team. Some people can work well in both production or UI, and they tend to move back and forth between projects.
018	Start by assessing project "needs"; what can I live with, what can I not live without, then a consideration of "who's available"; draw from a pool if available
019	The customer would first interact with an engagement manager, someone who was partially a sales person and partially a project manager who determined what the customer needed. And that engagement manager would then put together a team based on what they thought, what skills they needed.
020	Typically depending on the nature of the project, the technical staff may be sitting in different organizations. So depending on what you are trying to do, you may go to get this team to develop it or you maybe go get another team to develop it.

any given skill may or may not be needed on any particular project. One tactic for addressing this is to specialize in a limited set of software tools and to plan for training or hiring as new technologies are assimilated. Interpersonal skills also appear to be an essential component in project accomplishment, but not necessarily at the same time for all participants. One respondent related an anecdote of a superior technically proficient staff member who inadvertently offended a key customer. The response was to "buffer" valuable technical staff from direct client contact.

Table 5.7

Assuring the Full Range of Skills

	How do you assure that the team members have the collection of skills desired for participation on the project team?
001	Knowing the staff and their skills
003	Assign project manager then others-small enough not to need formal procedures
004	Know what tools will be used and learn new technical skills quickly when needed
005	Use skill assessment sheet; prioritize projects; personality as well as skills; project managers develop their "favorites"
006	Recruit from elsewhere in the company if there's a gap
010	Fill gaps from consultants, review strategic needs annually, some training
018	Needs someone with the broad range of knowledge about the project

DISCUSSION

Prior to conducting this investigation, it was expected that changes in job and tasks in developing e-commerce personnel and teams would be mirrored in the types of individual and team-level skills needed for the work. This is consistent with the various fit theories of personnel that emphasize matching the supply of worker talent to the demand of job tasks. More specifically, in contrast to traditional IT work, we would have expected Web-enabled e-commerce projects to require significant communications (and diplomacy) skills. Such communication skills should be important for integrating requirements across departments, for interacting smoothly with external stakeholders, and for sending both instructions and messages within the user interface. The need for such skills at the team level among at least some individuals was reflected in the data. However, we observed more specifically that organizations were looking for a higher level of sophistication in communication skills than normally considered or trained for in traditional MIS personnel. They were looking not only for clarity of expression but also for an ability to interact with meanings and intentions stated and unstated; to probe for common understanding. On the other hand, not all team members were viewed as needing to have high levels of communication and interpersonal skills. As long as the team had these, some individuals could focus on technical issues with others buffering their interactions.

On the other hand, we would have expected to find a high need for graphics and "content" skills to keep Web sites current, interesting to users, and consistent with changing marketing strategies and products. We did not find much of this. Those working on Web-enabled e-commerce projects did not generally include content specialists. The inference is that content remains within the domain of the functional area, marketing, logistics, and human resource management, while the Web-enabled e-commerce staff specializes in the mechanisms for distributing rather than creating content.

From a technical perspective, we would have expected the need for especially strong interface and usability engineering skills to assure that the software is easy to use, easy to learn, and predictable in function. The data support this need, though generally targeted to use of specific Web-supporting technologies and to the ability to improvise and solve problems as they arise.

Although the skills described by the respondents can be fit broadly into the Aladwani (2002) model of technical, business, and organizational categories, this study captured some of the more specific characteristics being sought—such as the ability to work in the face of previously un-solved problems. Additionally, although the listing of skills Aladwani presents likely reflects the collective skill set of an IT department, the fact that all individuals do not need to display the full range of skills is also an important observation.

In terms of creation of teams and project membership, some of the Web-enabled e-commerce groups were small enough that essentially all employees were involved in all but the smallest one-person projects. In this case, it seems that no team selection is required but rather that the initial hiring decision represents a one-time determination of skill needs (or represents gaps that are constant, at least in the short run). Even for larger work groups, little time and energy seemed to be spent on optimizing staffing for particular projects. Rather, managers would implicitly become familiar with the skills of individuals and assess the requirements for particular jobs, creating a match for a particular project. This is within the context of other assignments and who might be available.

CONCLUSION

Based on the results of interviews with eighteen e-commerce project managers and participants, a few skill areas appear to be emphasized in Web-enabled e-commerce projects. These include high-level communication skills with the purpose of interacting successfully with a broad array of stakeholders, including those outside the MIS technology management sphere—directors of business units—and those outside the organization such as suppliers or "organized customers," in particular, distributors. It is important to note that this emphasis on communication skills does not replace an emphasis on technical skills, although the particular technologies may shift from traditional mainframe skills to object-oriented environments and from straightforward application development to package installation and integration.

The study presented is based on a limited number of interviews and should, therefore, represent a partial but not necessarily complete picture of the range of approaches taken toward staffing e-commerce projects and programs in organizations. The variety of positions held by interviewees and the diversity of companies they represent aids in showing a broad range of responses, but does not guarantee that all possible responses are included. Being based on interviews, the tone and wording of the questions may vary slightly from one interview to the next. While working from a common protocol helps keep the interview questions within a reasonable range, it does not ensure that each question is interpreted identically by all respondents. The interviewees largely worked with supply chain and business-to-business e-commerce, and a fuller picture of staffing and governance of e-commerce projects will include a larger number of interviewees who work with direct to consumer e-commerce programs. No measures of central tendency are presented in this chapter. It is understood that interviews can form a solid base for determining a likely range of responses but that surveys and other methods are stronger at quantifying the tendencies of each value in a sample with inference to quantification of the population. This chapter does not present results regarding other management issues for e-commerce programs and projects that can affect personnel and skill needs such as the departmental reporting structure, performance evaluation, or financial compensation.

This chapter presents a look at e-commerce skills as they are actualized in organizations. While it does not measure the difference between e-commerce and traditional MIS projects, the findings do suggest that differing user characteristics—particularly, crossing organizational internal departmental and external boundaries—in turn cause some differences in staffing and skill demand.

APPENDIX 5.1. STAFFING E-COMMERCE PROJECTS

Preamble

- Who we are
- Why we are doing this interview
- How the results will be used; that the respondent may conclude any time; that we request permission to tape the proceedings; and what information will be shared and with whom.

Background and Initiation

(Individual characteristics—demographics, subjective norms, competencies and preferences, styles)

1. Your age (please check one)
   - ___ 20–29
   - ___ 30–39
   - ___ 40–49
   - ___ 50–59
   - ___ 60–69
   - ___ 70 or above

2. Your educational background (please check all that apply, and specify degrees earned)
   - ___ Undergraduate _____
   - ___ Graduate _____
   - ___ PhD _____
   - ___ Other _____

3. Do you have management responsibilities? (Are there other employees that report to you/that you supervise?)

4. Your place in the organization (IT department, line unit)

5. Your present position

6. Your work experience (position, start–end, type of projects)

Project Characteristics

1. Please tell us about the nature of e-commerce development projects you've worked on. What sort of technologies did you use?
2. What sort of deadlines and work arrangements? Other pressures?
3. What sort of outcomes were you aiming at?
4. How much did the projects change during the development process?
5. How autonomous was the working group?

Team Selection/Composition

1. How were individuals selected for these projects?
2. What sort of skills did they require for selection?
3. How did they handle publication-oriented skills versus information technology skills?
4. Was there a strategy of using highly specialized or more general folks?
5. How did you manage teams (did you have membership turnover; did you have specialists come and go)?
6. Did you use any part time/contractual/outsource/consultants?

Performance

1. Did you measure individual or team performance? If so, what sort of measures did you use?
2. Did you draw any conclusions regarding the effectiveness of your various staffing strategies? Were there any skills that proved more valuable (or less) than you expected?
3. What did they learn about staffing of these projects that they would take toward future projects?
4. What did they do or plan to do in the future that they would consider best practices?

Future Expectations

1. As technologies supporting e-commerce and business applications continue evolving, what implications do they see for staffing?

NOTE

1. We use the term "program" to refer to the overall organizational Web-enabled presence to one or more stakeholder groups, such as to customers or suppliers, and the term "project" to refer to the more specific tasks and jobs that when combined will lead to the fulfillment of the overall program. The term "program" is never meant as a file of commands in a "computer program," which is referred to as an application in this chapter.

REFERENCES

Aladwani, A.M. 2002. An exploratory investigation of requisite skills needed by developers of e-commerce systems. In *Proceedings of the Seventeenth International Conference on Informatics Education and Research.* Barcelona, Spain, December 13–15.

Burke, D., and Morrison, A. 2001. *Business @ the Speed of Stupid.* Cambridge, MA: Perseus.

Edwards, J.R. 1991. Person-job fit: A conceptual integration, literature review, and methodological critique. *International Review of Industrial and Organizational Psychology,* 6, 283–357.

Evaristo, R., and van Fenema, P.C. 1999. A typology of project management: Emergence and evolution of new forms. *International Journal of Project Management,* 17, 5, 275–281.

Gallivan, M.; Truex, D.P. III; and Kvasny, L. 2004. Changing patterns in IT skill sets 1988–2003: A content analysis of classified advertising. *Data Base,* 35, 3, 64–87.

Holzschlag, M.E. 2000. Turning chaos into order: Managing web projects. *Web Techniques,* 5, 1, 16–19.

Internet World Stats. 2009. Top 20 countries with the highest Internet users. Available at www.internetworldstats.com/top20.htm (accessed June 1, 2007).

Kristof, A.L. 1996. Person-organization fit: An integrative review of its conceptualizations, measurement, and implications. *Personnel Psychology,* 49, 1–49.

Lee, D.M.S.; Trauth, E.M.; and Farwell, D. 1995. Critical skills and knowledge requirements of IS professionals: A joint academic/industry investigation. *MIS Quarterly,* 19, 3, 313–340.

Livingstone, L.P.; Nelson, D.L.; and Barr, S.H. 1997. Person-environment fit and creativity: An examination of supply-value and demand-ability versions of fit. *Journal of Management,* 23, 2, 119–146.

McKee, J. 2001. Skill sets for the e-commerce professional. In *Proceedings of SSECP 2001: Skill Sets for the E-Commerce Professional.* Melbourne, Australia.

Nelson, R.R. 1991. Educational needs as assessed by IS and end-user personnel: A survey of knowledge and skill requirements. *MIS Quarterly,* 15, 4, 502–525.

Niederman, F., and Hu, X. 2003. Electronic commerce personnel in the age of clicks and mortar: Toward a framework of individual and project level skills. In E. Trauth (ed.), *Proceedings of the 2003 SIGMIS Conference on Computer Personnel Research,* Association of Computing Machinery, Philadelphia, PA, 104–110.

Quelch, J. A., and Klein, L. R. 1996. The Internet and International Marketing. *Sloan Management Review,* 37, 3, 60–75.

Rada, R. 1999. IT skills standards. *Communications of the ACM,* 42, 4, 21–26.

Schwarzkopf, A.B.; Mejias, R.J.; Jasperson, J.; Saunders, C.S.; and Gruenwald, H. 2004. Effective practices for IT skills staffing. *Communications of the ACM,* 47, 1, 83–88.

Trauth, E.; Farwell, D.; and Lee, D. 1993. The IS expectations gap: Industry expectations versus academic preparation. *MIS Quarterly,* 17, 3, 293–307.

U.S. Department of Commerce. 2004. Retail e-commerce sales in second quarter 2004 were $15.7 billion, up 23.1 percent from second quarter 2003, Census Bureau reports. *United States Department of Commerce News,* August 20. Available at www.census.gov/mrts/www/ecom.pdf (accessed October 8, 2004).

Wade, M.R., and Parent, M. 2001–2. Relationship between job skills and performance: A study of webmasters. *Journal of Management Information Systems,* 18, 3, 71–93.

Wenn, A., and Sellitto, C. 2001. Emerging technical standards: Towards an identification of skillsets needed by website developers. In *Proceedings of SSECP 2001: Skill Sets for the E-Commerce Professional.* Melbourne, Australia.

Werbel, J.D., and Gilliland, S.W. 1999. Person–environment fit in the selection process. In G.R. Ferris (ed.), *Research in Personnel and Human Resources Management,* 17, 209–243. Stamford, CT: JAI Press.

CHAPTER 6

FOCUSING ON WORK SYSTEMS TO UNDERSTAND AND ANALYZE INFORMATION SYSTEMS

STEVEN ALTER

Abstract: The work system method (WSM) was developed over many years to help business profes-sionals understand and analyze IT (information technology)-reliant work systems for themselves, thereby helping them to take more active and knowledgeable roles in system-related projects. It can be adapted or used directly to improve the quality of collaboration between business and IT professionals. This chapter presents basic ideas about work systems and explains how those ideas are related to WSM. It covers the concept of work system, the work system framework, work system life cycle model, the work system method, ideas for identifying issues and possibilities for change, the relevance of WSM for improving collaboration between business and IT professionals, and several areas of continuing research.

Keywords: Work System, Systems Analysis, Work System Framework, Work System Method

The idea of focusing on work systems to understand and analyze information systems emerged during a long-term research project aimed at developing systems analysis methods for business professionals. The project began in the early 1990s, motivated by difficulties in attaining genuine communication between a software firm and its customers about the use and impact of the software. The goal was to develop systems analysis methods that business professionals can use at whatever level of depth and detail was appropriate for their purposes.

The research unfolded iteratively using successive sets of group papers written by employed MBA and EMBA students about information systems in their own organizations. Based on initial results, it became apparent that general systems concepts combined with a typical coverage of technology and an exhortation to pay attention to performance indicators did not provide enough guidance. The students were more successful in addressing business issues if they focused first on the work and business objectives that were being supported, and second on the information system. Students who focused on the features and capabilities of software framed the question inappropriately because the main point from a business perspective is doing work more efficiently and effectively, not using hardware and software more efficiently and effectively.

"Work system" seemed a good term to focus their thinking and encourage them to consider information systems from a business viewpoint because the purpose of most information systems is to support a work system. Subsequent reading and searches on the Internet found that the term had been used many times in the past, but had not been defined carefully or used as an analytical concept. A notable use of the term occurred in 1977 in the first volume of *MIS Quarterly* in two articles by Bostrom and Heinen (1977a, 1977b). Later it was used by Sumner and Ryan (1994) to explain problems in CASE (computer-aided systems engineering) adoption. A number of sociotechnical researchers such as Trist and Mumford also used the term occasionally, but seemed not to define it in detail. In contrast, the work system approach defines work system carefully and uses it as a basic analytical concept.

THE CONCEPT OF A WORK SYSTEM

A work system is a system in which human participants and/or machines perform work using information, technology, and other resources to produce products and/or services for internal or external customers. Typical business organizations contain work systems that procure materials from suppliers, produce products, deliver products to customers, find customers, create financial reports, hire employees, coordinate work across departments, and perform many other functions. Almost all significant work systems in business and governmental organizations employing more than a few people cannot operate efficiently or effectively without using information technologies (IT). Most practical information systems (IS) research is about the development, operation, and maintenance of such systems and their components. In effect, the IS field is basically about IT-reliant work systems (Alter, 2003).

The work system concept is like a common denominator for many of the types of systems discussed in the IS practice and IS research. Operational information systems, projects, supply chains, and e-commerce Web sites can all be viewed as special cases of work systems.

- An information system is a work system whose processes and activities are devoted to processing information.
- A project is a work system designed to produce a product and then go out of existence.
- A supply chain is an interorganizational work system devoted to procuring materials and other inputs required to produce a firm's products.
- An e-commerce Web site can be viewed as a work system in which a buyer uses a seller's Web site to obtain product information and perform purchase transactions.

The relationship between work systems in general and the special cases implies that the same basic concepts apply to all of the special cases, which also have their own specialized vocabulary. In turn, this implies that much of the body of knowledge for the current information systems discipline can be organized around a work system core.

Specific information systems exist to support (other) work systems. Many different degrees of overlap are possible between an information system and a work system that it supports. For example, an information system might provide information for a nonoverlapping work system, as happens when a commercial marketing survey provides information to a firm's marketing managers. In other cases, an information system may be an integral part of a work system, as happens in highly automated manufacturing and in e-commerce Web sites. In these situations, participants in the work system are also participants in the information system, the work system cannot operate properly without the information system, and the information system's meaning and significance is based on its relationship to the work system.

The work system approach includes both a static view of a current (or proposed) system in operation and a dynamic view of how a system evolves over time through planned change and unplanned adaptations. The static view is summarized by the work system framework, which identifies the basic elements for understanding and evaluating a work system.

Figure 6.1   **The Work System Framework**

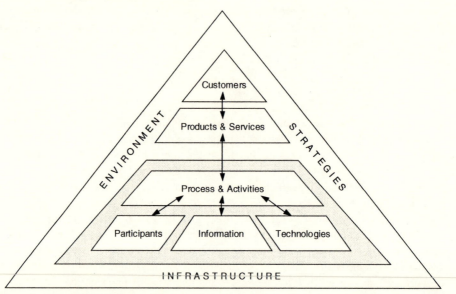

WORK SYSTEM FRAMEWORK

The nine elements of the work system framework (Figure 6.1) are the basis for describing and analyzing an IT-reliant work system in an organization. The work system framework is designed to emphasize business rather than IT concerns. It covers situations that might or might not include a tightly defined business process and might or might not rely heavily on IT. This framework is prescriptive enough to be useful in describing the system being studied by identifying problems and opportunities, describing possible changes, and tracing how those changes might affect other parts of the work system.

The basic idea of the framework first appeared in Alter (1995). An easily recognized triangular representation appeared in Alter (2002a, 2002b, 2003, 2006a). Figure 6.1 shows the latest version, which replaces the term "work practices" with "processes and activities," a term that is conversationally more natural for typical business professionals. Even a rudimentary understanding of a work system requires awareness of each of the nine elements. Four of these elements (processes and activities, participants, information, and technologies) constitute the work system. The other five elements fill out a basic understanding of the work system. The double-headed arrows in the work system framework express the need for alignment between the elements. The arrows also convey the path through which a change in one element might affect another element. For example, the arrows linking processes and activities to participants, information, and technology say that a change in the processes and activities might call for a change in any of these elements, and vice versa.

The definitions of the nine elements of a work system are given next.

1. Processes and Activities

Processes and activities include everything that happens within the work system. The term "processes and activities" is used instead of the term "business process" because many work systems do not contain highly structured business processes involving a prescribed sequence of steps, each of which is triggered in a predefined manner. Such processes are sometimes described as "artful processes" whose sequence and content "depend on the skills, experience, and judgment of the primary actors" (Hill et al., 2006, p. 665). In effect, business process is but one of a number of different perspectives for analyzing the activities within a work system. Other perspectives with their own valuable concepts and terminology include decision making, communication, coordination, control, and information processing.

2. Participants

Participants are people who perform the work. Some may use computers and IT extensively, whereas others may use little or no technology. When analyzing a work system the more encompassing role of work system participant is more important than the more limited role of technology user (whether or not particular participants happen to be technology users).

3. Information

Information includes codified and noncodified information used and created as participants perform their work. Information may or may not be computerized. Data not related to the work system are not directly relevant, making the distinction between data and information secondary when describing or analyzing a work system. Knowledge can be viewed as a special case of information.

4. Technologies

Technologies include tools (such as cell phones, projectors, spreadsheet software, and automobiles) and techniques (such as management by objectives, optimization, and remote tracking) that work system participants use while doing their work.

5. Products and Services

Products and services are the combination of physical things, information, and services that the work system produces. These may include physical products, information products, services, intangibles such as enjoyment and peace of mind, and social products such as arrangements, agreements, and organizations.

6. Customers

Customers are people who receive direct benefit from products and services the work system produces. They include external customers who receive the organization's products and/or services and internal customers who are employees or contractors working inside the organization.

7. Environment

Environment includes the organizational, cultural, competitive, technical, and regulatory environment within which the work system operates. These factors affect system performance even though the system does not rely on them directly in order to operate. The organization's general norms of behavior are part of its culture, whereas more specific behavioral norms and expectations about specific activities within the work system are considered part of its processes and activities.

8. Infrastructure

Infrastructure includes human, informational, and technical resources that the work system relies on even though these resources exist and are managed outside of it and are shared with other work systems. For example, technical infrastructure includes computer networks, programming languages, and other technologies shared by other work systems and often hidden or invisible to work system participants.

9. Strategies

Strategies include the strategies of the work system and of the department(s) and enterprise(s) within which the work system exists. Strategies at the department and enterprise level may help in explaining why the work system operates as it does and whether it is operating properly.

The work system framework can be used in a variety of ways:

- At the beginning of an analysis, a template called a work system snapshot (see below) can be used to clarify the scope of an existing or proposed work system; summarize the participants, information, and technologies; and identify products and services for primary and secondary customers.
- As the analysis proceeds, the work system framework can guide the analysis through the use of questions and templates related to individual work system elements. Broadly applicable characteristics and other properties of individual elements can support a deeper analysis.
- At the recommendation stage, the nine elements can be used to clarify exactly what changes are proposed and to sanity-check the recommendation. For example, a proposal to change technology without changing anything else is often incomplete.
- Throughout an analysis the work system framework can help the analyst focus on the system of doing work rather than just the software or hardware that is used by people who do the work.

WORK SYSTEM SNAPSHOT

The work system framework is the basis of a work system snapshot, which summarizes a work system on a single page by identifying its customers, products and services, processes and activities, participants, information, and technology. At the beginning of an analysis, creating and discussing a work system snapshot can be useful in clarifying and attaining agreement about the scope and purpose of the work system that is being analyzed. The environment, infrastructure, and strategy are not included in the work system snapshot in order to make it easier to use and to allow it to fit on one page. Those topics are considered as the analysis goes deeper. (At this level of summarization, the distinction between technology and technical infrastructure is unimportant.) Figure 6.2 shows a work system snapshot related to a hypothetical loan application and underwriting system that combines functional characteristics from a number of different real world systems.

Although more research is called for, research to date indicates that work system snapshots and a work system approach are useful for summarizing systems in organizations and for helping nontechnical individuals think about situations in system terms.

Work system snapshots are developed based on two deceptively simple guidelines:

- For purposes of the analysis, the work system is the smallest work system that has the problem or opportunity that motivated the analysis.

Figure 6.2   **Work System Snapshot for a Loan Application and Underwriting System for Loans to New Clients**

Customers	Products & Services
• Loan applicant • Loan officer • Bank's Risk Management Department and top management • Federal Deposit Insurance Corporation (FDIC) (a secondary customer)	• Loan application • Loan write-up • Approval or denial of the loan application • Explanation of the decision • Loan documents

Major Activities or Processes
• Loan officer identifies businesses that might need a commercial loan. • Loan officer and client discuss the client's financing needs and discuss possible terms of the proposed loan. • Loan officer helps client compile a loan application including financial history and projections. • Loan officer and senior credit officer meet to verify that the loan application has no glaring flaws. • Credit analyst prepares a "loan write-up" summarizing the applicant's financial history, providing projections, explaining sources of funds for loan payments, and discussing market conditions and applicant's reputation. Each loan is ranked for riskiness based on history and projections. Real estate loans all require an appraisal by a licensed appraiser. (This task is outsourced to an appraisal company.) • Loan officer presents the loan write-up to a senior credit officer or loan committee. • Senior credit officers approve or deny loans of less than $400,000; a loan committee or executive loan committee approves larger loans. • Loan officers may appeal a loan denial or an approval with extremely stringent loan covenants. Depending on the size of the loan, the appeal may go to a committee of senior credit officers, or to a loan committee other than the one that made the original decision. • Loan officer informs loan applicant of the decision. • Loan administration clerk produces loan documents for an approved loan that the client accepts.

Participants	Information	Technologies
• Loan officer • Loan applicant • Credit analyst • Senior credit officer • Loan committee and executive loan committee • Loan administration clerk • Real estate appraiser	• Applicant's financial statements for past three years • Applicant's financial and market projections • Loan application • Loan write-up • Explanation of decision • Loan documents	• Spreadsheet for consolidating information • Loan evaluation model • MS Word template • Internet • Telephones

Source: S. Alter, *The Work System Method: Connecting People, Processes, and IT for Business Results* (Larkspur, CA: Work System Press, 2006). All rights reserved.

- The work system's scope is not determined by the software that is used. (This is why a work system should not be called a "Lotus Notes system" or a "SAP system" just because it happens to use a particular brand of software.)

Despite the guidelines, many EMBA groups have difficulty agreeing on exactly what should and should not be included in a one-page work system snapshot that is produced at the beginning of a work system analysis. Sometimes they complain about how hard it is to produce something that seemingly should be easy to produce. An answer to such complaints is a reminder about the mess that would ensue if they or their organization tried to develop or install software without a negotiated agreement about what work system was to be improved. More experienced students often realize quickly that a few hours devoted to attaining agreement about a work system snapshot might have helped their firms avoid significant losses from misdirected projects that never attained their business goals.

WORK SYSTEM LIFE CYCLE MODEL

The dynamic view of a work system is summarized by the work system life cycle (WSLC) model, which shows how a work system may evolve through multiple iterations of four phases: operation and maintenance, initiation, development, and implementation (see Figure 6.3). As first presented in Alter (1992), the names of the phases were chosen to describe both computerized and noncomputerized systems, and to apply regardless of whether application software is acquired, built from scratch, or not used at all. The terms "development and implementation" have business-oriented meanings that are consistent with Markus and Mao's (2004) subsequent distinction between system development and system implementation. Note that the meaning of implementation in this context is quite different from the meaning of implementation in computer science, as in "I implemented the algorithm on the computer." Development encompasses the acquisition, configuration, and/or creation of resources needed for implementation in the organization. These resources include debugged software, installed hardware, documentation, procedure specifications, and training materials. Implementation involves more than producing debugged software or attaining initial usage in the organization. Implementation involves making desired work system changes operational in the organization. Most IT groups lack the authority and power to enforce work system changes in other functional areas. Whether or not projects are led jointly, executives who own the work system that is being created or improved should play an active role in the implementation.

The WSLC encompasses both planned and unplanned change. Planned change occurs through formal projects that encompass the four phases in a full iteration of the WSLC, that is, starting with an operation and maintenance phase, flowing through initiation, development, and implementation, and arriving at a new operation and maintenance phase. Unplanned change occurs through fixes, adaptations, and experimentation within any phase. The ideas in the work system method (WSM) can be used by any business or IT professional at any point in the WSLC. The steps in the WSM (described in the next section) are most pertinent in the initiation phase, as individuals think about the situation and as the project team negotiates the project's scope and goals.

The pictorial representation of the work system life cycle model places the four phases at the vertices of the rectangle. Forward and backward arrows between each successive pair of phases indicate the planned sequence of phase and allow the possibility of returning to a previous phase if necessary. To encompass both planned and unplanned change, each phase has an inward facing arrow to denote unanticipated opportunities and unanticipated adaptations, thereby recognizing the importance of diffusion of innovation, experimentation, adaptation, emergent change, and path dependence.

The phases in the WSLC can be summarized as follows:

Operation and Maintenance

Operation and maintenance is the ongoing operation of the work system after it has been implemented, plus small adjustments, corrections of flaws, and enhancements. Activities include:

- Operation of the work system and monitoring of its performance.
- Maintenance of the work system (which often includes at least part of the information systems that support it) by identifying small flaws and eliminating or minimizing them through fixes, adaptations, or workarounds.
- Ongoing improvement of processes and activities through analysis, experimentation, and adaptation.

Figure 6.3 **The Work System Life Cycle Model**

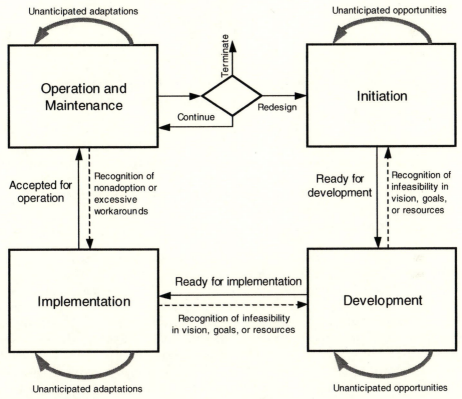

Initiation

Initiation is the process of defining the need for significant change in a work system and describing in general terms how the work system changes will meet the need. Activities include:

- Develop a vision for the new or revised work system.
- Develop operational goals.
- Allocate resources and clarify time frames.
- Evaluate the economic, organizational, and technical feasibility of planned changes.

Development

Development is the process of defining and creating or obtaining the tools, documentation, procedures, facilities, and any other physical and informational resources needed before the desired changes can be implemented successfully in the organization. Activities include:

- Determine detailed requirements for the new or revised work system (including requirements for information systems that support it).

- As necessary, create, acquire, configure, and/or modify procedures, documentation, training material, software, and hardware.
- Debug and test hardware, software, and documentation.

Implementation

Implementation is the process of making a new or modified system operational in the organization, including planning for the rollout, training work system participants, and converting from the old way of doing things to the new way. Activities include:

- Determine implementation approach and plan (pilot? phased? big bang?).
- Perform change management activities related to the rationale and positive or negative impacts of changes.
- Perform training on details of the new or revised information system and work system.
- Convert to the new or revised work system.
- Perform acceptance testing.

As an example of the iterative nature of a work system's life cycle, consider the sales system in a software start-up. The first sales system is the chief executive officer (CEO) selling directly. At some point the CEO cannot do it alone, several salespeople are hired and trained, and marketing materials are produced that can be used by someone other than the CEO. If the firm grows, the sales system becomes regionalized, and an initial version of sales tracking software is used. Later, the firm changes its sales system again to accommodate needs to track and control a larger sales force and predict sales several quarters in advance. A subsequent iteration might involve the acquisition and configuration of CRM software. The first version of the work system starts with an initiation phase. Each subsequent iteration involves deciding that the current sales system is insufficient; initiating a project that may or may not involve significant changes in software; developing the resources such as procedures, training materials, and software that are needed to support the new version of the work system; and finally, implementing the new work system.

The WSLC is fundamentally different from the frequently cited system development life cycle (SDLC). First, the SDLC is basically a project model rather than a system life cycle. Current versions of the SDLC may contain iterations, but they are basically iterations within a project. Second, the system in the SDLC is basically a technical artifact that is being programmed. In contrast, the system in the WSLC is a work system that evolves over time through multiple iterations. That evolution occurs through a combination of defined projects and incremental changes resulting from small adaptations and experimentation. In contrast to control-oriented versions of the SDLC, the WSLC treats unplanned changes as part of a work system's natural evolution.

WORK SYSTEM METHOD

The work system method (WSM) was developed for use by business professionals (and/or IT professionals) who need to understand and/or analyze a work system at whatever level of depth is appropriate for their particular concerns. It evolved iteratively starting around 1996. At each stage, the then-current version was tested informally by evaluating the areas of success and the difficulties experienced by MBA and EMBA students trying to use it for a practical purpose. A version called "work-centered analysis" that was presented in an information systems textbook (Alter, 1996) has been used in various ways by a number of universities as part of the basic explanation of systems in organizations, to help students focus on business issues, and to help student teams communicate. Ramiller (2002) reports on using a version of the work system framework within a method for "animating" the idea of business process within an undergraduate class. In a research setting, Petrie (2004) used the work system framework as a basic analytical tool in a Ph.D. dissertation examining thirteen e-commerce Web sites. Petkov and Petkova (2006) demonstrated the usefulness of the work system framework by comparing grades of students who did and did not learn about the framework before trying to interpret the same enterprise resource planning case study.

Results from analyses of real world systems by typical employed MBA and EMBA students indicate that a systems analysis method for business professionals must be much more prescriptive than soft system methodology (Checkland, 1999). While not a straitjacket, it must be at least somewhat procedural and must provide vocabulary and analysis concepts while at the same time encouraging the user to perform the analysis at whatever level of detail is appropriate for the task at hand. The various versions of WSM have all been organized around a general problem-solving outline that includes:

- Identify the problem or opportunity.
- Identify the work system that has that problem or opportunity (plus relevant constraints and other considerations).
- Use the work system framework to summarize the work system.
- Gather relevant data.
- Analyze, using design characteristics, measures of performance, and work system principles.
- Identify possibilities for improvement.
- Decide what to recommend.
- Justify the recommendation using relevant metrics and work system principles.

In contrast to systems analysis and design methods for IT professionals who need to produce a rigorous, totally consistent definition of a computerized system, the work system method:

- encourages the user to decide how deep to go;
- makes explicit use of the work system framework and work system life cycle model;
- makes explicit use of work system principles;
- makes explicit use of characteristics and metrics for the work system and its elements;
- includes work system participants as part of the system (not just users of the software);
- includes codified and noncodified information;
- includes IT and non-IT technologies; and
- suggests that recommendations specify how each element of the work system (not just the technology) should change.

WSM is built on the assumption that a single, totally structured analysis method is not appropriate for all situations because the specifics of a situation determine the nature of the understanding and analysis that is required. In some situations, a manager simply wants to ask questions to make sure someone else has done a thoughtful analysis. At other times, a manager may want to establish a personal understanding of a situation before discussing it with someone else. When collaborating with IT professionals, managers can use their understanding of a work system as a reference point for assuring that the IT professionals are fully aware of the business issues and goals that software improvements should address. From the other side, IT professionals can use the work system method at various levels of detail to confirm that they understand the business professionals who are the customers for their work.

The latest version of WSM recognizes five different roles in which WSM might be used (recognizing that the same person may play multiple roles). The scope and level of detail in the analysis differs across the roles and across different situations. In all cases, the analysis and design of a work system should include typical steps of identifying the problem and system, performing an analysis, and producing a justified recommendation. However, people in different roles should use the framework and related ideas at different levels of depth.

Level 1

Executives want their subordinates to perform thoughtful analysis of work systems but often are not directly involved in details. While participating in a discussion, they can use the work system framework to think about whether the work system and problem were defined, whether the analysis covered all elements of the work system, and whether the recommendation clarified how all elements of the work system would change.

Level 2

Strategists for work systems should think about those systems in big-picture terms. By organizing design characteristics, the work system framework has the potential for helping managers and business professionals perform the strategist role more effectively. (It is doubtful whether the strategist role is taken seriously in many systems analysis situations, especially since most tools and techniques focus on producing documentation and getting the details right.) Some design characteristics for strategists are related to work systems as a whole, such as flexibility, scalability, degree of centralization, and degree of virtuality. Others are related to specific elements of the work system framework, such as the complexity, variety, rhythm, and degree of structure in processes and activities. Yet other variables are related to the specific type of work system that is being analyzed. For example, if a work system is viewed as a service system, the strategy analysis might include characteristics implied by the service value chain framework (Alter, 2007), such as the extent of co-production, parameters of negotiations, and relative amount of effort in preparation vs. fulfillment of specific requests.

Level 3

Managers need to make sure that work systems operate efficiently and effectively. They need to understand operational details because they can neither control nor improve the results without a grasp of how the work system operates and how it satisfies the customer's wishes and needs. On the other hand, they do not need to start with high precision tools such as flow charts and database schemas. Instead, they can use a work system snapshot to summarize the work system and can go into greater depth by using a series of tools and templates that focus on specific work system elements or that look across a work system. For example, a template for a balanced scorecard identifies typical performance indicators for each element and provides space for identifying specific metrics and related performance gaps for each performance indicator.

Level 4

Implementers of work system changes need the same types of understanding required in the manager role, but also need to understand change management. The work system life cycle model and more detailed topics related to each part of it are potentially useful for them because the WSLC emphasizes the entirety of the work system change, rather than just software development and testing.

Level 5

Consultants and IT professionals need to understand enough about a work system to perform technical analysis and design tasks. When producing, configuring, and/or maintaining hardware and software the work system relies upon, IT professionals need to focus on a large number of computer- and network-related details that business professionals never need to know. In addition to understanding the parts of the work system that use IT directly, they should recognize that focusing solely on IT-reliant steps and activities creates blinders that limit their potential contribution and may lead to misunderstandings that undermine IT applications. Consequently, IT professionals are more successful if they can communicate effectively with people in strategist, manager, and implementer roles. All three frameworks might help them in their own understanding of the situation and in their communication with others.

WORK SYSTEM ISSUES AND POSSIBILITIES

As mentioned briefly above and explained in substantial depth in Alter (2006), WSM provides an organized way to pursue many different directions and metaphors for identifying issues and possible work system improvements. Although the details are beyond the scope of this article, it is worthwhile to identify some of directions.

Possibilities for Change

The purpose of analyzing a work system is to evaluate it and decide whether and how to improve it. Improving a work system is clearly not a board game like chess, but the idea of "moves" is useful in thinking about the range of possibilities for change. The moves in the system improvement game combine procedural, organizational, and technical changes that address problems and opportunities.

The elements of the work system framework can be used to organize a number of typical possibilities for change. WSM provides lists of typical possibilities for change related to each work system element. For example, changes in the process and activities might include:

- changing roles and division of labor;
- adding, combining, or eliminating steps;
- changing business rules and policies;
- eliminating built-in obstacles.

Performance Indicators

The balanced scorecard (Kaplan and Norton, 1996) is a commonly used management tool. The underlying idea is that a firm's performance should be evaluated based on factors other than just financial performance. At the corporate level, a balanced scorecard often contains performance indicators related to four perspectives: finance, customers, internal business processes, and learning and growth. According to the logic of the balanced scorecard, management should identify objectives, measures of performance, targets, and initiatives in each area.

It is possible to apply the idea of a balanced scorecard for a work system rather than an entire firm. At this level, application of a balanced scorecard approach starts with identifying relevant areas of performance related to work system elements. In any particular situation, at least several areas of performance for at least several elements probably will be relevant.

Ideally, WSM users should evaluate whether the work system is achieving targets for all significant metrics. They should also estimate the extent of improvement that is likely to occur after the recommendations are implemented. In many situations they cannot do a thorough job in either area. First, many analysis efforts quickly find that important metrics have not been tracked. In other words, whether or not targets have been established, no one knows whether those targets are being met. Under those circumstances, estimates of the likely performance impact of recommended changes are no more than guesses. Anyone using WSM under those circumstances is left with a quandary about how to describe current performance and how to estimate the impacts of recommended changes. In many cases it is impractical to accept lengthy delays to set up performance tracking. If action is required regardless of whether desired information is available, the WSM user needs to proceed cautiously based on estimates that may not be supported by facts. Unlike quality management methods that require the tracking of metrics over time, WSM is designed to allow the analysis to proceed whether or not complete information is available. Obviously, the analysis is much more solid and convincing if performance information is available and is used effectively.

Work System Strategies and Design Characteristics

Strategies express big-picture choices about how resources are deployed to meet goals. A work system's strategies are conscious rationales under which it operates. Thinking about work system strategies focuses on why a work system operates one way or another, not just the details of how it happens to operate. For example, each of the following strategies, or a version of its opposite, might be appropriate for a particular work system:

- Automate work to the extent possible. (Opposite: Do everything manually.)
- Structure work and minimize application of judgment to the extent possible. (Opposite: Rely on judgment and avoid structuring work.)
- Automate information processing, but assure that system participants can use judgment in making decisions. (Alternatives: process information manually; enforce decision rules.)

The idea of work system strategies can help WSM users visualize alternatives that may not be obvious. Experience with WSM has shown that it is comparatively easy to recommend small, incremental changes in work systems, such as eliminating an unnecessary step or computerizing information that is currently stored on paper. To make it easier to imagine and describe changes in a work system's rationale, WSM encourages (optional) use of checklists of typical strategies and design characteristics for each work system element and for the work system as a whole.

Work System Risk Factors and Stumbling Blocks

Risk factors are recognized factors whose presence in a situation increases the risk that a work system will perform poorly or will fail totally. For example, lack of participant experience and participant dissatisfaction are risk factors because they often affect performance negatively. Similarly, some work systems contain stumbling blocks, features of the work system's design or of its environment whose presence tends to interfere with efficient execution of work. Examples of built-in stumbling blocks include unnecessary inspections or signoffs that absorb time and cause delays without adding value.

The presence of risk factors and stumbling blocks is a warning sign that should lead to corrective action if possible. If a risk factor or stumbling block that has a significant effect cannot be eliminated, at minimum its effect should be mitigated if possible. For example, if there is no way to avoid having inexperienced people do the work, it may be possible to introduce tighter inspections and close mentoring. Similarly, if there is no way to eliminate inspections that are required for purposes outside of the work system, perhaps there is a way to do the inspections more efficiently. To make it easier to mitigate a work system's risk factors and stumbling blocks, WSM encourages (optional) use of checklists of typical risk factors and stumbling blocks for each work system element and for the work system as a whole.

Work System Principles

The idea of defining work system principles and incorporating them within WSM came from observing difficulties encountered by users of earlier versions of WSM. The work system elements provided a useful outline for identifying and describing a work system, but many teams had difficulty searching for improvements other than relatively obvious changes such as recording data that were not being recorded or sharing data that were not being shared. They seemed to need guidelines for evaluating both the current system's operation and the likely impacts of any proposed improvements. Providing a set of work system principles seemed a plausible way to support their analyses, but it was not clear what those principles should be.

The current version of WSM provides a set of twenty-four principles that apply to almost any work system. These are principles related to a work system in operation rather than principles about how to create or improve a work system. The twenty-four principles combine sociotechnical principles (e.g., Cherns, 1976) with additional ideas from TQM (total quality management), reengineering, computer science, ethics, and other sources. Use of the current version of the principles by MBA and EMBA students has confirmed their plausibility and potential usefulness in identifying possible alternatives and in sanity-checking a recommended set of changes. To date, however, the principles have not been validated formally, and it is likely that the current principles are not universal, especially since the principles are based on values and assumptions that may not be shared. Furthermore, it is not obvious that the number twenty-four strikes the best trade-off between insufficient guidance from too few principles and overwhelming guidance from too many.

IMPROVING COLLABORATION BETWEEN BUSINESS AND IT PROFESSIONALS

Although it was developed to help business professionals think about systems for themselves, the work system approach is also potentially relevant for improving collaboration between business and IT professionals. There is widespread agreement about the importance of user involvement in system development and maintenance, yet the level and quality of user involvement is often inadequate. Users often have difficulty saying what they want. Even if the software totally reflects what they requested, it often omits important capabilities that they failed to request. At a different organizational level, but in a similar vein, misalignment between business and IT is an ongoing source of frustration and inefficiency. As reported in *MIS Quarterly Executive,* annual surveys of Society of Information Management (SIM) executives in 2003, 2004, and 2005 all identified "IT and business alignment" as the most pressing management concern (Luftman, 2005; Luftman et al., 2006; Luftman and Mclean, 2004). The 2003 and 2005 surveys asked about key enablers and inhibitors of alignment. For both years, the enabler "IT understands the firm's business environment" ranked first. In 2005, the inhibitor "business communication with IT" ranked first.

These issues have been discussed for several decades, and the same issues will surely appear for years to come. Focusing on work systems and attaining a mutual understanding of how work systems should be improved might be an approach for improving the efficiency and quality of collaboration between business and IT professionals. Obviously, it is necessary to compile details needed for programming and software configuration. However, many business professionals find discussions of software-related details about as pleasurable as visiting the dentist. In addition, IT-centered discussions may miss many important big picture issues that can engage business professionals and that should be discussed before launching into technical details. For example, jumping quickly to "tell me what you want this software to do" might miss big-picture issues such as whether current processes and activities are too structured or not structured enough, whether processes and activities are too complex or not complex enough, and whether the rhythm of the work might change for the better. Improvements at the detailed level will yield marginal results if big-picture issues are ignored.

View of Systems

If the goal is to improve business results, focusing on the work systems that generate those results is more direct than focusing on the details and usage of hardware and software. Analysis that business professionals engage in should encompass not only technology but also processes and activities, human participants in work systems, information, and the products and services that are produced for internal or external customers.

Definition of Success

If the real goal is to improve business results, the success of projects should be measured based on improvement in work system performance, rather than on the production and/or installation of software on time and within budget. Maintaining control of programming projects requires measurement of whether programming work is completed on time and within budget. However, measuring the development of IT tools is quite different from measuring whether desired changes in processes and activities or business results occurred. IT projects end when the hardware and software operate correctly. Projects that focus on work systems end when business professionals have adopted new ways of doing work. Some of the new processes and activities may be essential for work system success even though they seem unrelated to software and hardware requirements.

Empowerment

A path toward better user involvement and business/IT alignment is to empower business professionals by providing frameworks, terminology, and methods that can help them contribute more effectively to IT-related projects. Many firms have standard templates and cost/benefit methods for evaluating projects and allocating budgets, but far fewer have organized methods for doing the analysis and design work that precedes a project proposal. The relative dearth of such methods is obvious when my incoming

EMBA students turn in a brief assignment describing whether business professionals in their firms use any defined methods for analyzing and designing typical business systems, such as systems for finding sales leads, systems for hiring employees, and systems for providing customer service. The EMBA students who work in IT are familiar with process and data modeling methods used in their IT groups, but neither they nor non-IT EMBAs usually say they are aware of any frameworks or methods used by typical business professionals in their own firms for thinking about IT-reliant systems. The main exceptions tend to be current or former employees of consulting companies or people who went through Six Sigma training primarily related to statistical quality control.

CONTINUING RESEARCH

The work system approach overlaps with many aspects of the IS field and addresses many important issues across the entire work system life cycle. Progress to date calls for additional research in a large of number of areas. Four areas with the highest potential value include the following.

1. Testing and Improving the Work System Method

Although work system concepts make sense, the usefulness of the work system approach and WSM has been validated only informally. The effectiveness and impact of both work system ideas and WSM should be tested in both pedagogical and real-world settings. This testing should identify the aspects of the method that are most and least effective and should suggest related improvements. WSM should be compared to other methods such as soft system methodology. The results of the testing should be used to develop improved versions.

2. Incorporating a Service Metaphor

Services comprise nearly 75 percent of the U.S. economy (Horn, 2005). Recognizing the large percentage of its revenues that services produce, IBM has promoted a major initiative to encourage the development of "services science" along with the development of instructional programs in SSME (services science, management, and engineering). The July 2006 edition of the *Communications of the ACM* contained a special section on services science that included thirteen papers such as Chesbrough and Spohrer (2006), Bitner and Brown (2006), and Maglio et al. (2006). Editorial notes in *Information Systems Research* (Rai and Sambamurthy, 2006) covered similar territory with special emphasis on opportunities for IS scholars.

Growing interest in services science constitutes a challenge for the further development of WSM. Perhaps it would be possible to develop a special version of the work system method that would focus on analyzing services. For example, perhaps that version would be based on a different version of the work system framework (Figure 6.1) or would provide a new framework specifically related to services. Preliminary efforts (Alter, 2007) in this direction have generated a new framework, the service value chain framework, and a new tool, service responsibility tables, that may be incorporated into or used in conjunction with future versions of WSM. As with WSM in its current state, the service-related ideas require formal testing.

3. Developing System Interaction Theory

Interactions between systems constitute a common source of difficulty and complication in building, implementing, and maintaining systems in organizations. In some cases, the interactions are direct, such as in supplier–customer interactions or dynamically negotiated allocations of shared resources. In other cases, the interactions are quite indirect, such as when the activities or policies in one system are disruptive to another system, or when design or configuration choices for one system cause subsequent problems in another system. Although there is a substantial body of knowledge related to systems analysis and design for information systems, most of the literature in that area focuses on analyzing a specific information system. Comparatively little attention focuses on direct and/or indirect interactions and conflicts between systems.

Efforts to date (e.g., Alter, 2006b) indicate that it may be possible to develop a new system interaction theory that builds upon or complements existing areas of organization- and system-related theory, including coordination theory (Malone and Crowston, 1994), loose coupling theory for organizations (Orton and Weick, 1990), coupling concepts from computer science, concepts from supply chain management, and WSM. Preliminary efforts have generated a set of design issues–related system interactions, a typology of different forms of system interactions, and common pitfalls of system interactions.

4. Developing Sysperanto

Many, and possibly most, business professionals lack an organized vocabulary for thinking about systems in organizations. Sysperanto is being developed as an ontology that codifies concepts and knowledge useful in describing and analyzing systems in organizations. Sysperanto's architecture is organized around the nine elements of the work system framework and the observation that information systems, projects, supply chains, e-commerce, and other important types of systems can be modeled as special cases of work systems (Alter, 2005). These supertype-subtype relationships provide an opportunity to organize relevant concepts economically based on the conjecture that most, but not all, properties for a specific work system type are inherited by more specialized work system types. The types of properties in Sysperanto include components and phenomena (nouns), actions and functions (verbs), characteristics (adjectives), performance indicators (adverbs), and generalizations, among others. For any particular type of work system, the properties are organized within "slices" for a specific element. The slices are specific groups of properties that are associated with a particular perspective on a work system element or the entire work system. For example, the slices for understanding processes and activities include business process, communication, and decision making, among others. Each slice provides an umbrella for a number of related terms that constitute the vocabulary for looking at a work system from a particular viewpoint. If Sysperanto is developed successfully, aspects of it might be built into procedures and/or tools that help people think about systems in organizations and help them sanity-check recommended changes. It might also contribute to the development of a body of knowledge for the IS field.

REFERENCES

Alter, S. 1992. *Information Systems: A Management Perspective.* Reading, MA: Addison-Wesley.
———. 1995. How should business professionals analyze information systems for themselves? In E.D. Falkenberg and W. Hesse (eds.), *Proceedings of the IFIP International Working Conference on Information System Concepts: Towards a Consolidation of Views,* 284–299. London: Chapman and Hall.
———. 1996. *Information Systems: A Management Perspective,* 2d ed. Menlo Park, CA: Benjamin-Cummings.
———. 2002a. The collaboration triangle. *CIO Insight,* 9 (January), 21–26. Available at www.cioinsight.com/article2/0,1397,16484,00.asp (accessed August 1, 2007).
———. 2002b. The work system method for understanding information systems and information systems research. *Communications of the AIS,* 9, 9, 90–104. Available at http://cais.isworld.org/articles/default.asp?vol=9&art=6 (accessed August 1, 2007).

————. 2003. 18 reasons why IT-reliant work systems should replace "the IT artifact" as the core subject matter of the IS field. *Communications of the AIS,* 12, 23, 365–394. Available at http://cais.isworld.org/articles/default.asp?vol=12&art=23 (accessed August 1, 2007).

————. 2005. The architecture of Sysperanto, a model-based ontology of the IS field. *Communications of the Association for Information Systems,* 15, 1, 1–40.

————. 2006a. *The Work System Method: Connecting People, Processes, and IT for Business Results.* Larkspur, CA: Work System Press.

————. 2006b. System interaction theory. Working paper presented to the JAIS Theory Development Workshop at the International Conference on Information Systems. Milwaukee, WI, December 10–13.

————. 2007. Service responsibility tables: A new tool for analyzing and designing systems. In *Proceedings of the Thirteenth Americas Conference on Information Systems* (AMCIS'07). Keystone, CO, August 10–12.

Bitner, M.J., and Brown, S.W. 2006. The evolution and discovery of services science in business schools. *Communications of the ACM,* 49, 7 (July), 73–79.

Bostrom, R.P., and Heinen, J.S. 1977a. MIS problems and failures: A socio-technical perspective. Part I: The causes. *MIS Quarterly,* 1, 3, 17–32.

————. 1977b. MIS problems and failures: A socio-technical perspective. Part II: The application of socio-technical theory. *MIS Quarterly,* 1, 4, 11–28.

Checkland, P. 1999. *Systems Thinking, Systems Practice: Includes a 30-Year Retrospective.* Chichester, UK: Wiley.

Cherns, A. 1976. Principles of socio-technical design. *Human Relations,* 2, 9, 783–792.

Chesbrough, H., and Spohrer, J. 2006. A research manifesto for services science. *Communications of the ACM,* 49, 7, 35–40.

Hill, C.; Yates, R.; Jones, C.; and Kogan, S.L. 2006. Beyond predictable workflows: Enhancing productivity in artful business processes. *IBM Systems Journal,* 45, 4, 663–682.

Horn, P. 2005. The new discipline of services science. *BusinessWeek,* January 21. Available at www.businessweek.com/technology/content/jan2005/tc20050121_8020.htm (accessed August 1, 2007).

Kaplan, R.S., and Norton, D.P. 1996. Using the balanced scorecard as a strategic management system. *Harvard Business Review* (January/February), 75–85.

Luftman, J. 2005. Key issues for IT executives for 2004. *MIS Quarterly Executive,* 4, 2, 269–285.

Luftman, J., and McLean, E.R. 2004. Key issues for IT executives. *MIS Quarterly Executive,* 3, 2, 89–104.

Luftman, J.; Kempaiah, R.; and Nash, E. 2006. Key issues for IT executives 2005. *MIS Quarterly Executive,* 5, 2, 27–45.

Maglio, P.P.; Srinivasan, S.; Kruelen, J.T.; and Spohrer, J. 2006. Service systems, service scientists, SSME, and innovation. *Communications of the ACM,* 49, 7, 81–85.

Malone, T.W., and Crowston, K. 1994. The interdisciplinary study of coordination. *ACM Computing Surveys,* 26, 1, 87–119.

Markus, M.L., and Mao, J.Y. 2004. Participation in development and implementation: Updating an old, tired concept for today's IS contexts. *Journal of the Association for Information Systems,* 5, 11–12, 514–44.

Orton, J.D., and Weick, K.E. 1990. Loosely coupled systems: A reconceptualization. *Academy of Management Review,* 15, 2, 203–223.

Petkov, D., and Petkova, O. 2006.The work system model as a tool for understanding the problem in an introductory IS project. In *Proceedings of the Twenty-Third Conference for Information Systems Educators* (ISECON'06). Dallas, Texas, November 4.

Petrie, D.E. 2004. Understanding the impact of technological discontinuities on information systems management: The case of business-to-business electronic commerce. Ph.D. diss., Claremont Graduate University.

Rai, A., and Sambamurthy, V. 2006. Editorial notes: The growth of interest in services management: opportunities for information system scholars. *Information Systems Research,* 17, 4, 327–331.

Ramiller, N. 2002. Animating the concept of business process in the core course in information systems. *Journal of Informatics Education and Research,* 3, 2, 53–71. Available at www.sig-ed.org/jier/v3n2/JIERv3n2_article6.pdf (accessed August 1, 2007).

Sumner, M., and Ryan, T. 1994. The impact of CASE: Can it achieve critical success factors? *Journal of Systems Management,* 45, 6, 16–22.

CHAPTER 7

SOFTWARE QUALITY EVALUATION

State of the Art, Practice, and Directions

PAOLO SALVANESCHI

Abstract: *The aim of the chapter is to provide an integrated view of the approaches, technologies, and problems related to the quality evaluation of software products. The research and application area includes a variety of methods: quality models and related standards, metrics, testing, inspection methods, and model-based approaches. Great research effort has been allocated to software metrics, even if they have had a limited impact in engineering practice. All of these methods may be useful in evaluating the quality of software products, but an integrated view is not easily available from the literature. Moreover, from the practitioner point of view, the key point is not the identification of "the best metric" but the ability to exploit in a coherent framework every available measure (quantitative or qualitative, static or execution-based), depending on the existing technical and managerial constraints. The chapter organizes the knowledge of the area through a conceptual framework taken from other engineering disciplines. The framework is composed of the following parts: a tree of quality attributes; a definition of quality requirements; a set of measures; an algorithm able to generate values of high-level attributes from measures; a number of product models (abstractions of the software components to be measured); and a process model (the product at various development stages in time). Finally, the evolution of the state of the art and the application to current professional practice are discussed.*

Keywords: *Software Quality Evaluation, Software Measurement, Software Quality Models*

Software quality evaluation is an important theme in information systems. Information technology (IT) managers are increasingly involved in quality requirements both for the development of software applications and for the acquisition of software products and services.

The quality requirements of modern systems are increasingly wide and complex. The pervasiveness of software stresses the usability and the security of products. The complexity of the distributed systems requires careful consideration of efficiency. Maintainability and portability of applications are increasingly significant due to long service life.

The meaning of the term "software quality" is extending from the old meaning of "correct and sufficient functionality" to a broad set of different characteristics. Besides this requirement, the quality evaluation of software products is a controversial area in software engineering practice (Voas, 2003).

A great amount of research effort has been devoted to the definition of so-called software metrics, even if the engineering practice impact of this effort has been limited. Surprisingly (for a self-proclaimed "engineering" discipline), the experimental approach (formulate the hypothesis, design the experiment, get data, validate them, interpret them, draw conclusions) has been significantly addressed only recently (Perry et al., 2000).

As pointed out in Fenton and Neil (2000) some classical statements concerning the applicability of typical metrics are not confirmed by the experiments. For example, Fenton and Neil show that size-based metrics are poor predictors of defects, and static complexity metrics, such as cyclomatic complexity, are not significantly better predictors. Moreover, complexity metrics are strongly correlated with much simpler size metrics. They also show that the count of prerelease defects is a very bad predictor of in-service defects (the popularly believed assertion that modules with a high incidence of faults detected during prerelease testing are likely to have a higher incidence of defects in operation is not confirmed by experiments).

The state of the art and the practice of software-product quality control are quite fragmented. A quality control procedure may include the following techniques:

- Collection and evaluation of measures (the so-called metrics)
- Testing
- Product inspections
- Use of formal models for deriving properties (e.g., queuing network models for performance evaluation). This approach is usually confined to specialized areas of software engineering.

Even if all of these techniques may be useful for evaluating the quality of software products, it is not easy to derive a reference landscape from literature and to appreciate the roles and relationships of each technique. Furthermore, from the practitioner point of view, a quality control procedure should integrate the techniques for a unique purpose: to support managerial decision making during the software life cycle.

From this point of view, we should take into account the following requirements:

- Quality is a broad definition that includes a number of different aspects. Following the International Organization for Standardization (ISO) 9126 (ISO/IEC 9126–1, 2001) classification, it includes six different characteristics, each of which is composed of a number of subcharacteristics. This means that we should require a number of specialized techniques for evaluating each attribute.
- Quality is context situated. The quality of a system depends not only on the characteristics of the system itself but also on the current context of use.
- Quality is life-cycle situated. It is useful to evaluate the same characteristic in various phases of the development cycle. For instance, early evaluation at the design phase may prevent significant costs of code changes.
- Quality control requires partial evaluations of attributes of a complex structure of interacting heterogeneous components. Some attributes may be critical, while others may be noncritical. This means also that software components may not be equally relevant for a specific quality attribute. For example, efficiency may be critical for a database and a communication mechanism, while the same attribute may be unimportant for other components.
- Quality management requires a pragmatic view. This requires the management of a risk vs. cost approach and the integration of different techniques to achieve the best results, given the existing constraints.

An interesting question is why the discipline of software quality evaluation is so difficult. In our opinion, at least the following characteristics contribute to the difficulty:

1. Measuring quantities for evaluating, controlling, or forecasting properties of things is a core issue for both engineering and science. It requires a strong scientific approach. Civil engineering is based on the laws of physics and exploits a number of theories and models built on the principles of physics. Theories and models are validated using the scientific experimental method. Software engineering in many cases (e.g., a new software design method) is a technology that is not scientifically validated, but is simply submitted to the market forces and becomes part of the discipline after de facto wide use. However, if you want, for example, to measure some internal software properties to forecast the maintenance effort, you need to deal with the whole complexity of a scientifically validated model to be used for engineering purposes.

2. Quality evaluation requires a system view. It requires not only the availability of well-founded specific technologies but also suitable engineering approaches to integrate and exploit them. A software product may have a number of different interacting properties. Furthermore, a software product is usually part of a larger system including data, hardware components, humans, and organizational rules.

Given the above considerations, we will try to integrate the existing approaches and technologies in a reasonable engineering framework, so that readers can locate each technique in a unified landscape. The practitioner as well as the researcher can use this landscape for a better comprehension of the state of the art, the current practice, and the possible directions of evolution.

The first part of the chapter defines the engineering reference framework by using an approach common to other engineering fields. It also defines the scope of the survey and the issues that are not considered, even if they are related to software quality evaluation. The second part gives the references to the main technologies involved in software quality evaluation, and locates them in the engineering framework. The third part discusses some specific aspects related to the evaluation process. Finally, some suggestions are given for practitioners, and research directions are discussed.

THE REFERENCE FRAMEWORK

Quality evaluation of software-intensive systems includes two different approaches: product quality evaluation and process quality evaluation. The process quality approach is based on the assumption that well-defined and organized processes are the basis for the development of good quality products. On the contrary, product quality evaluation is a technical procedure whose aim is the assessment of a specific product against a set of quality requirements.

We will not examine the area of process quality evaluation but will concentrate our overview on product quality.

The evaluation of product quality includes the technical content of the measurement procedure and the evaluation process (process phases, deliverables, organizational aspects). We discuss only some considerations related to the measurement process (the aspects more closely linked to technical problems), while we do not explore the organizational issues in depth.

A final limitation of our overview concerns the relation between software and management information systems (MIS). The quality evaluation of an MIS exceeds the problems related to the quality of the software part, encompassing other aspects such as the quality of data or the quality of the organizational procedures. We focus only on the software part of an MIS.

As previously mentioned, we need a framework in which to locate and establish the relations among the various knowledge chunks that may contribute to the quality evaluation of a software product. Other engineering disciplines (e.g., civil engineering) may provide useful guidance in defining the conceptual framework. An interesting presentation of the concepts underlying the civil engineering discipline may be found in Blockley (1980). Tekinerdogan (2000) discusses the engineering approach and applies it to the design of software architectures.

According to other engineering fields, we say that the technical part of a procedure used for evaluating the quality of a software product (e.g., based on ISO 9126) should typically be composed of the following items:

- A tree of attributes linking low-level measures to high-level abstractions (a definition of "quality")
- A definition of quality requirements
- A set of measures
- An algorithm able to generate values of high-level attributes from measures
- A numbers of product models (abstractions of the software product to be measured)
- A process model (the product at various development stages in time).

Software "quality" is defined as a set of attributes of the software product. The "quality" attribute is a broad and vague concept. For this reason it is divided into a list of more specific attributes, usually organized into a hierarchical structure. A good example is the ISO 9126 hierarchy of quality characteristics and subcharacteristics (the so-called IS0 9126 "quality model"; note that the word "model" in this case does not have the usual engineering meaning of an abstract description, through some mathematical formalism, of a product).

The hierarchy of attributes drives the requirements definition (typically nonfunctional requirements). Clearly, the required value of each attribute is not the same for each product. For instance, a high maintainability value is relevant for a product with a long life but not for a program to be used only once for a specific application. The requirements of a software product should include a "quality profile" based on the context of use.

At the bottom level of the model is a set of characteristics to be measured on the software artifact. Usually the set of concepts related to one of these measurable characteristics (measured quantity, scale, measurement procedure, associated formulas, etc.) is called "metric."

An algorithm is used to compute the values of high-level attributes, given a number of measured values. A simple example of this algorithm may be an interpretation function for each measure, mapping of row data to a common quantity space of merit values, and a computation (e.g., a weighted average) integrating a number of merit values into a unique score.

It is assumed that the measurement procedure can be executed (with specific constraints) on the deliverables of each development phase. This is particularly relevant for anticipating problems. For instance, the evaluation of nonfunctional requirements at the end of the design phase may reduce the risk of a significant reworking at the end of the development. This means that the quality control procedure uses an underlying process model. Each phase of the process delivers a set of documents, and each set describes the same product at different levels of abstraction. The first three components of the framework (the tree of attributes, the set of measures, and the algorithm) may be, in principle, applied to each set of documents. The procedure must enforce some constraints (e.g., a structural complexity metric is not applicable to a requirements document).

Finally, each quality evaluation procedure assumes the existence of a product model. The simpler product model is a hierarchy of software components. The hierarchy is generally used as a way to manage the multiplicity of objects to be measured and to focus the effort (some components may be more critical and may require a deeper measurement effort). This part of the framework is significantly less developed in software engineering than in other engineering fields. For example, the assessment of structural properties of civil engineering artifacts exploits a large number of mathematical models, from very simple qualitative descriptions to highly sophisticated finite elements models. Software engineers use quality-oriented product models for specific purposes, but they are not widely used.

THE MEASUREMENT TECHNOLOGIES

In the following paragraphs, we give an overview of the methods, technologies, and problems related to the quality evaluation of software systems and locate them in the engineering framework presented before.

Tree of Attributes

The attributes tree has been largely explored. Many "quality models" are available from the literature. The original work of McCall et al. (1977) provided a first definition of the term "software quality." Many variants of the definition are used in practice. The ISO 9126 document (ISO/IEC 9126–1, 2001) provides a standard reference to this issue. The standard classifies six quality attributes: functionality, reliability, usability, efficiency, maintainability, and portability. They are further classified into twenty-seven subattributes. Note that the ISO model is a tree, whose attributes do not interact, while the original McCall model includes positive and negative interactions between them. This is a simplification of the real case. However, in the most common cases of quality evaluation, each attribute is considered in isolation, even if studies of interactions are available. For instance, Cranor and Garfinkel (2005) include a broad set of contributions discussing the interaction between usability and security (a subattribute of functionality, according to the ISO standard).

Measures

Measuring software is sometimes considered a matter of metrics. In fact, a quality evaluation procedure may use various techniques: metrics, testing, and inspections.

A large number of metrics have been proposed and studied. The guidelines associated with the ISO standard (ISO 9126–2/3/4, 2001) include a long list of possible metrics. Specific metrics have been developed for measuring different characteristics in different documents of the development cycle. Fenton and Pfleeger (1997) present a set of classical metrics and, more significantly, apply the scientific approach to the measurement process (correct use of scales, experimental design, data collection, statistic tests, and validation). An application of this approach and some case studies, derived from the EU-funded SCOPE project, are described in Bache and Bazzana (1994).

Testing is a commonly used technology but is usually not integrated with other quality control techniques. Note that the result of a test case may be considered a measure having a Boolean (pass/fail) value. A broad literature on this topic is available. For an overview of the state of the art of testing, see Harrold (2000). Testing usually refers to functionality even if it can be applied to other attributes (e.g., efficiency). Testing is a dynamic technique requiring the availability of code. In some cases, it is also applied at the design phase, through the development of executable prototypes. An example is the implementation of a prototype for efficiency estimation at the design phase.

Inspections are also a well-known technique. Checklists provide a structured way of applying inspections to many types of documents. Each checklist consists of a number of questions. Each question has a number of specified replies (e.g., "yes" or "no" or a value in a qualitative scale). Note that applying checklists may require the availability of an expert assessor and may imply a degree of subjectivity. Extensive examples of inspections through checklists may be found in Bache and Bazzana (1994) and Spinelli et al. (1995).

The important point is that, while a number of techniques are available, there is a need to combine them (even relatively simple ones) to build management decision-support tools. It seems to us that the key point is not the identification of "the best quantitative measure" but the ability to exploit in a coherent framework every available measure (quantitative or qualitative, with a reasonable degree of objectivity or dependent on expert judgment, static- or execution-based), depending on the existing technical and managerial constraints. Key points for engineers and managers seem to be the framework and the integration, not the single metric.

Quality Requirements

The quality of a software product is a context-dependent concept. It depends on the intended uses of the product and on risk evaluation (software that may lead to large financial losses in case of failure will be tested more accurately than other less critical applications).

Basili and Rombach (1988) introduced the concept of goal in the software measurement process (the goal, question, metric paradigm). The concept is part of the approach proposed by the ISO standards (ISO/IEC 15939, 2007) and the PSM (Practical Software and Systems Measurement) methodology, supported by the U.S. Department of Defense (U.S. DOD, 2003). Through the definition of goals, we may define where to spend the (limited) available resources. Some attributes may be critical, while others may be irrelevant.

This leads to the definition of a "quality profile" of a software product. A quality profile is part of the requirements document and defines the expected level of each quality attribute (functional and nonfunctional requirements). The level may be defined using the following two approaches:

- A quality value (e.g., in a qualitative scale). This is a global value, applied to all the intended uses of the product. The meaning may be the level of adherence to a set of the best practices adopted in the market for similar products. An example of this type of quality profile is described in Spinelli et al. (1995).
- A set of scenarios defining specific uses. For each use, it is possible to give a specific required value of the quality attribute and to measure it.

The concept of scenario is widely used to manage the context issue. A requirements document exploiting this concept has to classify and accurately write all of the relevant scenarios related to the whole set of quality attributes (not only functionality). Scenarios may also be used for quality requirements evaluation not only at the code level but also at the design level (Bass et al., 2001; Folmer et al., 2003).

The two approaches may be combined for the definition of different quality requirements of the same product. See the example presented in Salvaneschi (2005a).

Interpretation and Integration Algorithms

The plan of measures (through metrics, test cases, or inspections) has to be linked to the attributes tree. More measures (leaves of the attributes tree) may contribute to the value of a single quality attribute. Usually, the global "quality" of a software product is not computed. Instead a measured quality profile to be compared with the required quality profile is generated (a required value for each attribute or subattribute). For a discussion related to the definition of the quality profile, see Voas (2003).

The set of values derived from a number of measures is the input for the computation of each quality attribute score. Some measures are quantitative values; others may be based on qualitative evaluations. For example, you can derive measures related to maintainability from the design and code documents (modularity measures, ratio comments/lines of code, and an expert evaluation of the design document). If you want to evaluate the global maintainability, you need to take the following steps. The first is the interpretation of each measured value. Is a given value of comments/lines of code ratio bad or good? Note that the interpretation function is not necessarily linear (a low value of comments/lines of code is bad, but an extremely high value is also bad). The second step requires answering questions of the following type: if the architectural design is very good, code modularity is medium, and the code is not sufficiently commented, how do you rate maintainability? This rating may be done through a form of evidential reasoning where each interpreted value provides evidence for a global quality value. The reasoning may be codified through a set of rules (or a set of decision tables). This approach can manage both quantitative and qualitative measures and host different types of rules (e.g., you can manage the relevance of each measure or focus on the criticality of a cluster of measures) with a degree of flexibility higher than, for example, averaging the measured values. While the procedure is somewhat arbitrary, it is nevertheless useful to provide a global quality profile that can be used to present the results and discuss them. The global profile may be complemented by the more relevant specific quantitative measures. An example of this type of computation is described in Piazzalunga et al. (2005).

Process Models

Some quality attributes may be measured at various stages of development. This means that the attributes tree and the set of measures should be adapted to the orthogonal view of a process model. For each phase of the process, we define the set of delivered documents. For each set we instantiate an applicable subset of the attributes and measures tree. Obviously not all possible measures are applicable at each phase. For instance, specific metrics are available to evaluate the design modularity or the complexity of the code control flow. There are various reasons for evaluating the software quality at different stages of the development process:

- Some attribute is essentially handled at a specific phase. For instance, the ability to support the evolution of the software product is essentially related to the architectural design.
- It may be of interest to anticipate the evaluation. For instance, the efficiency evaluation during the design phase may prevent significant reworking due to late discovery of efficiency problems during the final test. This also means that the same attribute may be evaluated at the end of different phases with different uncertainty degrees. You can estimate a performance parameter at the end of the design phase and get a better measure of it at the end of the coding phase.

Measurement frameworks, including multiple quality evaluations at the end of the main phases of a linear development cycle, are presented in Bache and Bazzana (1994) and Spinelli et al. (1995).

Product Models

The use of product models is one of the main differences between software quality engineering, and other engineering disciplines (the other main difference being the limited use of the scientific experimental method).

For example, if you examine the approach used by civil engineers for evaluating the earthquake resistance of buildings, you may find attributes and measures as well as hierarchies of buildings models. Models are used to infer properties from measured values. Engineers manage a variety of models. For instance, a building may be modeled as a unique object, and you can infer properties (seismic resistance) from qualitative attributes and simple rules. A more complex and expensive model describes the physical system as a set of interconnected objects. Modeling the behavior requires, in this case, the availability of quantitative measures and some computation based on the definition of typical failure mechanisms. See Salvaneschi et al. (1997) for a more detailed discussion. In general, the prediction of the seismic behavior of existing buildings is obtained through the following components: a definition of the seismic input, a model (representing both structure and behavior) of the seismic resistance of the building, and a number of model attributes whose values are measurable on the physical artifact. The structural part of the model allows the assignment of attributes to parts of the building. Through the behavioral part, one can apply the seismic input and, depending on the measured attributes, compute the expected damage. This approach is applied to a variety of situations and includes many specialized models. A tall steel building is different from a two-floor masonry one. Civil engineers have a long history of theoretical and experimental studies related to specific classes of artifacts.

Product models are usual ingredients of quality evaluation in engineering. The modeling of software products is largely used in many areas of software engineering (see, e.g., Unified Modeling Language [UML] models or conceptual models in database design). On the contrary, the use of product models specifically developed for software quality evaluation is uncommon and highly fragmented.

In the following, we present an overview of application and research areas relevant for the development of a more mature use of quality-oriented product models. The areas are:

- ISO standards and related projects;
- Formal models;
- Patterns for quality evaluation; and
- Aspect-oriented development.

The ISO 9126 approach assumes that the software product is a unique object. In the SCOPE project (Bache and Bazzana, 1994), the product is composed of nonexecutable components (e.g., design documents) and the executable system. The latter is modeled as a hierarchy of subsystems and modules. Another example is the PSM procedure (U.S. DOD, 2003) that uses a hierarchical representation of components. The product model hierarchy is generally used as a way to manage the multiplicity of objects to be measured. The approach used in Spinelli et al. (1995) for evaluating and explaining the quality profile of a large automation system introduces a different point of view. The software product is modeled through a hierarchy of components (an abstract structural model).

The model is used to focus the quality profile and the measurement effort. In fact, quality requirements are seldom uniform over the whole product (e.g., high efficiency may be required in graphic display functionality, but not in batch print functionality; maintainability is more necessary in functions that are more likely to evolve over time).

Specialized product models based on formal modeling languages are used in software quality evaluation for specific purposes. Examples are reliability models (Musa et al., 1987), where the whole software component is modeled as a stochastic process, and performance models (Balsamo et al., 2002), used to predict values of performance parameters through, for instance, the use of stochastic Petri nets or queuing network models. These performance models are behavioral models that can be derived at the earliest stages of the software life cycle, namely, software architecture and software specification, allowing the study of this important nonfunctional attribute before implementation.

Formal languages have been studied to describe programs and designs and derive properties through mechanical reasoning. An overview of this field may be found in Jackson and Rinard (2000).

Another significant application area of formal models is model-based testing. The term refers to test case derivation from a model (e.g., a finite state machine) representing software behaviors. Even in this case, the test selection is based on different precode artifacts, such as requirements, specifications, and design models. See Bertolino et al. (2005) for an overview of the approach and Whittle et al. (2005) for an application of the approach to the real problem of testing telecommunications systems. The latter authors propose a methodology for creating a state machine-based test model from a collection of scenarios (given as UML interaction diagrams). An interesting point of this study is the use of an engineering approach mixing semiformal models, formal models, and heuristic rules.

Product models based on formal languages have had, until now, a limited impact on the software engineering profession. Looking at the state of the art of other engineering disciplines, qualitative and simple models complement more complex and formal ones, so that the engineer can tune the modeling effort depending on the specific problem (e.g., the criticality level of software components).

From this point of view, patterns (e.g., design patterns) can play a significant role. Patterns can be interpreted as empirically validated models of a qualitative nature. Usually, design patterns are interpreted as a tool to design new systems reusing predefined and tested structural and behavioral models. Design patterns also can be interpreted as mechanisms responsible for quality values. Finding suitable patterns (and also suitable values of attributes associated with them) may be interpreted as evidence for values of quality attributes. This approach is used in the SEI "quality attribute design primitives" method (Bass et al., 2000).

Finally, an interesting research area that can make significant contributions to the modeling of mechanisms responsible for quality values is aspect-oriented software development (AOSD).

The basic idea is to support the multidimensional analysis, design, and programming of complex systems by complementing the traditional hierarchical view with additional orthogonal models. For example, at the design level, these models describe properties scattered throughout the designed modules (designed using a "dominant" view). They define the intersections between different views and support the integration of views into a unique code. AOSD may lead to a better understanding, classification, and modeling of structures and behaviors related to each quality attribute. A comprehensive survey of aspect-oriented analysis and design approaches may be found in AOSD-Europe (2005).

All of these approaches contribute to "quality-oriented product modeling" research. Nevertheless, product models are not common ingredients of quality evaluation practice, and there is a limited effort to develop useful engineering models of this type for specialized types of software.

We clarify the concept of "quality-oriented software model" using an example taken from the work of Balducci et al. (2005).

The aim is to measure the security strength of the copy protection mechanism reached by software through hardware dongle. Dongles are usually USB (Universal Serial Bus) keys or small boxes to be attached to the host parallel port. The copy-protected software interacts with the dongle and progresses in its execution only if the dongle answers appropriately. A library provides access to the dongle functions. Different ways of using the library affect the security strength of the protection. For instance, the copy-protected software tries to uniquely identify the key and confirm that it is a "real" one. The cryptographic function in the dongle is used as the basis for a challenge-response protocol between the host software and the dongle. It is fundamental that the challenge be unpredictable, for example, by being generated with a secure random number generator. These suggestions may be organized as the defense pattern "cryptographic challenge-response" that improves the security of your software. The research developed a quality-oriented model able to predict the security strength of the protection in terms of the estimated amount of time a hacker would need to break it. The model is composed of the following parts.

A Defense Pattern Catalogue

This is the structural part of the model. A set of measurable attributes is associated with each pattern. For instance the "cryptographic challenge-response" pattern has the following attributes: number of different caller addresses; challenge distribution; number of cryptographic keys.

An Attack Pattern Catalogue

An attack pattern catalogue defines the possible inputs to the model. For example, a possible attack may be "locate the dongle checks starting from the library calls and modify the code with a hexadecimal editor."

A Flow Diagram

A flow diagram for each attack pattern represents the experimental knowledge of how to conduct an attack in the catalogue. This is the behavioral part of the model. The flow diagram computes the time required to successfully execute the attack and is influenced by the values of the defense pattern attributes. It includes parameters that have to be tuned experimentally. The result of the computation is the measure in minutes of how long an attacker will need to successfully conduct an attack depending on defense attributes. In fact, the behavioral model is more complex, because a real attack may use multiple attack patterns. This is modeled through an AND/OR graph (an attack tree).

We can see from the short description of the example that metrics (the attributes of the defense patterns) are only one of the ingredients. In the example we find all of the components of a typical engineering model (see the seismic engineering example above): input, structural and behavioral description, measurable attributes, and output computation. We also note that, while the approach is general (e.g., you can use it in Web application security), the model is specific to a well-defined type of software, such as in the buildings example from the seismic engineering domain.

MEASUREMENT PROCESS ISSUES

The technical content of a measuring procedure is only an aspect of the measurement process. A guideline for implementing the whole process is the set of ISO/IEC 14598 documents (ISO/IEC 14598–1,2,3,4,5,6,

1998–2001). They provide support for planning, managing, and documenting the measurement activities, according to three different views: developers, acquirers, and third party evaluators.

As mentioned before, an in-depth discussion of the organizational issues related to the measurement process is outside the scope of this chapter. We highlight only some aspects that are more strictly related to the technical content of the measurement task.

A first aspect is the experimental approach to software quality measurement. This is a very important point. Many claims related to the prediction of quality characteristics through suitable measures lack empirical studies organized as scientific experiments. Doing an experimental evaluation requires a well-defined sequence of steps:

1. Definition of purpose (hypothesis) and scope of the experiment. We have to clearly define the aims of the experiment (e.g., a comparison of the usability of two types of software components), and we have to set the limits.
2. Design of the context for the experimental scenario. This may include the software component to be measured, the tools, the involved actors, their roles and tasks. If, for example, a set of users is required, they must be selected according to the defined context and the aims of the test. The number of users has to be chosen to provide a wide enough sample to support the statistical analysis of data. The task to be executed by each user (sequence of steps, input data, output data) must be defined.
3. Design of the measurement apparatus. We must define the quality attributes, the metrics, and their relationships. For each metric, we need to state name, description, scale, and procedures for collecting the data and computing the value.
4. Measurement execution and data collection.
5. Processing for statistical significance. Data must be processed to assure their statistical significance (e.g., a metric is the result of the computation of a mean value of raw data, and it is required to compare two mean values coming from two different experimental design cases).
6. Computation of the quality attributes score.
7. Results presentation, interpretation, and explanation.

A roadmap of the empirical research in software engineering is presented in Perry et al. (2000). An example of an experimental comparison of the usability of two ICT (information and communication technology) products is presented in Piazzalunga et al. (2005).

A second aspect discusses the role of measures. A typical role of software measurement is the quantitative prediction of quality properties (e.g., a prediction of the maintenance effort from measurable software attributes such as cohesion and coupling of modules or size of modules). In many cases, this has proved a difficult task. The essential reason is that maintainability depends on a number of sociotechnical parameters that are difficult to model and measure. See Fenton and Neil (2000) for an in-depth discussion. Even if the development of predictive models is a difficult task, this is not the only possible and fruitful use of software measurement. In the following, we list a number of situations in which you can successfully manage a measuring procedure, even if a quantitative model able to compute predictions based on a robust understanding of cause-effect relations is not available.

Prediction

Prediction is based on stable environments and availability of historical data. If these assumptions hold, it is possible to use metrics to derive predictions that are not general but may be statistically useful for a specific organization. In this case, it is again true, for example, that the maintenance effort depends on a number of unknown parameters (people skill, time pressure, technical environment, application type, etc.), but it may be reasonably assumed that these parameters are stable.

Risk Management

A car may be used only if an agency periodically assesses the car's safety through a set of measures. This is considered useful even if there is no quantitative model able to predict, from the car's measures, the number of future car accidents. The idea is a risk-based classification. An analogous approach may classify the modules of a software system using, for instance, some "intricacy" metrics (known to have a significant impact on the maintainability effort). The classification may be used for an acceptance procedure based on the risk concept. Modules exceeding an "intricacy" threshold are rejected. In this case, we are not able to quantitatively predict the effect of the "intricacy" on the future maintenance effort. Nevertheless, we prefer to avoid future significant risks for our organization, and the measurement procedure may support the decision process.

Monitoring

Measures may be used to maintain the value of key software attributes within defined thresholds. This has been used, for instance, to control the performance of software maintenance outsourcers. Even in this case, we are not able to predict the maintenance effort. We simply know that a set of attributes could influence the future maintenance effort and we want to prevent the quality attributes of the software delivered by the maintenance outsourcer from worsening. The critical point is that well-founded experimental studies should be available to demonstrate that, in our specific type of software and environment, the chosen set of quality attributes is strongly correlated to the maintenance effort.

SUGGESTIONS FOR PRACTITIONERS AND RESEARCH DIRECTIONS

The research effort has been focused for a long time on two components of the engineering framework already presented: metrics and the tree of attributes. The impact on engineering practice has been very limited until now. The failure of excessive expectations and the overselling of commercial tools for metrics have had a negative effect in some cases. While testing is a common practice, measuring software properties is an uncommon practice. This is also related to poor practice in defining and managing the nonfunctional requirements of software systems. In many cases, performance or usability problems of large and complex systems are discovered after delivery.

We suggest that the following research aspects are important for improving the state of the art and for technology transfer to the software engineering profession:

1. Specialize the Research

If we consider the field of seismic engineering, the growth of available engineering knowledge was not only based on news and better theories but also on thorough experimental studies of specific engineering artifacts (e.g., classes of bridges or buildings). Specialization also produced significant improvements in other areas of software engineering. See, for example, the research in design patterns. Software engineers may now use books of structural and behavioral models proven useful for designing classes of software systems (e.g., management information systems, real time systems, or communication components). We think that the same approach should be effective in the area of software quality evaluation. Our research must specialize in studying not only specific quality attributes (e.g., security) but also specific types of software (e.g., the software for copy protection previously mentioned).

2. Do Experimental Studies

In the past, some claims regarding the applicability of metrics were not based on the availability of results from thorough experimental studies. The research should be more strongly founded on the approach of experimental software engineering.

3. Improve the Role of Quality-Oriented Software Product Models

We suggest that (1) quality-oriented software product models are important ingredients of a quality evaluation procedure; (2) the evaluation of a product of significant complexity may require various models of different types; and (3) quality-oriented product models have not been sufficiently explored. There is a need to investigate the modeling issue by itself (e.g., the role of models, types of models, levels of abstraction, catalogues of models, and need for multiple models), experiment with the use of models, and develop reusable classifications and examples. A discussion of the role of models in software quality evaluation and some case studies are presented in Salvaneschi (2005b).

Even if significant research is required, a number of technologies and methods are available and may significantly improve current practice. Some suggestions for practitioners follow.

Integrate the Measurement Process and the Other Software Processes

Pay attention to a careful definition of nonfunctional requirements. The aim is to include a complete quality profile of the product in the requirements document. Define a quality control plan that takes into account not only the functional verification but also the nonfunctional aspects. Anticipate the control activities through quality evaluation in the early development phases.

Integrate the Measurement Technologies

A quality control plan may integrate various techniques (metrics, testing, inspections, use of prototypes, formal models). The introduction of new quality control technologies may be based on the traditional test plan. The test plan may be improved, adding new control technologies and extending it to the early phases of development.

The approaches that integrate the technologies and manage different levels of complexity and cost are very important to support exploitation in real cases. The case studies included in Bache and Bazzana (1994), Spinelli et al. (1995), and Salvaneschi (2005b) may be useful examples.

Use the Experimental Approach

Practitioners should learn and use the experimental approach. Exploiting the available techniques of software measurement requires not only the choice of reasonable metrics but also the ability to design the measurement experiment, assess the significance of the results, and correctly interpret them.

REFERENCES

AOSD-Europe. 2005. Survey of Aspect-Oriented Analysis and Design Approaches. Available at www. aosd-europe.net.

Bache, R., and Bazzana, G. 1994. *Software Metrics for Product Assessment.* New York: McGraw-Hill.

Balducci, F.; Jacomuzzi, P.; and Moroncelli, C. 2005. Security measure of protected software: A methodology and an application to dongles. Master thesis (in Italian), Turin Polytechnic.

Balsamo, S.; Di Marco, A.; Inverardi, P.; and Simeoni, M. 2002. Software performance: State of the art and perspectives. Technical report, Dipartimento di Informatica, Università dell'Aquila.

Basili, V.R., and Rombach, H.D. 1988. The TAME project: Towards improvement-oriented software environments. *IEEE Transactions on Software Engineering,* 14, 6, 758–773.

Bass, L.; Klein, M.; and Bachmann, F. 2000. Quality Attribute Design Primitives, Technical Note, CMU/SEI-2000-TN-017.

Bass, L.; Klein, M.; and Moreno, G. 2001. Applicability of General Scenarios to the Architecture Tradeoff Analysis Method. CMU/SEI-2001-TR-014, ESC-TR-2001–014.

Bertolino, A.; Marchetti, E.; and Muccini, H. 2005. Introducing a reasonably complete and coherent approach for model-based testing. *Electronic Notes in Theoretical Computer Science,* 116 (January 19), 85–97.

Blockley, D. 1980. *The Nature of Structural Design and Safety.* Chichester, UK: Ellis Horwood.

Cranor, L.F., and Garfinkel, S. (ed.). 2005. *Security and Usability: Designing Secure Systems That People Can Use.* Sebastopol, CA: O'Reilly & Associates.

Fenton, N.E. and Pfleeger, S.L.1997. *Software Metrics: A Rigorous and Practical Approach.* Boston: PWS Publishing Co.

Fenton, N.E., and Neil, M. 2000. Software metrics: A roadmap. In A. Finkelstein (ed.), *The Future of Software Engineering 2000: Twenty-second International Conference on Software Engineering.* 357–370. New York: ACM Press.

Folmer, E.; Van Gurp, J.; and Bosch, J. 2003. Scenario-based assessment of software architecture usability. In *Proceedings of ICSE 2003 Workshop: Bridging the Gap between Software Engineering and Human-Computer Interaction.* Portland, Oregon, 61–68. Portland: IFIP.

Harrold, M.J. 2000. Testing: A roadmap. In A. Finkelstein (ed.), *The Future of Software Engineering 2000: Twenty-second International Conference on Software Engineering,* 61–72. New York: ACM Press.

ISO/IEC 14598–1,2,3,4,5,6. 1998–2001. Information technology, Software product evaluation, Parts 1–6.

ISO/IEC 15939. 2007. Software Engineering, Software measurement process.

ISO/IEC 9126–1 2001. Standard, Software Engineering, Product Quality, Part 1: Quality Model.

ISO/IEC 9126–2/3/4. 2001. Software engineering, Product quality, External Metrics; Internal Metrics; Quality in Use Metrics.

Jackson, D., and Rinard, M. 2000. Software analysis: A roadmap. In A. Finkelstein (ed.), *The Future of Software Engineering 2000: Twenty-second International Conference on Software Engineering,* 133–145. New York: ACM Press.

McCall, J.A.; Richards, P.K.; and Walters, G.F. 1977. Factors in Software Quality, RADC TR-77–363. Rome Air Development Center Reports, Griffiths Air Force.

Musa, J.D.; Iannino, A.; and Okumoto, K. 1987. *Software Reliability: Measurement, Prediction, Application.* New York: McGraw-Hill.

Perry, D.E.; Porter, A.A.; and Votta, L.G. 2000. Empirical studies in software engineering: A roadmap. In A. Finkelstein (ed.), *The Future of Software Engineering 2000: Twenty-second International Conference on Software Engineering,* 345–355. New York: ACM Press.

Piazzalunga, U.; Salvaneschi, P.; and Coffetti, P. 2005. The usability of security devices. In L. Cranor and S.L. Garfinkel (eds.), *Designing Secure Systems That People Can Use,* 209–234. Sebastopol, CA: O'Reilly Media.

Salvaneschi, P. 2005a. The quality matrix: A management tool for software quality evaluation. In Peter Kokol (ed.), Proceedings of *IASTED International Conference on Software Engineering.* Innsbruck, 394–399. Calgary: ACTA Press.

———. 2005b. Towards model-based quality evaluation of software products. Paper presented at the Third World Congress for Software Quality, Munich, September 26–30.

Salvaneschi, P.; Cadei, M.; and Lazzari, M. 1997. A causal modelling framework for the simulation and explanation of the behaviour of structures. *Artificial Intelligence in Engineering,* 11, 3 (July), 205–16.

Spinelli, A.; Pina, D.; Salvaneschi, P.; Crivelli, E.; and Meda, R. 1995. Quality measurement of software products: An experience about a large automation system. In P. Nesi (ed.), *Objective Software Quality,* LNCS 926, 192–206. Berlin: Springer Verlag.

Tekinerdogan, B. 2000. Synthesis-Based Software Architecture Design. PhD Thesis, Department of Computer Science, University of Twente, March.

U.S. Department of Defense (U.S. DOD). 2003. Practical Software and Systems Measurement. A Foundation for Objective Project Management, v.4.0. Available at: www.psmsc.com.

Voas, J. 2003. Trusted software's holy grail. *Software Quality Journal,* 11, 1 (May), 9–17.

Whittle, J.; Chakraborty, J.; and Krüger, I. 2005. Generating simulation and test models from scenarios. Paper presented at the Third World Congress for Software Quality, Munich, September. 26–30.

CHAPTER 8

MACOM: MULTIAGENTS COGNITIVE MAP APPROACH FOR INFORMATION SYSTEMS PROJECT RISK MANAGEMENT

KUN-CHANG LEE AND NAM-HO LEE

Abstract: *Project risks encompass both internal and external factors, characterized by unplanned problems and events. These factors are interrelated, influencing others in a causal way. In fact, most information technology companies evaluate project risk by roughly measuring the related factors, ignoring the important fact that there are complicated causal relationships among them. More effective mechanisms must be developed to systematically judge all factors related to project risk. In order to accomplish this, our study adopts a cognitive map (CM)–based mechanism. The CM represents the causal relationships in a given object and/or problem and describes tacit knowledge hidden in the problem domain. CMs have proven especially useful in solving unstructured problems with many variables and causal relationships. However, simply applying CMs to project risk management is not enough because most causal relationships are hard to identify and measure exactly. To overcome this problem, we have borrowed a mutiagent metaphor in which CM is represented by a use of mutiagents, and project risk is explained through the interaction of the mutiagents. Such an approach presents a new computational capability for resolving complicated decision problems. Our own proposed system is called MACOM (multiagent cognitive map) where CM is represented by a set of mutiagents, each embedded with basic intelligence in order to determine its causal relationships with other agents in decision-making situations. Using the MACOM framework, we demonstrate that the task of resolving the information systems (IS) project risk management can be systematically solved, and in this way IS project managers can be given robust decision support.*

Keywords: *Cognitive Map, Multiagent Cognitive Map, Swarm Simulation, Information System Project, Project Risk, Node Value*

Many uncertainties exist in information systems (IS) projects, including project size estimates, schedules, quality, and resource allocation. Such uncertainties have always been at the heart of risk management (Boehm, 1991; Charette, 1989; Karolak, 1996) in systems analysis and development. In general, uncertainty management is best managed across an organization's total portfolio (Kitchenham and Linkman, 1997), by allowing resources to be adjusted or reallocated among several projects in order to enhance the likelihood of project success. However, a serious problem with this type of project management is that resources are limited, and many ongoing projects may need those resources at a specific time.

Project risks encompass both internal and external factors (Bandyopadhyay et al., 1999). For example, human resources that are important to the success of a project may move on before the project is completed. Political intrusions are an example of external risk factors. Project risk factors are characterized by the occurrences of unplanned problems and events (Buhl et al., 2004; Wognum et al., 2004), and are interrelated so that they influence each other in a causal way. Project risk management is subject to human error and nonsystematic practices. A more effective mechanism must be developed, in which all factors related to project risk can be systematically judged and causal relationships considered systematically. Decision makers can then view project risk from a holistic perspective that encompasses all of the possible causal influences among factors, measure project risk more objectively, and set up more robust decision-making strategies.

To accomplish this research purpose, we have adopted a cognitive map (CM)–based mechanism. The CM is a representation of the causal relationships that exist among the decision elements of a given object and/or problem and describe experts' tacit knowledge. CM is composed of:

1. concept nodes (i.e., variables or factors) that represent the factors describing a target problem;
2. arrows that indicate causal relationships between two concept nodes; and
3. causality coefficients on each arrow that indicate the positive (or negative) strength with which a node affects another node.

Its main virtue lies in the ability to see whether one node has an influence on the state of another. CM has been used very successfully in the fields of administrative science and management science—for example, as an application in addressing organization issues (Bougon et al., 1977; Eden et al., 1979; Ross and Hall, 1980), a strategic planning simulation (Eden and Ackerman, 1989; Lee et al., 1998), economics and politics (Craiger and Coovert, 1994; Taber, 1994), and negotiation (Kwahk and Kim, 1999). CM is also used in various information system and information technology areas—for example, in geographic information systems (Liu and Satur, 1999; Satur and Liu, 1999), network management (Ndousse and Okuda, 1996), and electronic circuit analysis (Styblinski and Meyer, 1991). Recently, CM has been used in more complex business decision areas such as business process reengineering (George and Michael, 2004). Another interesting application of CM is found in Chinese Chess (Chen and Huang, 1995).

Simply applying CM to project risk management is not enough, however, because most existing causal relationships are hard to identify and measure exactly. In order to overcome this problem, we use a mutiagent metaphor in which each factor is represented by an agent, and a CM explaining project risk is explained by the interaction of the mutiagents. Mutiagent systems are a new paradigm in many fields, in which multiple computational entities, called "agents," interact with one another. The power of mutiagent systems does not lie in a single agent, but rather in the mutual interactions and emerging global outcomes, which overcome the limited properties and capabilities of single agents (Privosnik et al., 2002). Mutiagent systems use the concept of swarm simulation to induce emergent behavior from the interactions of multiagent (Rouff et al., 2004). In swarm simulations, each agent interacts with other agents to satisfy its own goals, but multiple agents interact based on simple action strategies, leading to logical and stable behavioral outcomes called "emergent behaviors" (Liu and Passino, 2002; Weiss, 1999), which convey meaningful information to decision makers.

Our proposed CM, which we call MACOM (multiagent cognitive map), is represented by a set of multiagent that are embedded with basic intelligence in order to determine causal relationships and causalities in decision-making situations. The MACOM for resolving project risk management is designed as follows:

First, CM is described using a set of multiagent in which each agent represents a node, and the agent is autonomously capable of determining causal relationships as well as causality given information that decision makers interpret from the project risk problem.

Second, since MACOM is composed of multiple agents, interactions among multiagent in MACOM are able to address project risk management issues more effectively. One advantage of this approach is that the proposed MACOM can behave more intelligently using a swarm simulation mechanism (Rouff et al., 2004), whereas multiagent working together in an iterative manner display emergent behaviors that are derived from the complicated interactions among multiple agents over a certain period. The emergent behaviors deduced by MACOM reveal important implications for decision makers who are trying to handle project risk issues.

Third, decision makers who use MACOM do not need to supply complete information in order to build an appropriate CM for a specific decision-making problem. Partial information relating to some project risk factors is a good starting point for MACOM to be able to construct an appropriate CM. This is because the swarm simulation mechanism in which MACOM locates the best configuration of concept nodes, causal relationships, and causality coefficients leads to an appropriate CM suitable for the target-project risk-management problem. From the perspective of a mutiagent simulation, the final CM can be viewed as an emergent behavior or equilibrium status after a number of iterations among agents given conditions set by a target problem.

In order to prove the validity of the proposed approach, the proposed MACOM was applied to a real data set extracted from a multinational information technology (IT) company. For the experimental platform of MACOM, we adopted the Netlogo (2006) environment where decision makers can build their own multiagent simulation mechanism for various decision problems. The results revealed the robustness of the proposed approach in organizing various types of risk-reducing strategies. The next section of the chapter addresses the theoretical background for this study. In the third section, we describe the proposed MACOM, using an illustrative example and its related experiments.

THEORETICAL BACKGROUND

MACOM is based on two concepts:

1. cognitive map, and
2. particle swarm optimization.

In addition, MACOM represents expert knowledge by using CM. Finally, we elaborate on project risk assessment to help readers understand it more clearly.

Cognitive Map

As mentioned previously, a CM is composed of concept nodes, their causal relationships, and causality coefficients. CMs have proven especially useful in dealing with situations in which a number of decision-making factors are interrelated causally and must be considered simultaneously, not ignoring certain factors during the problem-solving process (Lee and Lee, 2003; Liu and Satur, 1999; Noh et al., 2000; Numata et al., 1997; Park and Kim, 1995; Wellman, 1994; Zhang et al., 1989, 1994). The IS project risk-management problem also includes qualitative and quantitative factors, which makes the CM approach quite useful in resolving the related decision problems.

Usually, CM allows a set of identified causality coefficients to be organized in a causality coefficient matrix (or adjacency matrix), enabling a what-if and/or goal-seeking simulation to be created on its basis. This simulation enables decision makers to identify the most relevant decision factors for enhancing outcomes. The advantages of the CM simulation are many: first, activation of specific nodes can result in a chain of effects on the other nodes through positive or negative causal relationships defined in the CM, until equilibrium is attained. Second, a variety of what-if sensitivity simulations can be performed according to the decision maker's intent. Through these simulations, decision makers can identify the relevant decision variables and their acceptable values, ensuring they obtain the intended results.

The CM allows experts to draw causal pictures of their problems. We view the CM as a dynamic system that settles down to a specific stable state. The causal dynamic system represented by CM responds to external stimuli, and we interpret its equilibrium-seeking behavior as a CM-based simulation or inference. Let us consider the CM-based simulation using the illustrative CM in Figure 8.1. We assume a concept node vector beforehand. There are six concept nodes in Figure 8.2. We can define a concept node vector as follows: $N = (N_1, N_2, N_3, N_4, N_5)$, where each concept node represents a concept in Figure 8.1. Based on the CM in Figure 8.1, we can build a causality coefficient matrix, E, as seen in Figure 8.2.

Using this causality coefficient matrix, we can test the effect of "increase of project duration (time)" on all of the concept nodes in CM by setting the first concept node vector N_1 as follows:

$$N_1 = (1\ 0\ 0\ 0\ 0).$$

Multiplying this by E, we obtain the second concept node vector N_2.

$$N_1 \times E = (0\ 1\ 0\ 0\ 0) \rightarrow (0\ 1\ 0\ 0\ 0) \qquad \text{(inference 1)}$$
$$(1\ 1\ 0\ 0\ 0) = N_2$$

The arrow indicates the threshold operation using 1/2 as a threshold value (Kosko, 1992), which is the most popular CM-based inference. We can use different values for the threshold operation, but will derive the same results with the same meaning unless the threshold values lie in the interval $[-1, 1]$. If the causality coefficient is less than 1/2, it becomes 0; otherwise, it equals 1. Applying 1/2 threshold to the result of $N_1 \times E$ yields inference result 1, which is not the same as N_1. Therefore, we need to design the second concept node vector N_2 contains $N_1 = 1$ because we are testing the effect of increase of project duration (time), which is the first concept node. Then inference result 2 is derived as follows:

$$N_2 \times E = (0\ 1\ 1\ 0\ 0) \rightarrow (0\ 1\ 1\ 0\ 0) \qquad \text{(inference 2)}$$
$$(1\ 1\ 1\ 0\ 0) = N_3$$

Since inference results 1 and 2 are not the same, we need to develop a third concept, node vector N_3, by inserting $N_1 = 1$ into the vector of inference result 2. Multiplying N_3 by E yields inference result 3, as follows.

$$N_3 \times E = (0\ 1\ 1\text{–}1\ 1) \rightarrow (0\ 1\ 1\ 0\ 1) \qquad \text{(inference 3)}$$
$$(1\ 1\ 1\ 0\ 1) = N_3$$

$$N_4 \times E = (0\ 1\ 1\text{–}1\ 1) \rightarrow (0\ 1\ 1\ 0\ 1) \qquad \text{(inference 4)}$$
$$(1\ 1\ 1\ 0\ 1) = N_4$$

Figure 8.1   **Illustrative CM**

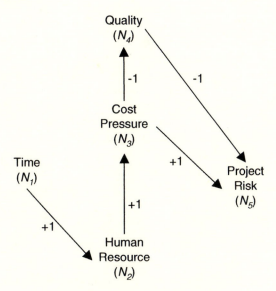

Figure 8.2   **Causality Coefficient Matrix of CM in Figure 8.1**

$$E = \begin{matrix} & \begin{matrix} N_1 & N_2 & N_3 & N_4 & N_5 \end{matrix} \\ \begin{pmatrix} 0 & 1 & 0 & 0 & 0 \\ 0 & 0 & 1 & 0 & 0 \\ 0 & 0 & 0 & -1 & -1 \\ 0 & 0 & 0 & 0 & 1 \\ 0 & 0 & 0 & 0 & 0 \end{pmatrix} & \begin{matrix} N_1 \\ N_2 \\ N_3 \\ N_4 \\ N_5 \end{matrix} \end{matrix}$$

Finally, we reach a state of equilibrium where inference 4 equals inference 3. As a result, inference 4, or (1 1 1 0 1), is a fixed point of the CM dynamic system described in Figure 8.1. The CM has associatively inferred the answer $\{N_1, N_2, N_3, N_5\}$ given the what-if question $\{N_1\}$. This simple CM tells us clearly that increase of project duration (time) leads to increase of human resource in the project, causing additional labor cost. As a result, it can be said that project risk may increase.

CM should also determine its causality coefficients. Traditionally, CM does not induce causality coefficients through more sophisticated learning algorithms, though a questionnaire survey was taken (Lee and Lee, 2003). Many IT consulting firms have entered bids to win specific IS projects, and these bid results are stored in the case base for reference. Potential IS project risks start to occur at the point of bid and proposal. The CMs used to analyze IS project risk management can use these past bid results to identify appropriate causality coefficients. We propose using a swarm simulation, which will allow MACOM to determine its causality coefficients.

Particle Swarm Optimization

The particle swarm optimization (PSO) is a parallel evolutionary computation technique developed by Kennedy and Eberhart (2001) based on the social behavior metaphor. Their standard textbook on PSO treats both the social and computational paradigms. The PSO algorithm is initialized with a population of random candidate solutions, conceptualized as particles. Each particle is assigned a randomized velocity and is iteratively moved through the problem space. It is attracted toward the location of the best fitness achieved so far by the particle itself and by the location of the best fitness achieved so far across the whole population (global version of the algorithm). The PSO algorithm includes some tuning parameters that greatly influence algorithm performance, often stated as the exploration-exploitation trade-off: Exploration is the ability to test various regions in the problem space in order to locate a good optimum, hopefully the global one. Exploitation is the ability to concentrate the search around a promising candidate solution in order to locate the optimum precisely. Despite recent research efforts, the selection of the algorithm parameters remains empirical to a large extent. A complete theoretical analysis of the algorithm has been given by Clerc and Kennedy (2002). Based on this analysis, the authors derived a reasonable set of tuning parameters, as confirmed by Eberhart and Shi (2000). Clerc and Kennedy (2002) contain a good deal of mathematical complexity, however, and deriving simple user-oriented guidelines from it for parameter selection in a specific problem is not straightforward. The present work gives some additional insight into the topic of PSO parameter selection. It is established that some of the parameters add no flexibility to the algorithm and can be discarded without loss of generality. Results from the dynamic system theory are used for a relatively simple theoretical analysis of the algorithm, which results in graphical guidelines for parameter selection. The user can thus make well-informed decisions according to the desired exploration-exploitation trade-off: either favoring exploration by a thorough sampling of the solution space for a robust location of the global optimum at the expense of a large number of objective function evaluations or, on the contrary, favoring exploitation that results in a quick convergence but possibly a nonoptimal solution. Unsurprisingly, the best choice appears to depend on the form of the objective function. In our case, the particle swarm optimization mechanism is used to determine the causal relationships among the concept nodes and the causality coefficients that produce emergent behavior in the IS project risk-management problem.

Decision-Making Mechanism Using Expert Knowledge

The proposed MACOM represents expert knowledge on project risk. There are many ways of representing expert knowledge, including rule-based systems (Hatzilygeroudis and Prentzas, 2004; Cohen and Shoshany, 2002; Tseng and Huang, 2006), neural networks (Kengpol and Wangananon, 2006; Wang et al., 2004), and case-based reasoning (Fu and Shen, 2004; Kowalski et al., 2005). However, MACOM uses CM as a vehicle of representing expert knowledge on project risk by using concept nodes, causal relationships among them, and causality coefficients. The main advantage of using the MACOM is that it combines the knowledge-representation mechanism and the inference mechanism in a single framework in which expert knowledge can be codified and visualized via CM, and appropriate inference procedures can be performed on the basis of the CM.

Project Risk Assessment

There are many uncertainties in software development processes and products, such as uncertainties in estimating project size, schedule, and quality, and in determining resource allocation (Chin-Feng and Yuan-Chang, 2004). It is suggested in the literature (Keil, 1995) that in order to reduce an organization's exposure to failure in an IS project, managers should assess risks early and update risk evaluation constantly throughout the software development process.

Figure 8.3 **Simple MACOM**

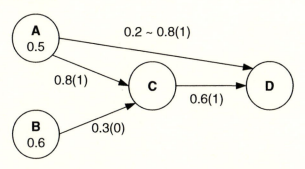

Many studies argue that IS project risk is dependent on a number of factors such as organizational change as well as political factors in the organization (Ewusi-Mensah and Przasnyski, 1994), users' level of understanding and attitude (Keider, 1984; Robey and Farrow, 1982), uncertain user requirements and changes in the requirement (Boehm, 1991; Schmidt et al., 2001), intrinsic complexities of the project (Barki et al., 1993; Kemerer and Sosa, 1988), and project planning and control (Jones and McLean, 1970; Keider, 1984). The diversity of the factors that can affect project risk causes subjective ways of managing the project's risk factors (Chin-Feng and Yuan-Chang, 2004), leading to human-intensive and opaque project risk methods. To avoid such problems, we propose a new type of project risk-management method by using the MACOM.

MACOM

The proposed MACOM works in a mutiagent framework, extracting tacit knowledge from domain experts in the form of a CM and making inferences with respect to the input case. In this study, domain is related to IS project risk assessment.

Inference Mechanism of MACOM

Since a concept node in MACOM is represented by an agent, all of the causal relationships and causality coefficients are determined autonomously, on the basis of the characteristics of the constraints imposed by the target problem. As noted previously, MACOM can adjust the causality coefficients in accordance with the changing properties of the target problem, enabling very robust decision support for decision makers. Time t can also be considered more freely within MACOM. Let us assume a simple MACOM consisting of four concept nodes, A, B, C, and D, and causality coefficients with time lag. In Figure 8.3, the causality coefficients along the path from A to D can be determined flexibly from 0.2 to 0.8 with time lag 1, while the causality coefficient along the path from A to C is 0.8 with time lag 1. Other causality coefficients can be interpreted similarly. The longest time lag is expected in the causal relationship from A to D through C.

When the two concept nodes A and B initiate events such as "$A = 0.5$" and "$B = 0.6$," then the MACOM is calculated as shown in Table 8.1, where function f indicates a node output function used at each concept node to produce the output value that will be transferred to the connected concept nodes as input. The node output function f can have different forms in accordance with

the characteristics of the problem. For example, the function is defined as $f(x) = \dfrac{1}{1 + e^{-x}}$ when the

Table 8.1

Calculation of Node Values

Time lag	Node			
	A	B	C	D
0	0.5	0.6	$f(0.6 \times 0.3)$	n/a
1	0.5	0.6	$C_0 + f(0.5 \times 0.8)$	$D_0 + f(0.5 \times [0.2, 0.8] + C_0 \times 0.6)$
2	0.5	0.6	$C_0 + f(0.5 \times 0.8)$	$D_1 + f(C_1 \times 0.6)$

node output function is intended to follow sigmoid function and thus produce more stable output value within [0, 1]. $f(x) = \begin{cases} 1, & x \geq \partial \\ 0, & x < \partial \end{cases}$ (where δ is the threshold value) is another candidate for the node output function, where threshold value δ is usually set to 0.5 in literature related to the CM inference (Kosko, 1992; Lee and Kwon, 2006; Lee and Lee, 2003). However, in this example, the node output function is designed to follow $f(x) = x$ because x is usually a weighted sum of the input values multiplied with corresponding causality coefficients. The time lag between B and C is zero, so concept node C reacts to event $B = 0.6$ immediately, without time lag. Meanwhile, concept node D is not affected by the changes or events in other, preceding nodes at time = 0, because its time lag between node C is 1, and changes in the node value of C will influence D after time lag 1. Therefore, D does not have any value at time = 0.

At time = 1, C is affected by event $A = 0.5$ (note that the causality coefficient from A to C is 0.8 with time lag 1). The output value of C at time = 1 is computed as $f(x)$. At the same time, event A = 0.5 will affect D at time = 1 with causality coefficient ranges [0.2, 0.8]. Therefore, at time = 1, D is affected directly by event $A = 0.5$, and indirectly by event $B = 0.6$ through C. At time = 2, D is affected by event $A = 0.5$ through C. In this chain of cause-effect relationships among nodes, MACOM can make inferences about the given target problem.

Particle Swarm Optimization in MACOM

In our study, the swarm simulation is used to determine the causal relationships among the concept nodes and the MACOM causality coefficients that produce emergent behavior in the IS project risk-management problem. In other words, the main components of MACOM are determined by past experiences and supervised learning processes. The determination of causal relationships and causality coefficients is of major significance in project risk management because MACOM encompasses tacit knowledge through supervised learning. For example, project managers (PMs) may want some factors to lie within certain prespecified boundaries. The MACOM learns these boundaries through swarm simulation.

In our case, the swarm simulation is constructed to find the causal relationships and causality coefficients that will minimize the error function. Say that C_i denotes the ith concept node of MACOM, and A_i represents actual value of the ith concept node C_i, $1 \leq i \leq N$. MACOM is interested in restricting the values of the concept nodes in bounds such as $A_i^{min} \leq A_i \leq A_i^{max}$, $i = 1$, ..., N, where the upper bound A_i^{max} and lower bound A_i^{min} are predetermined by the IS project experts. In MACOM, a concept node C_i is represented by an agent, and therefore a complete CM is regarded as a set of multiagent that are dynamically interrelating with each other, affecting other agents through dynamically changing causality coefficients through time. Therefore, the main objective of MACOM is to find a causality coefficient matrix, $E = \lfloor E_{ij} \rfloor i, j = 1, \ldots, N$, that leads the CM to a steady state at which the output concept nodes lie in their prespecified bounds, while the causality coefficients retain their physical meaning. In this way, MACOM finds the causality coefficient matrix $E = \lfloor E_{ij} \rfloor i, j = 1, \ldots, N$, by imposing constraints given by the past instances of IS projects. To do this, the following objective function (see Equation 1.1) is considered provided

that the number of output concept nodes is m, $A_{out} = \lfloor A_{out_i} \rfloor$, $i = 1, \ldots, m$ represents the actual

value vector of output concept nodes, and $\hat{A}_{out} = \lfloor \hat{A}_{out_i} \rfloor$, $i = 1, \ldots, m$ the computed value vector

of output concept nodes. $\hat{A}_{out}$ is obtained by multiplying output concept node vector C_{out} by E,

and organizing the corresponding computed values into a vector consisting of m output concept

nodes, where vector $C_{out} = \begin{bmatrix} 0, & i \neq j \\ C_{out_i} & i = j \end{bmatrix}$, $i = 1, \ldots, N$, and $j = 1, \ldots, m$.

$$\sum_{i=1}^{m} \left(A_{out_i} - \hat{A}_{out_i} \right)^2 \tag{1.1}$$

is obtained through application of the procedure in Equation 1.2

$$A_{out_i}(k+1) = A_{out_i}(k) + \sum_{\substack{j=1 \\ j \neq i}}^{N} A_{out_i}(k) \bullet E_j, i = 1, \ldots, m \tag{1.2}$$

where k stands for the iteration number, and E_{ji} is the causality coefficient of the causal relationship connecting concept node C_j to concept node C_i, and it follows the uniform distribution $[-1, 1]$. In the swarm simulation, therefore, the causality coefficient matrix E is computed by minimizing the objective function as in Equation 1.1 under the constraints $A_i^{min} \leq A_i \leq A_i^{max}$, $i = 1, \ldots, N$. In the process of building the MACOM, decision makers can impose a certain set of constraints—for example, if two concepts C_i and C_j are negatively related, then the corresponding causality coefficient E_{ij} should range within $[-1, 0]$. Otherwise, E_{ij} should belong to $[0, 1]$.

The proposed PSO algorithm is composed of two main steps. Step 1 begins a search from a certain starting point located in $\Re^n$ representing a set of relations among the nodes. If it finds that no solution is capable of minimizing the objective function, then Step 2 begins where evolution is made and another new point is selected, and the local search in Step 1 resumes.

Stage 1. Search Local Optimal

Step 1a: Select random vector $E_{initial}$ in $\Re^n$ Space.
Step 1b: Search E_k that minimize objective function $[1, 1]$ near $E_{initial}$ Vector
Step 1c: If $A_{out_i}(k+1) \geq A_{out_i}(k)$, then step Stage 1, otherwise repeat Step 1b

Stage 2. Evolution

Step 2a: Select $E_{initial}$ that satisfy $A_{out_i}(k+1) \geq A_{out_i}(k)$ in $\Re^n$ Space
Step 2b: Repeat Step1b
Step 2c: Repeat Step 1c

Termination rule: after N number of evolutions, if $A_{out_i}(k+1) - A_{out_i}(k) \leq \partial$ then stop.

Experiment

Target Problem

In general, many IT consulting firms have tried to win IS project bids that seemed to secure a certain level of profitability with minimum risk. However, client companies issuing IS projects are often vulnerable to many fluctuations and factors that could lead to abrupt changes in project requirements and/or financial terms. It is widely accepted in IS project fields that every IS project has pros and cons in terms of profits and risks. Without question, IT consulting firms want IS projects that can guarantee high profits and low risks, though this is very hard to realize in reality. This chapter reviews IS project-bid processes first, after which we search for an opportunity to take advantage of MACOM. Before submitting a proposal to a client company, a risk manager usually scrutinizes the proposal, assessing and minimizing possible risk factors. Specifically, risk managers comment on financial conditions and compare the client's requirements, including contract type, client status, and so on. In this process, risk managers depend heavily on their past experience and qualitative judgment. MACOM can complement this judgment by combining relevant quantitative and qualitative factors related to IS project risk management, and analyzing them from a holistic point of view.

Data Gathering

To prepare MACOM, we must consider a number of past instances of IS project risk management. For this purpose, we gathered them from a multinational IT consulting firm located in Seoul, South Korea. To ensure data quality, ten experts who have had over ten years of experience as IS project and risk managers were interviewed, and then twenty-four main factors believed through experience to affect project risk significantly were selected. Table 8.2 shows the twenty-four factors, which are categorized as input and output factors. Input factors are those that can be obtained before starting the IS project, while output factors are the final output of the MACOM inference. The factors are regarded as concept nodes of CM, and are treated as agents in MACOM afterward. By interviewing the ten experts, we obtained partial information about the causal relationships among the twenty-four factors, as shown in Table 8.3. Since some of the causality coefficients are restricted by the experts, we used different linguistic variables (positive, negative, slightly positive, slightly negative, etc.), whereby positive means that the causality coefficient falls within [0, 1], negative [0,–1], strongly positive [0.5, 1], weakly positive [0, 0.5], strongly negative [–0.5,–1], and weakly negative [0,–0.5].

A time lag exists between concept nodes in accordance with the time-variant characteristics of causal relationships. When the time lag is zero, it means that changes in a node will affect the connected nodes immediately. When the time lag is 1, it means that there is a time gap between the related concept nodes. Therefore, some changes in the preceding nodes will affect the connected

Table 8.2

Relevant Factors Related to Assessing the IS Project Risk

Number	Factors	Description	Type
1	Consultant skill	Average careers of engaged consultants	Input
2	Customer IT infrastructure	Hardware, network, software, IT training	Input
3	Customer satisfaction	Customer's satisfaction for the project	Input
4	Customer participation	Customer's involvement in project	Input
5	Top management sponsorship	Top management's support for this project	Input
6	PM experience	Career of project manager	Input
7	Customer's change adoption	Cultural flexibility for the change	Input
8	Customer's requirement	Customer's additional requirement	Input
9	Extension volume	Expected extension or customization volume	Input
10	Clear R&R definition	How clearly defined are roles and responsibilities	Input
11	Customer relationship	Historical relationship with this client	Input
12	Project risk	Anticipated project risk	Output
13	Contingency	Contingency for this project	Input
14	Solution mapping ratio	Functional mapping ratio between S/W and requirements	Input
15	Customer project experience	Customer's experience for IT project	Input
16	Contractual risk	Contractual risks that cause legal problem	Input
17	Profit	Total margin of project	Input
18	Financial risk	Financial risk such as revenue recognition issue and collection issue	Input
19	Project duration	Total project duration	Input
20	Contract type	Time & material, or fixed price	Input
21	Terms & conditions (T&C)	How T&Cs are favorable for us	Input
22	Bidding margin	Calculated margin in bidding	Input
23	Competition in bidding	How many competitors are involved in this deal	Input
24	Reference	Reference sites for similar project	Input

nodes after the specified time lag. The swarm simulation will be performed on the basis of such initial information, leading to the final MACOM.

The factors identified in the interviews are regarded as concept nodes in CM. Therefore, we need node values for attributes that each factor can have, because the node values will be used in MACOM as events or stimuli that are likely to affect the other connected agents (i.e., nodes). For the purpose of identifying the node values, we performed focus-group interviews with five experts currently working as active project managers. The results are summarized in Table 8.4.

MACOM requires a training data set before starting the swarm simulation in order to determine the causality coefficient matrix. We asked the first ten experts to assess possible IS project risks for the ten specific samples, with the results described in Table 8.5. Project risk is located in the far right column, meaning that it is an outcome variable in this training data set.

Table 8.3

Partial Information About the Causal Relationships Among the IS Project Risk Factors

From node #	To node #	Relation	Time lag
1	11	Weakly positive	0
	14	Strongly positive	0
2	7	Weakly positive	0
	13	Weakly negative	0
3	12	Strongly negative	1
4	3	Weakly positive	0
	7	Strongly positive	0
5	4	Strongly positive	0
	7	Strongly positive	0
6	3	Strongly positive	0
	4	Strongly positive	0
	8	Strongly negative	0
	10	Strongly positive	0
	11	Strongly positive	0
	12	Strongly negative	0
7	9	Strongly negative	0
8	9	Strongly positive	0
9	13	Strongly positive	1
10	13	Strongly negative	1
11	12	Strongly negative	1
	16	Weakly negative	0
13	12	Strongly positive	0
14	3	Weakly positive	0
	9	Strongly negative	0
	13	Strongly negative	0
15	7	Weakly positive	0
	10	Weakly positive	0
16	12	Strongly positive	1
17	18	Strongly negative	0
18	12	Strongly positive	0
19	7	Weakly positive	1
	13	Weakly positive	1
20	12	Strongly negative	1
	18	Strongly negative	0
21	18	Strongly negative	0
22	13	Strongly negative	0
	17	Strongly positive	0
23	21	Strongly negative	0
	22	Strongly negative	0
24	12	Strongly negative	0
	13	Strongly negative	0

Swarm Simulation

By using the training data set in Table 8.5, we performed a swarm simulation with 1,243 iterations, obtaining a minimum error value of 0.645. The swarm simulation was performed in the Netlogo (2006) environment (Figure 8.4). At the final iteration stage, the final causality coefficient is obtained and the final MACOM is produced accordingly, as depicted in Figure 8.5.

Table 8.4

Node Values

Number	Node name (factor)	Attributes	Node value
1	Consultant skill	Average level: 6	1.0
		Average level: 5	0.5
		Average level: 4	0.0
2	Customer IT infra	Top level	1.0
		Not bad (average)	0.5
		Needs improvement	0.0
3	Customer satisfaction	Very satisfied	1.0
		Satisfied	0.5
		No complain	0.0
		Not satisfied	−0.5
		Much to complain about	−1.0
4	Customer participation	Aggressive	1.0
		Average	0.0
		Passive	−1.0
5	Top management (C-Level) sponsorship	Very interested in project	1.0
		Interested in project	0.7
		Very low-level involvement	0.4
		No involvement from top management	0.0
6	PM experience	More than 12 years	1.0
		More than 7 years	0.7
		More than 5 years	0.4
		Under 5 years	0.1
7	Customer's change adoption	Very flexible	1.0
		Flexible	0.5
		Normal	0.0
		Inflexible	−0.5
8	Customer's requirements	Unreasonable requirements that cannot be handled	1.0
		Unreasonable requirements that can be handled	0.5
		Reasonable requirements	−0.5
9	Extension volume (package S/W extension)	More than 50 percent of standard functionality	1.0
		Around 30 percent	0.6
		Around 10 percent	0.2
10	Clear R&R definition	Very clearly defined	1.0
		Clearly defined	0.5
		Not clear	0.0
11	Customer relationship	Very good	1.0
		Good	0.6
		Not good	0.2
		Bad	−0.6
		Very bad	−1.0
12	Project risk	Green	0.2
		Yellow	0.2–0.4
		Red	0.4
13	Contingency	n/a (because mediation attributes between Yes attribute and result)	n/a
14	Solution mapping ratio	Approximately 80 percent	1.0
		Approximately 60 percent	0.7
		Approximately 40 percent	0.4
		Below 30 percent	0.1
15	Customer project experience	Same size project experience	1.0

(continued)

Table 8.4 *(continued)*

Number	Node name (factor)	Attributes	Node value
		Project experience weaker than this project	0.5
		No project experience	0.0
16	Contractual risk	Very high	1.0
		High	0.5
		Medium	0.0
		Low	−0.5
		Very low	−1.0
17	Profit	n/a	n/a
18	Financial risk	Collection risk	1.0
		Revenue recognition issue	0.7
		No expected problem	0.0
19	Project duration	More than 2 years	1.0
		Around 1 year	0.7
		Around 6 months	0.4
		Around 3 months	0.1
20	Contract type	Time & material	1.0
		Fixed price	0.5
21	Terms & conditions	Meet our policy	1.0
		Do not meet our policy, but have the same case in the past	−0.5
		Several critical items that do not meet our policy	−1.0
22	Bidding margin	More than 40 percent	1.0
		Around 30 percent	0.7
		Around 20 percent	0.4
		Around 10 percent	0.1
		Below 10 percent	0.0
23	Competition in bidding	High	1.0
		Medium	0.5
		Almost no competition	0.0
24	Reference	Have reference in same industry	1.0
		Have reference in other industry	0.5
		Don't have any reference in any industry	0.0

Problem Solving

On the basis of the MACOM as shown in Figure 8.5, the next job is a problem-solving task to estimate the IS project risk. For the purpose of illustration, suppose that we are going to submit a proposal for an IS project having the conditions as summarized in Table 8.6.

This IS project is related to implementation of a CRM (customer relationships management) package. The expected ratio of software solution mapping to user requirements is under 50 percent. The client company, which is in the telecommunications industry, started its business as a public company. Cultural flexibility is expected to be low, and the company is big, so a great deal of competition will be necessary to win this deal. A reference to application of the same CRM package is not reported in South Korea, and it seems that this IS project may be the first CRM package implementation project in the telecommunications industry in that country. The problem is to determine how much project risk may be involved in this IS project. To solve this problem, we applied MACOM, with a project risk value assessed as−0.17 or 0.42 after normalization (see the "current" row in Table 8.7). This is relatively high and should be reduced by adjusting the controllable input factors. Another round of simulation is needed to

Table 8.5

Training Data Set

	Attributes	1	2	3	4	5	6	7	8	9	10
1	Consultant skill	1.0	0.5	0.7	0.3	0.5	0.5	1.0	0.7	0.7	0.5
2	Customer IT infra	1.0	1.0	0.5	0.5	0.7	1.0	0.7	0.8	0.8	1.0
3	Customer satisfaction	0.0	0.0	0.0	0.0	0.0	0.0	0.0	0.0	0.0	0.0
4	Customer participation	1.0	−1.0	−0.5	−1.0	−1.0	0.7	0.7	0.5	0.2	1.0
5	Top management sponsorship	1.0	0.0	0.7	0.0	0.0	1.0	1.0	0.0	0.5	1.0
6	PM experience	1.0	0.7	0.5	0.7	0.7	0.7	1.0	0.7	0.7	1.0
7	Customer's change adoption	1.0	−0.5	−0.2	0.0	−0.2	0.7	0.8	0.0	−0.2	1.0
8	Customer's requirements	0.5	1.0	1.0	0.5	1.0	0.5	−0.5	−0.5	1.0	−0.5
9	Extension volume	0.6	1.0	0.6	0.6	1.0	0.6	0.2	0.6	1.0	0.2
10	Clear R&R definition	1.0	0.5	0.5	0.5	0.5	1.0	1.0	1.0	0.4	1.0
11	Customer relationship	1.0	0.0	0.0	0.0	0.0	1.0	1.0	0.0	−0.2	1.0
13	Contingency	0.0	0.0	0.0	0.0	0.0	0.0	0.0	0.0	0.0	0.0
14	Solution mapping ratio	1.0	0.6	0.7	0.6	0.5	1.0	1.0	0.8	0.5	1.0
15	Customer project experience	1.0	1.0	0.5	0.5	0.5	1.0	1.0	0.5	1.0	1.0
16	Contractual risk	−1.0	0.5	0.0	0.0	0.5	−0.5	−1.0	−0.5	1.0	−1.0
17	Profit	0.0	0.0	0.0	0.0	0.0	0.0	0.0	0.0	0.0	0.0
18	Financial risk	0.0	0.0	0.0	0.0	0.0	0.0	0.0	0.0	0.7	0.0
19	Project duration	0.5	0.7	0.7	0.5	0.7	0.7	0.6	0.6	0.7	0.7
20	Contract type	1.0	0.5	0.5	0.5	0.5	0.5	1.0	0.5	0.5	1.0
21	T&C	1.0	−0.5	−0.5	−0.5	−1.0	1.0	1.0	1.0	−0.5	1.0
22	Bidding margin	0.7	0.4	0.4	0.1	0.0	0.4	0.4	0.4	0.4	0.4
23	Competition in bidding	0.0	1.0	0.2	1.0	1.0	0.7	0.2	0.7	1.0	0.5
24	Reference	0.5	0.0	1.0	0.0	0.0	1.0	1.0	1.0	0.0	1.0
12	**Project risk**	**0.00**	**0.52**	**0.34**	**0.73**	**1.04**	**0.52**	**0.20**	**0.36**	**0.68**	**0.22**

reduce project risk even more. The controllable input factors for this IS project were believed to include seven factors:

1. Consultant skill
2. PM experience
3. Clear definition of roles and responsibilities (R&R)
4. Contractual risk

Figure 8.4 **Swarm Simulation**

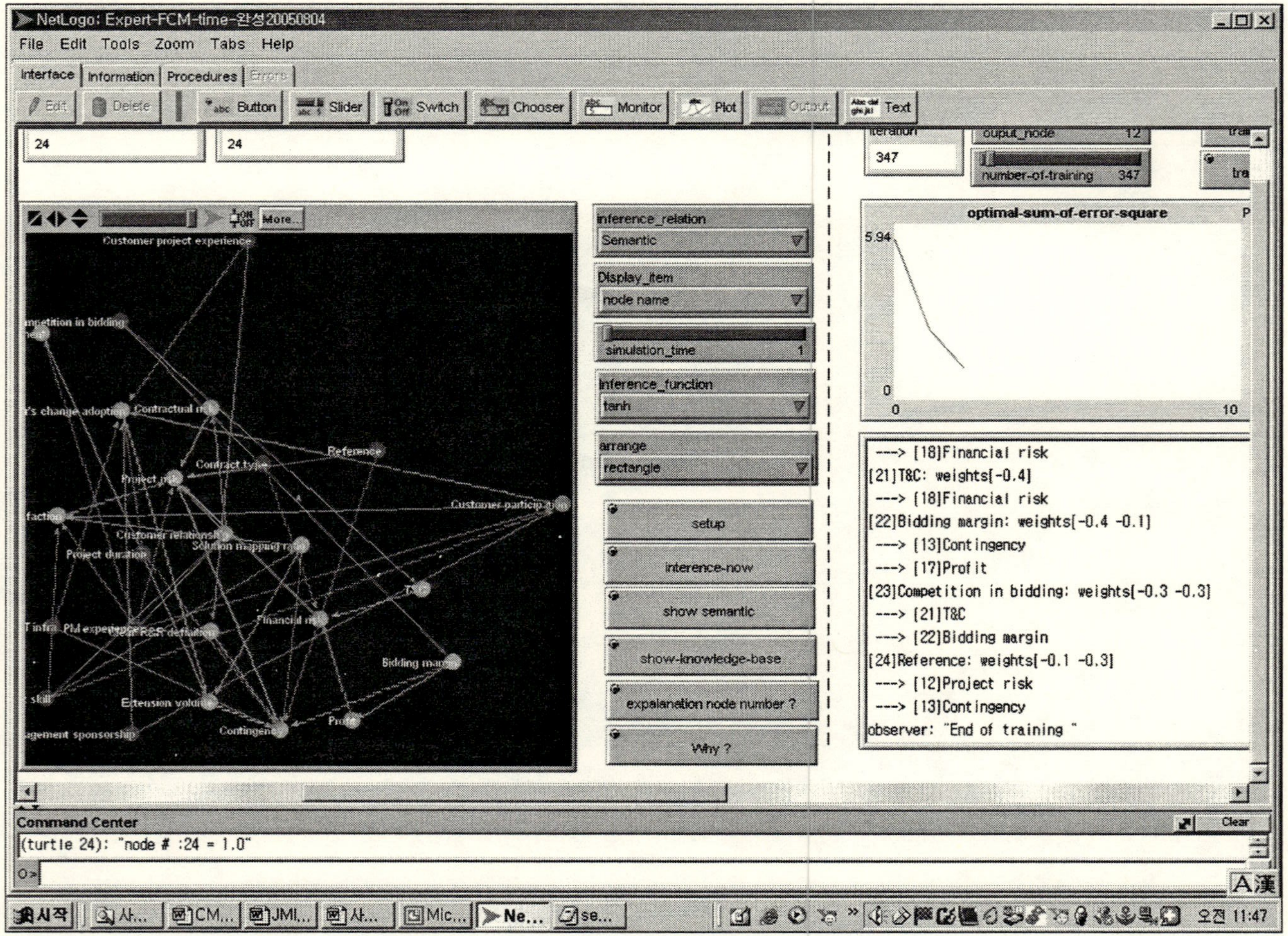

Figure 8.5 The Final MACOM Obtained by Swarm Simulation

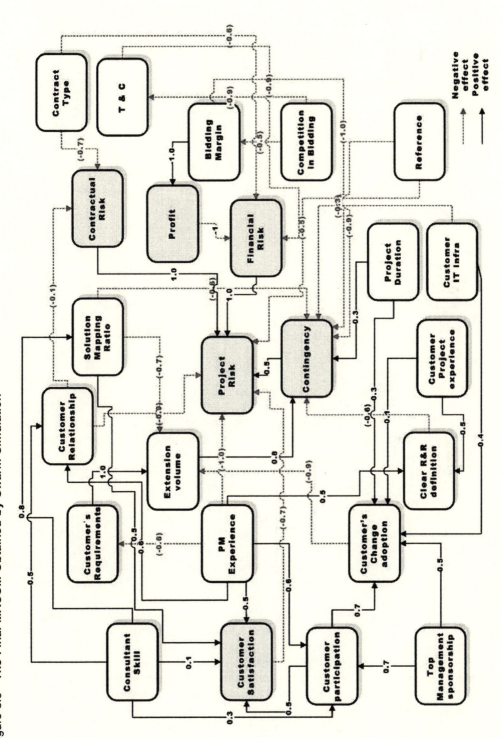

Table 8.6

Information about an Illustrative IS Project

Factors	Value
Consultant skill	Average level: 0.65 (0.7)
Customer IT infra	Top level (0.8)
Customer participation	Under average (0.2)
Top management sponsorship	A little bit interest (0.5)
PM experience	More than 7 year (0.7)
Customer's change adoption	Not so flexible (−0.2)
Customer's requirements	Unreasonable requirement (1.0)
Extension volume	More than 50% (1.0)
Clear R&R definition	Something needs to be defined clearly (0.4)
Customer relationship	Not good (0.2)
Solution mapping ratio	Around 50% (0.5)
Customer project experience	Same size experience (1.0)
Contractual risk	Very high (1.0)
Financial risk	Revenue recognition issue (0.7)
Project duration	Around 1 year (0.7)
Contract type	Fixed price (0.5)
Terms & conditions	Do not meet our policy (−0.5)
Bidding margin	Around 20% (0.4)
Competition in bidding	High (1.0)
Reference	No reference (0.0)

5. Contract type
6. Terms and conditions
7. Bidding margin

MACOM was applied to find the most promising combination of feasible values for these seven controllable factors. After 500 experiments, MACOM recommended four alternatives, as summarized in Table 8.7.

When interpreting each node value based on Table 8.4, alternative 1 requires more clear R&R definition on statement of work and recommends the change of contract type from *Fixed Price* type to *Time and Material* type. However, increasing the bidding margin seems difficult, because this alternative recommends assigning a similar level of consultants and a project manager. The normalized project risk of alternative 1 is 0.15, which is noticeably less than the original project risk of 0.42. Similarly, alternative 2 also recommends change of contract type and a very clear definition of R&R, provided that we can assign a lower level of consultant and project manager to increase the bidding margin. The normalized project risk is 0.17. Alternative 3 does not recommend changing contract type, but it does require that the best quality consultant and project manager should be assigned, so that the terms and conditions become very favorable. The normalized project risk is 0.09. Alternative 4 suggests a low margin on the condition that the quality of the consultant and project manager is increased, and both contract type and terms and conditions become favorable. The normalized project risk is 0.23.

In summary, the bidding strategy for this IS project can be described as follows. First, alternative 1 is recommended if the decision maker wants a high margin strategy. Second, alternative 2 can be considered a strategy for securing a favorable contract condition. Third, if the decision maker seeks the strategy of supplying the best quality consultants, then alternatives 3 and 4 can be considered. Fourth, if project risk is the greatest concern, then alternative 3, which shows the lowest project risk (0.09), is the most highly recommended.

Table 8.7

Four Alternatives Induced by MACOM for Reducing the IS Project Risk

Alternative	Consultant skill	PM experience	Clear R&R	Contractual risk	Contract type	T&C	Bidding margin	Project risk	Normalized risk value
Current	0.7	0.7	0.4	1.0	0.5	0.5	0.4	-0.17	0.42
1	0.7	0.6	0.6	0.6	0.9	0.1	0.8	-0.70	0.15
2	0.5	0.4	0.9	0.1	0.9	0.2	0.6	-0.66	0.17
3	1.0	1.0	0.4	0.5	0.4	1.0	0.6	-0.83	0.09
4	1.0	0.9	0.9	0.5	0.8	0.6	0.3	-0.54	0.23

CONCLUSION

The proposed MACOM was used to assess IS project risks by considering all the relevant internal factors and external factors. Decision makers must investigate various strategies for reducing the possible project risks involved in a specific IS project, while considering all the interrelationships of the relevant internal and external factors. Many approaches have been proposed, most of which are based on the subjective judgment of so-called project risk managers. This chapter proposed the MACOM CM to allow all possible combinations of causal relationships between risk-related factors and causality coefficients to be examined, and not restricted by the rigid requirements of the conventional cognitive map. MACOM can also incorporate possible constraints on the causal relationships among factors and causality coefficients into its inference mechanism.

To prove the usefulness of MACOM, we used a real IS project from a multinational IT consulting company. The case consisted of twenty-four factors and related attributes. By applying the swarm simulation, the final MACOM was induced successfully. MACOM was applied to the case to seek various types of strategies for reducing project risk. We identified four alternatives and organized three risk-reducing strategies. We believe that the proposed methodology can be used to trigger related research in other decision-making problems. Further research topics remain. First, the swarm simulation mechanism used for producing MACOM needs to be improved algorithmically. Second, more sophisticated constraints needs to be incorporated into the MACOM to represent the complexity of the problems more flexibly. Third, the MACOM should be accessed on the Web to allow decision makers to use it to assess IS project risks more conveniently

ACKNOWLEDGMENTS

This work was supported by grant No. B1210–0502–0037 from the University Fundamental Research Program of the Ministry of Information and Communication in the Republic of Korea.

REFERENCES

Bandyopadhyay, K.; Mykytyn, P.; and Mykytyn, K. 1999. A framework for integrated risk management in information technology. *Management Decision,* 37, 5, 437–444.

Barki, H.; Rivard, S.; and Talbot, J. 1993. Toward an assessment of software development risk. *Journal of Management Information Systems,* 10, 2, 203–225.

Boehm, B.W. 1991. Software risk management: Principles and practices. *IEEE Software,* 8, 1, 32–41.

Bougon, M.; Weick, K.; and Binkhorst, D. 1977. Cognition in organizations: An analysis of the Utrecht jazz orchestra. *Administrative Science Quarterly,* 22, 606–639.

Buhl, H.; Kenett, R.S.; Lombardo, S.; and Wognum, P. 2004. Methods to collect and analyze organizational change management data: The BEST approach. Paper presented at the European Network for Business and Industrial Statistics (ENBIS) Fourth Annual Conference on Business and Industrial Statistics, September 20–22, Copenhagen, Denmark.

Charette, R.N. 1989. *Software Engineering Risk Analysis and Management.* New York: McGraw-Hill.

Chen, M.E., and Huang, Y.P. 1995. Dynamic fuzzy reasoning model with fuzzy cognitive map in Chinese chess. In *Proceedings of the IEEE International Conference on Neural Networks,* 3, 27, 1353–1357.

Chin-Feng, F., and Yuan-Chang, Y. 2004. BBN-based software project risk management. *Journal of Systems and Software,* 73, 193–203.

Clerc, M., and Kennedy, J. 2002. The particle swarm: Explosion, stability, and convergence in a multi-dimensional complex space. *IEEE Transactions on Evolutionary Computation,* 6, 58–73.

Cohen, Y., and Shoshany, M. 2002. A national knowledge-based crop recognition in Mediterranean environment. *International Journal of Applied Earth Observation,* 4, 75–87.

Craiger, P., and Coovert, M. 1994. Modeling social and psychological processes with fuzzy cognitive maps. In *Proceedings of the Third IEEE Conference on Fuzzy System,* 3, 1873–1877.

Eberhart, R.C., and Shi, Y. 2000. Comparing inertia weights and constriction factors in particle swarm optimization. In *Proceedings of the 2000 IEEE Congress on Evolutionary Computation,* 84–88. San Diego, CA.

Eden, C., and Ackermann, F. 1989. Strategic options development and analysis (SODA)—Using a computer to help with the management of strategic vision. In G.I. Doukidis, F. Land, and G. Miller (eds.), *Knowledge-Based Management Support Systems,* 198–207. New York: Halstead Press.

Eden, C.; Jones, S.;and Sims, D. 1979. *Thinking in Organizations.* Macmillan, London.

Ewusi-Mensah, K., and Przasnyski, Z. 1994. Factors contributing to the abandonment of information systems development projects. *Journal of Information Technology,* 9, 185–201.

Fu, Y., and Shen, R. 2004. GA based CBR approach in Q&A system. *Expert Systems with Applications,* 26, 167–170.

George, X., and Michael, G. 2004. Fuzzy cognitive maps in business analysis and performance driven change. *IEEE Transactions on Engineering Management,* 51, 3, 56–88.

Hatzilygeroudis, J., and Prentzas, J. 2004. Integrating (rules, neural networks) and cases for knowledge representation and reasoning in expert systems. *Expert Systems with Applications,* 27, 63–75.

Jones, M.M., and McLean, E.R. 1970. Management problems in large-scale software development projects. *Industrial Management Review,* 11, 3, 1–15.

Karolak, D.W. 1996. *Software Engineering Risk Management.* Los Alamitos, CA: IEEE Computer Society Press.

Keider, S.P. 1984. Why systems development projects fail. *Journal of Information Systems Management,* 1, 3, 33–38.

Keil, M. 1995. Pulling the plug: software project management and the problem of project escalation. *MIS Quarterly,* 19, 4, 421–447

Kengpol, A., and Wangananon, W. 2006. The expert system for assessing customer satisfaction on fragrance notes: Using artificial neural networks. *Computers and Industrial Engineering,* 51, 4, 567–584.

Kemerer, C.F., and Sosa, G.L. 1988. Barriers to successful strategic information systems. *Planning Review,* 16, 5, 20–23.

Kennedy, J., and Eberhart, R.C. 2001. *Swarm Intelligence.* San Francisco: Morgan Kaufmann.

Kitchenham, B., and Linkman, S. 1997. Estimates, uncertainty, and risk. *IEEE Software,* 14, 3, 69–74.

Kosko, B. 1992. *Neural Networks and Fuzzy Systems.* Englewood Cliffs, NJ: Prentice Hall.

Kowalski, Z.; Meler-Kapcia, M.; Zielinski, S.; and Drewka, M. 2005. CBR methodology application in an expert system for aided design ship's engine room automation. *Expert Systems with Applications,* 29, 2, 256–263.

Kwahk, K.Y., and Kim, Y.G. 1999. Supporting business process redesign using cognitive maps. *Decision Support Systems,* 25, 2, 155–178.

Lee, K.C., and Kwon, S.J. 2006. The use of cognitive maps and case-based reasoning for B2B negotiation. *Journal of Management Information Systems,* 22, 4, 337–376.

Lee, K.C., and Lee, S. 2003. A cognitive map simulation approach to adjusting the design factors of the electronic commerce Web sites. *Expert Systems with Applications,* 24, 1, 1–11.

Lee, K.C.; Han, J.H.; Song, Y.U.; and Lee, W.J. 1998. A fuzzy logic-driven multiple knowledge integration framework for improving the performance of expert systems. *International Journal of Intelligent System in Accounting, Finance and Management,* 7, 213–222.

Liu, Y., and Passino, K.M. 2002. Biomimicry of social foraging bacteria for distributed optimization: Models, principles, and emergent behaviors. *Journal of Optimization Theory and Applications,* 115, 3, 603–628.

Liu, Z.Q., and Satur, R. 1999. Contextual fuzzy cognitive map for decision support in geographic information systems. *IEEE Transactions on Fuzzy Systems,* 7, 5, 495–507.

Ndousse, T.D., and Okuda, T. 1996. Computational Intelligence for distributed fault management in networks using fuzzy cognitive maps. In *Proceedings of the IEEE International Conference on Communications: Converging Technologies for Tomorrow's Applications* (ICC'96), Dallas, TX, 1558–1562.

Netlogo. 2006. Available at http://ccl.northwestern.edu/netlogo/ (accessed February 4, 2006).

Noh, J.B.; Lee, K.C.; Kim, J.K.; Lee, J.K.; and Kim, S.H. 2000. A case-based reasoning approach to cognitive map-driven tacit knowledge management. *Expert Systems with Applications,* 19, 4, 249–259.

Numata, J.; Hane, K.; Bangyu, L.; and Iwashita, Y. 1997. Knowledge discovery and sharing in an information system. In *Proceedings of the Portland International Conference on Management of Engineering
Technology (PICMET'97), 27–31 July, Portland, OR,* 713–716.

Park, K.S., and Kim, S.H. 1995. Fuzzy cognitive maps considering time relationships. *International Journal
of Human Computer Studies,* 42, 2, 157–168.

Privosnik, M.; Marolt, M.; Kavcic, A.; and Divjak, S. 2002. Evolutionary construction of emergent properties in multi-agent systems. In *Proceedings of the Eleventh Mediterranean Electrotechnical Conference*
(MELECON'02), 7, 9, 327–330.

Robey, D., and Farrow, D.L. 1982. User involvement in information systems development: A conflict model
and empirical test. *Management Science,* 28, 1, 73–85.

Ross, L.L., and Hall, R.I. 1980. Influence diagrams and organizational power. *Administrative Science Quarterly,* 25, 57–71.

Rouff, C.; Vanderbilt, A.; Hinchey, M.; Truszkowski, W.; and Rash, J. 2004. Properties of a formal method
for prediction of emergent behaviors in swarm-based systems. In *Proceedings of the Second International
Conference in Software Engineering and Formal Methods* (SEFM'04), 28, 30, 24–33.

Satur, R., and Liu, Z.Q. 1999. A contextual fuzzy cognitive map framework for geographic information
systems. *IEEE Transactions on Fuzzy Systems,* 7, 481–494.

Schmidt, R.; Lyytinen, K.; Keil, M.; and Cule, P. 2001. Identifying software project risks: An International
Delphi study. *Journal of Management Information Systems,* 17, 4, 5–36.

Styblinski, M.A., and Meyer, B.D. 1991. Signal flow graphs vs fuzzy cognitive maps in application to qualitative circuit analysis. *International Journal of Man-Machine Studies,* 35, 2, 175–186.

Taber, R. 1994. Fuzzy cognitive maps model social systems. *AI Expert,* 9, 7, 19–23

Tseng, T.L., and Huang, C.C. 2006. Rough set-based approach to feature selection in customer relationship
management. *Omega,* 35, 4, 365–383.

Wang, X.; Qu, H.; Liu, P.; and Cheng, Y. 2004. A self-learning expert system for diagnosis in traditional
Chinese medicine. *Expert Systems with Applications,* 26, 557–566.

Weiss, G. 1999. *Multiagent Systems: A Modern Approach to Distributed Artificial Intelligence.* Cambridge,
MA: MIT Press.

Wellman, M. 1994. Inference in cognitive maps. *Mathematics and Computers in Simulation,* 36, 2, 137–148.

Wognum, P.; Krabbendam, J.; Buhl, H.; Ma, X.; and Kenett, R.S. 2004. Improving enterprise system support—
A case-based approach. *Advanced Engineering Informatics,* 18, 4, 241–253.

Zhang, W.R.; Chen, S.S.; and Bezdek, J.C. 1989. P0012: A generic system for cognitive map development
and decision analysis. *IEEE Transactions on Systems, Man and Cybernetics,* 19, 1, 31–39.

Zhang, W.R.; Wang, W.; and King, R.S. 1994. A-Pool: An agent-oriented open system shell for distributed
decision process modeling. *Journal of Organizational Computing,* 4, 2, 127–154.

PART III

TECHNICAL SYSTEMS FOCUS: PROJECTS

CHAPTER 9

USE OF MODELING TECHNIQUES IN INFORMATION SYSTEMS DEVELOPMENT PROJECT TEAMS

Theoretical and Empirical Insights

PETER F. GREEN AND ALASTAIR ROBB

Abstract: *Numerous studies have investigated information systems development methodologies and practices over the past decade. However, relatively few have focused on the characteristics of project teams and how the project teams operate to create, configure, or assemble the systems under investigation. Furthermore, even fewer studies have considered the way in which analysts (modelers) create models to collaborate and share knowledge about requirements within the project teams. This situation is in stark contrast to the fact that the fundamental organizational unit used to conduct information systems development is the project team. This study used data gathered on how modelers working in project teams used grammars within a CASE (computer-aided systems engineering) tool environment to test a model based on ontological, task, individual, and contextual factors in an effort to explain the decision to use or not use a combination of grammars for modeling. The results found a strong association between recognition of ontological incompleteness in the grammars provided by the tool and the decision to use a combination of grammars. Moreover, the odds of a project team using grammars in combination are approximately 2 to 1, which is significantly reduced from the 5 to 1 odds of a similar occurrence reported for individual analysts (modelers) who did not work in project teams. Qualitative evidence highlighted the influence of corporate modeling standards and specialization on the use of sets of grammars within project teams. This result, in particular, is reinforced by recent findings by Kautz et al. (2007). An integrating mechanism (e.g., central model repository) was seen as highly significant in achieving high levels of consistency among the models generated by the project team. However, the influence of minimal ontological overlap among the grammar set used by the team was not seen as a significant influence on the decision to use combinations of grammars, although significant contextual factors may have confounded this outcome.*

Keywords: *Representation Theory, Project Teams, Information Systems Development, Conceptual Modeling*

The aim of this chapter is to respond in part to a recent call by Kautz et al. (2007) for more research on the occurrence and interaction of problems and practices in information systems development at different contextual levels to understand and assess (the gap between) "observed practice" and "good practice." This chapter responds to this call by focusing on the use of conceptual modeling grammars by modelers, but specifically those modelers working in the context of information systems development (ISD) project teams. As Faraj and Sambamurthy (2006) highlight, teams are the fundamental organizational unit through which information systems (IS) projects are executed. They go on to point out that the effectiveness of the ISD project team is challenged particularly by the fact that knowledge required for the completion of the IS project tasks is distributed across team members, who must thus discover effective ways of collaboration, knowledge sharing, and problem solving to tap the expertise of each team member.

A major task undertaken by the analysts/designers in these teams is to develop a model(s) of a perception(s) of a portion of the world. These so-called conceptual models have been found to be very conducive to articulating knowledge and perceptions about real-world domains. In many instances these models are then used as a basis to develop, or configure, or assemble components into an automated system intended to simulate or support the real-world area under investigation (Wand and Weber, 2002). These models are specified using "a *grammar* (i.e., a set of constructs and rules to combine those constructs), a *method* (i.e., procedures by which the grammar can be used), a *script* (i.e., the product of the modeling process), and a *context* (i.e., the setting in which the modeling occurs)" (Davies et al., 2006, p. 359).

Accordingly, this sharing of knowledge through the development of models to represent the requirements of an ISD project by analysts (modelers) within the context of a project team environment is the focus of the work reported in this chapter. Furthermore, as Kautz et al. (2007) point out, these projects typically take place in environments supported by powerful tools such as computer-aided systems engineering (CASE) tools.

Another objective of this work is to determine, in part, whether representation theory (e.g., Wand and Weber, 1995) provides some insightful basis through which to understand how analysts (modelers) working with numerous grammars provided in powerful CASE environments manage to share their knowledge effectively with the other members of the project team through the models they create. Indeed, the number of modeling grammars in general has proliferated exponentially (e.g., Olle et al., 1991; Fitzgerald, 1998). This trend has continued into other areas of modern modeling such as object-oriented analysis (Coad and Yourdon, 1990), enterprise systems interoperability (OASIS, 2003), workflow design (Jablonski and Bussler, 1996), and business process modeling (Curtis et al., 1992).

In the light of such proliferation, an increased need for theory has arisen to give some guidance and insight to practitioners to assist them in the use of such grammars (Moody, 2005). This situation has been accentuated by the provision of powerful CASE environments to support the use of these grammars.

If models are the way in which analysts (modelers) working in project teams share their knowledge, then how do analysts (modelers) use the grammars available in large powerful CASE tools to construct their models? Why do they choose to use the grammars that they do? How do they coordinate the use of modeling grammars within their team environments to construct models that lead to effective capture and sharing of requirements concerning the project? The overall research question of this chapter then is:

> What factors influence the decision of analysts (modelers) working in project teams to use (not use) grammars in combination within a CASE tool environment to create models to capture and share the knowledge of project requirements with other team members?

Over the years, we have contributed to this stream of research by providing a theory-based understanding of how and why modelers individually use grammars in their design and analysis of information systems. We have used principally representation theory, which is based on the Bunge-Wand-Weber (BWW) representation model (Wand and Weber, 1990, 1993, 1995) for this work. In most instances, we have attempted to validate our analyses through qualitative and/or quantitative research methods in order to be able to reflect on the validity and usefulness of our selected theory.

Some criticisms aimed at our work over the years (e.g., Wyssusek, 2006) have focused on the fact that representation theory is based originally on Bunge's (1977) ontology, which assumes a realist view of the world. Many colleagues argue a subjectivist view of the world (Burrell and Morgan, 1979) and argue that therefore it is not appropriate to use representation theory because of its underlying assumptions. A strong contention of this chapter is that the usefulness of the theory and its extensions should be judged on the basis of the insights obtained from the analysis and its empirical results, as opposed to the correctness or appropriateness of the assumptions underlying the theory for the context in which it is applied. So, indeed, we argue for a perspective of methodological pragmatism (Rescher, 1973) on the validity of theory—namely, that a theory proves itself valid and useful by being successfully applied in research practice.

The work reported in this chapter is set in the context of analysts (modelers) in project teams using traditional and structured modeling grammars (as opposed to, say, object-oriented or high-speed techniques). Indeed, one might question the usefulness of choosing traditional and structured modeling grammars, as implemented in an automated tool environment, as an appropriate setting in which to examine how modelers use grammars to construct and share models in project team environments. Yet, most recently, Davies et al. (2006) confirm that among the top six modeling grammars used most frequently by practitioners today are the traditional grammars of systems flowcharting and the structured grammars of entity-relationship (ER) diagramming, data flow diagramming, and structure charts. Moreover, as Kautz et al. (2007) argue, even though there have been numerous changes in information technologies and techniques over the years, the underlying, persistent decision-making characteristics of ISD have not significantly changed. Consequently, this is seen as an appropriate setting in which to test the usefulness of representation theory and the resultant decision-making model. Accordingly, the work in this chapter is concerned with whether the theory and resulting model can provide insight into the choice of grammars provided by an automated tool and be used by analysts (modelers) when working on ISD projects in project teams. While one might question the degree to which automated modeling tools are used (e.g., Butler, 2000; Howard and Rai, 1993), there is evidence to suggest that these tools continue to be used and to have a positive impact on systems development effectiveness in those sites where they are used (Iivari, 1996). Indeed, Davies et al. (2006) report that while a relatively simple automated tool such as Microsoft Visio is generally most frequently used, more sophisticated tools such as Rational Rose, Oracle Developer, and AllFusion ERwin Data Modeler remain relatively frequently used in practice today.

This chapter unfolds in the following manner. The second section provides an overview of the related work in the area of representation theory and ISD in project teams. It also argues that the usefulness of the theory and its analysis should be judged on the basis of the insights it gives, rather than on the basis of the assumptions or methodology underlying the theory. The next section explains how representation theory can be applied to the grammars provided in a CASE tool environment. Specifically, in this work, the environment examined provides traditional and structured grammars for analysts (modelers) to use. The section goes on to present a model of decision-making factors potentially used by analysts (modelers) when making their decision within a project team environment of which grammars to use to create their models. It also presents hypotheses from this model. The fourth section presents and discusses the results, and the final section summarizes the chapter and reviews potential limitations of the work.

BACKGROUND

Throughout the 1980s, the 1990s, and into the new millennium, it has become increasingly apparent to many researchers that without a theoretical foundation, incomplete evaluative frameworks of factors, features, and facets continue to proliferate (Bansler and Bodker, 1993). Furthermore, without a theoretical foundation, one framework of factors, features, or facets is as justifiable as another for use (e.g., Floyd, 1986; Karam and Casselman, 1993; Kautz et al., 2004).

Wand and Weber (e.g., 1990, 1993, 1995) have investigated the branch of philosophy known as ontology as a foundation for understanding the process in developing an information system. Ontology is a well-established theoretical domain within philosophy dealing with models of reality (Shanks et al., 2003). Wand and Weber (e.g., 1990, 1993, 1995) and Weber (1997) have extended an ontology described by Bunge (1977) and applied it to the modeling of information systems. In doing so, these researchers have produced three models of information systems' structure and behavior: the representation model, the state-tracking model, and the good decomposition model (Wand and Weber, 1995). The work presented here is focused on the representation model. Its fundamental premise is that any modeling grammar must be able to represent all things in the real world that might be of interest to users of information systems; otherwise, the resultant model is incomplete, and the analyst(s) (modelers) will somehow have to augment the model(s) (Weber, 1997). The representation model's set of constructs that attempt to describe the structure and behavior of the world are explained in Table 9.1 Wand and Weber (1993) clarify two major situations that may occur when a grammar is analyzed according to the representation model: construct deficit (or ontological incompleteness) and clarity (i.e., construct overload, construct redundancy, and construct excess). In particular, the concept of construct deficit is used in this chapter to analyze the grammars provided within an automated tool. A grammar exhibits construct deficit unless there is at least one grammatical construct for each construct in the representation model. The main premise associated with construct deficit is that users of a grammar will tend to employ additional means of articulation in order to compensate for the deficit (e.g., via additional grammars, free text, or other means) (Weber, 1997).

The representation model, its associated analytical procedure, and the predictions that can be made on the basis of the analysis have become known as representation theory.

Related Work

Table 9.2 presents a summarized review of the substantial amount of related work concerning representation theory and its use in various modeling domains, for example, traditional, structured, data-oriented, object-oriented, process modeling, activity-based costing, enterprise resource planning (ERP) systems, enterprise systems interoperability, other ontologies, use cases, and reference models. For an in-depth review of the related literature, see Green et al. (2005).

Most of the work reported in Table 9.2 has involved analysis of grammars using the representation model only. Moreover, much of the work has been analytical in nature, with few of the studies validating their results through qualitative and/or quantitative empirical tests.

Some criticisms have been leveled over the years at the use of representation theory, namely, limited empirical testing (Wyssusek, 2006; Wand and Weber, 2006), a lack of coverage caused by the representation model focusing only on the representational algebra ("grammar") of a technique, and a lack of understandability of the BWW constructs (Rosemann et al., 2004). Certainly, the work to date has attempted to mitigate each of these criticisms. For instance, a number of authors have undertaken empirical tests of the "validity" of predictions stemming from representation

Table 9.1

Constructs in the Bunge-Wand-Weber (BWW) Representation Model

Ontological construct	Explanation
Thing*	A thing is the elementary unit in the BWW ontological model. The real world is made up of things. Two or more things (composite or simple) can be associated into a composite thing.

Property*
  Intrinsic
  Nonbinding mutual
  Binding mutual
  Emergent
  Hereditary
  Attributes
	Things possess properties. A property is modeled via a function that maps the thing into some value. A property of a composite thing that belongs to a component thing is called an *hereditary property*. Otherwise it is called an *emergent property*. Some properties are inherent properties of individual things. Such properties are called *intrinsic*. Other properties are properties of pairs or many things. Such properties are called mutual. *Nonbinding mutual properties* are those properties shared by two or more things that do not "make a difference" to the things involved; for example, order relations or equivalence relations. By contrast, *binding mutual properties* are those properties shared by two or more things that do "make a difference" to the things involved. *Attributes* are the names that we use to represent certain properties of things (normally abstract properties).

Class	A class is a set of things that can be defined via their possessing a single property.
Kind	A kind is a set of things that can be defined only via their possessing two or more properties.
State*	The vector of values for all property functions of a thing is the state of the thing.
Conceivable state space	The set of all states that the thing might ever assume is the conceivable state space of the thing.

State law:
  Stability condition
  Corrective action
	A state law restricts the values of the properties of a thing to a subset that is deemed lawful because of natural laws or human laws. The *stability condition* specifies the states allowed by the state law. The *corrective action* specifies how the value of the property function must change to provide a state acceptable under the state law.

Lawful state space	The lawful state space is the set of states of a thing that comply with the state laws of the thing. The lawful state space is usually a proper subset of the conceivable state space.
Event	An event is a change of state of a thing.
Process	A process may be regarded either as an intrinsically ordered sequence of events on, or states of, a thing.
Conceivable event space	The event space of a thing is the set of all possible events that can occur in the thing.
Transformation*	A transformation is a mapping from one state to another state.

Lawful transformation
  Stability condition
  Corrective action
	A lawful transformation defines which events in a thing are lawful. The *stability condition* specifies the states that are allowable under the transformation law. The *corrective action* specifies how the values of the property function(s) must change to provide a state acceptable under the transformation law.

(continued)

Table 9.1 *(continued)*

Ontological construct	Explanation
Lawful event space	The lawful event space is the set of all events in a thing that are lawful.
History	The chronologically ordered states that a thing traverses in time are the history of the thing.
Acts on	A thing acts on another thing if its existence affects the history of the other thing.
Coupling Binding mutual property	Two things are said to be coupled (or interact) if one thing acts on the other. Furthermore, those two things are said to share a *binding mutual property* (or relation); that is, they participate in a relation that "makes a difference" to the things.
System	A set of things is a system if, for any bipartitioning of the set, couplings exist among things in the two subsets.
System composition	The things in the system are its composition.
System environment	Things that are not in the system but interact with things in the system are called the environment of the system.
System structure	The set of couplings that exist among things within the system, and among things in the environment of the system and things in the system, is called the structure.
Subsystem	A subsystem is a system whose composition and structure are subsets of the composition and structure of another system.
System decomposition	A decomposition of a system is a set of subsystems such that every component in the system is either one of the subsystems in the decomposition or is included in the composition of one of the subsystems in the decomposition.
Level structure	A level structure defines a partial order over the subsystems in a decomposition to show which subsystems are components of other subsystems or the system itself.
External event	An external event is an event that arises in a thing, subsystem, or system by virtue of the action of some thing in the environment on the thing, subsystem, or system.
Stable state*	A stable state is a state in which a thing, subsystem, or system will remain unless forced to change by virtue of the action of a thing in the environment (an external event).
Unstable state	An unstable state is a state that will be changed into another state by virtue of the action of transformations in the system.
Internal event	An internal event is an event that arises in a thing, subsystem, or system by virtue of lawful transformations in the thing, subsystem, or system.
Well-defined event	A well-defined event is an event in which the subsequent state can always be predicted given that the prior state is known.
Poorly defined event	A poorly defined event is an event in which the subsequent state cannot be predicted given that the prior state is known.

Source: Wand and Weber (1993), Weber (1997), with minor modifications.

* Indicates a fundamental ontological construct. All other constructs are derived from these constructs.

Table 9.2

Related Work Using Representation Theory

| Study | Study focus — Business systems analysis grammar | | | | | Representation theory aspect | | | | |
	Traditional — Structured	Data-centered	O-O	Process	Other	Deficit	Clarity	Good decomposition	Overlap	Empirical tests
Wand and Weber 1989	• LDFD	• ER				•				
Wand and Weber 1993; 1995		• ER				•				
Weber 1997		•				•	•			
Keen and Lakos 1994			• LOOPN++			•	•			
Weber and Zhang 1996		•				•	•			• 10 interviews
Green 1997	•	•				•	•		Only described MOO & MOC	• 203 surveys & 24 interviews
Parsons and Wand 1997			•			•	•			
Wand, Storey, and Weber 1999		•				•	•			
Rosemann and Green 2000					• Activity-based costing	•	•			
Green and Rosemann 2000				• ARIS		•	•			
Bodart, Patel, Sim, and Weber 2001		•				•	•			• 3 experiments; 200 participants

(continued)

Table 9.2 (continued)

| | Study focus | | | | | | Representation theory aspect | | | | |
| | Business systems analysis grammar | | | | | | Deficit | Clarity | Good decomposition | Overlap | |
Study	Traditional Structured	Data-centered	O-O	Process	Other						Empirical tests
Opdahl and Henderson-Sellers 2001			• OML					•			
Green and Rosemann 2001				• ARIS			•	•			• 12 surveys & 4 interviews
Green and Rosemann 2002					• Enterprise interoper- ability			•			
Sia and Soh 2002					• ERP systems		•	•			
Shanks, Tansley, Nuredini, Tobin, and Weber 2002		•	• UML class				•	•			• Experiment 20 participants
Opdahl and Henderson-Sellers 2002			• UML	• ARIS & UML			•	•			
Rosemann and Green 2002			•				•	•			
Davies, Green, and Rosemann 2002					• Other ontology		•	•			
Davies, Green, Milton, and Rosemann 2003					• Other ontology		•	•			
Fettke and Loos 2003					• Reference models		•	•			

Study		Techniques	Method
Green, Rosemann, and Indulska 2005	•	• ebXML	• 11 interviews
Recker, Indulska, Rosemann, and Green 2005		• BPMN	
Irwin and Turk 2005		• UML-Use Case	
Burton-Jones and Meso 2006		• UML	• Experiment 57 students
Rosemann, Recker, Indulska, and Green 2006		• 12 process modeling techniques	
Green, Rosemann, Indulska, and Manning 2007		• Enterprise interoperability	• Analysis only
Zhang, Kishore, and Ramesh 2007		• MibML	
This work	•		• Interview + survey data in project teams

theory (e.g., Bodart et al., 2001; Burton-Jones and Meso, 2006; Gemino and Wand, 2005; Wand and Weber, 1989), while others have undertaken efforts to provide procedural guidelines for the application of the theory (e.g., Rosemann et al., 2004).

However, the most consistent criticism lies in the selection of Bunge's (1977) ontology on which to base the representation model (Hirschheim et al., 1996). These critics claim that, as Bunge's ontology assumes an objectivist, realist view of the world (Burrell and Morgan, 1979), users of the resultant representation model and representation theory must be imposing a similar view and set of assumptions on their work. Indeed, many systems development researchers see the world as being "socially constructed" (Berger and Luckmann, 1966). The world exists as it is *perceived* by humans. In other words, the world is a *constructed perception* by humans. These researchers advocate the use of research techniques for systems development based on a social relativist or interpretivist set of philosophical assumptions. This chapter argues, however, that representation theory is *not* being used to analyze modelers' *perceptions* of the requirements; rather, it is being used to analyze the *goodness of representation* of the perceptions being converted into models by *other people*.

But more important, as Gemino (2005) points out, a theory that is used by researchers to analyze and help their understanding of modeling in its various domains should not be tested on the basis of its underlying *assumptions* (e.g., realist versus subjectivist) but rather on whether its application leads to "useful" insights. Gemino (2005, p. 318) goes on to explain that "useful can be defined as results confirming both the differences (between modeling techniques) identified and their significant impact on participants' performance." For this view, he relies on the work of Alchian (1950) and Friedman (1953) when comparing economic theories " . . . the entirely valid use of 'assumptions' in *specifying* the circumstances for which a theory holds is frequently, *and erroneously,* interpreted to mean the assumptions can be used to *determine* the circumstances for which a theory holds, and has, in this way, been an important source of the belief that a theory can be tested by its assumptions" (Friedman, 1953, p. 19). In line with this view, this chapter argues that it is the useful insights a theory gives that should be used to evaluate the appropriateness of the theory for its application in a particular context. Or, in Weber's (1997, p. 24) words: "Who wants to debate recipes without first having tasted the cooking?"

ISD in Project Teams

Numerous studies have investigated ISD (or configuration, or assembly of modules) methodologies and practices over the past decade (Baskerville et al., 2007; Kautz et al., 2007). However, relatively few have focused on the characteristics of project teams and how the project teams operate to create, configure, or assemble the systems under investigation. Furthermore, even fewer studies have considered the way in which analysts (modelers) work in collaborating and sharing knowledge about requirements using models within the project teams. This situation is in stark contrast to the fact that most IS developments (configurations or assemblies) are conducted by project teams (Faraj and Sambamurthy, 2006).

Kirsch (1996) investigated the application of control theory to a complex, nonroutine task: the management of ISD in teams. He found that the theory provided an incomplete explanation. Moreover, his work focused only on the control of the development projects and not on the ways in which the team analysts (modelers) worked. Janz et al. (1997) investigated the effects of process reengineering and "downsizing" on the systems development process conducted by teams. They found that, while employee autonomy may lead to increased levels of satisfaction and motivation, the level of team development and an organization's learning capacity may be more important in achieving improved work outcomes. This study looked at how participants in the ISD project team worked, but it did not focus on the knowledge-sharing activities of analysts (modelers) using models within the teams.

Roberts et al. (2005) investigated the effect of varying project complexity on the group interaction processes of small IS project teams. They found significantly higher expectations, group integration, communication, and participation while working on less complex projects. While this study focused on project team interaction, it did not look at how modelers within the team interacted using their models of requirements. Tiwana and McLean (2005) studied how individually held expertise in ISD teams resulted in creativity at the team level during the development process. They found that integrating individually held tacit and explicit knowledge about the problem domain and the technology at the team level was central to achieving team creativity. This finding provides significant motivation for the current study to investigate the knowledge-sharing activities of analysts (modelers) within teams using their models developed either using single or combination grammar sets within a CASE tool environment. Finally, Faraj and Sambamurthy (2006) investigated leadership practices in information systems project teams. While this factor is critical to the performance of IS project teams, it does not explain how analysts (modelers) within the teams create their models of requirements knowledge.

ANALYSIS, MODEL, AND HYPOTHESES

A "standard" representation model analysis of the target grammars as they are implemented within a CASE tool providing traditional and structured grammars was performed. The grammars were implemented in a popular CASE tool used by ISD project teams in the late 1990s with a well-established user base in Australasia—Excelerator V1.9 from Intersolv, Inc. Nine traditional and structured graphical grammars in the tool were identified and analyzed, namely, system flowchart (SF), program flowchart (PF), logical data flow diagram (LDFD), structure chart (STC), state transition diagram (TRD), structure diagram (STD), structured decision table (SDT), entity-relationship attribute (ERA), and data model diagram (DMD). Table 9.3 provides a section of the analysis undertaken according to selected core and fundamental constructs of the representation model. The complete discussion of analysis results is omitted for the sake of brevity and, instead, a detailed explanation of the application of the analysis to the ERA grammar is provided as an example. The complete version of the analysis is available from the authors on request. Where a mapping was interpreted by the researcher, an "(I)" follows the result in Table 9.3. An interpretation mapping starts with the grammatical construct and determines which (if any) ontological constructs correspond (Weber, 1997).

Applying the Analysis to the Entity-Relationship Attribute (ERA) Grammar

A *class* is represented by a data entity. For example, a CUSTOMER entity on an ERA represents customers that share the common, single property of being customers of the company of interest. A type of *state law* is represented by the cardinality constraints on a data relationship. It constrains the values of the *binding mutual property* (or *coupling*) of the things by specifying how many "replications" of this property each of the coupled things must (or can) have. Optionality constraints only exist in ERAs because ERAs do not represent individual things. Rather, the data entity represents *classes* of things. Optionality simply says that some individual things in a coupled class may or may not participate in the coupling. A *coupling* (or *binding mutual property*) is represented by a data n-ary relationship. While there are no specific constructs for thing or property of a thing in

Table 9.3

Portion of the Grammar Analysis

Ontological construct	System flowchart (SF)	Program flowchart (PF)	Data flow diagrams (LDFD)	Structure chart (STC)	State transition diagrams (TRD)	Structure diagrams (STD)	Structured decision tables (SDT)	Entity-relationship attributes (ERA)	Data model diagrams (DMD)
Thing*	No construct in SF, Described by REC in XLDict.(I)	No construct in PF, Described by REC in XLDict.(I)	No construct in LDFD, Described by REC in XLDict (I)	No construct in STC Described by REC in XLDict.(I)		No construct in STD, Described by REC in XLDict(I)		No construct in ERA, Described by REC in XLDict.(I)	No construct in DMD, Described by REC in XLDict.(I)
Property* Intrinsic Nonbinding Mutual Emergent Hereditary Attributes	No construct in SF, Described by ELE in XLDict(I)	No construct in PF, Described by ELE in XLDict(I)	No construct in LDFD, Described by ELE in XLDict.(I)	1. Data Couple 2. ELE in XLDict.(I)		No construct in STD, Described by ELE in XLDict.(I)		No construct in ERA, Described by ELE in XLDict(I)	No construct in DMD, Described by ELE in XLDict.(I)
Class	1. Media objects(I) 2. People objects		1. Data store 2. Data flow 3. External entity	1. System device(I) 2. Global data store				Entity	Entity
State*		Flowline(I)	1. Data flow(I) 2. Control flow(I)	Data couple(I)	State	Connection(I)			
State law:									
Stab. condition		Condition		1. Decision diamond, and 2. Control couple		Select		Cardinality of relationship	1. Cardinality 2. Binary relationships
Corr. action		Process; I-O process		Function		Function; Inclusive alternative			

Event	In flowline → (process/I-O process) → Out flowline	1. At functional primitive level, in data flow–process–out data flow 2. External entity → data flow 3. External entity → control flow(signal) 4.Control flow(signal)–control transform–control flow (prompt)	At lowest level, in data couple–function–out data couple	1. State–transition vector–state vector 2. "Naked" transition vector 3. Condition	1. At lowest level, in connection–function–out connection(l) 2. Release condition 3. Terminating activity			
Transformation*	Process rectangle	At functional primitive level, process	Function	Action	At the lowest level, function, inclusive alternative, parallel activity	Action		
Coupling: Binding mutual property							1. N-ary relationship 2. Associative entity(l)	1. Binary relationship
Stable state*	Flowline(l)	1. Data flow(l) 2. Control flow(l)	Data couple(l)	States on TRD	Connection(l)			

Source: Wand and Weber (1995).
*Indicates a fundamental ontological construct.

Table 9.4

Grammar Analysis Summary

Construct	SF	PF	LDFD	STC	TRD	STD	SDT	ERA	DMD
Thing	X	X	X	X		X		X	X
Property	X	X	X	X		X		X	X
Class	X		X	X				X	X
Kind								X	X
State		X	X	X	X	X			
Conceivable state space									
State law: mono-property		X		X		X			
Lawful state space									
Event		X	X	X	X	X			
Process	X	X	X	X	X	X			
Conceivable event space									
Transformation		X	X	X	X	X	X		
Lawful transformation		X		X	X	X	X		
Lawful event space									
History									
Acts on								X	X
Coupling								X	X
System								X	X
System composition	X		X	X				X	X
System environment			X	X				X	X
System structure								X	X
Subsystem	X	X	X	X	X	X		X	X
System decomposition	X	X	X	X	X	X	X	X	X
Level structure	X	X	X	X	X	X	X	X	X
External event	X	X	X	X	X	X	X		
Stable state		X	X	X	X	X			
Unstable state									
Internal event		X	X	X	X	X			
Well-defined event		X	X	X	X	X			
Poorly defined event									

ERA diagrams, the data dictionary augments the grammar by providing integrated record definitions (through the REC construct) and data item definitions (through the ELE construct). The REC construct is interpreted as representing a *thing,* while the ELE construct is interpreted as a *property.* If a data element describes the *interaction* (or *coupling*) of two or more entities, Yourdon (1989) prescribes that the "naked" relationship between the entities should be replaced with an *associative entity.* An associative entity can be assigned attributes (data elements) of its own, and it can participate in further relationships. The associative entity is an artificial mechanism by which n-ary ($n > 2$) relationships in the real world are represented in the model as a series of binary relationships. It represents a number of *binding mutual properties* (or *couplings*).

Table 9.4 shows that certain ontological constructs do not have a grammatical representation in any of the nine grammars, namely, *conceivable state space, lawful state space, conceivable event space, lawful event space, history, unstable state,* and *poorly defined event.* One possible implication of this result could be that the representation model is misspecified or wrong. Yet, any conclusion with regard to this implication should be made only after substantial testing of the theory has been performed in this, and other settings. By contrast, another possible implication is that not having representations for these ontological real-world concepts at the time of modeling the information systems solution will cause problems for the system at later stages of the development life cycle.

Figure 9.1   **Factors Influencing the Decision to Use Grammars in Combination in Project Teams**

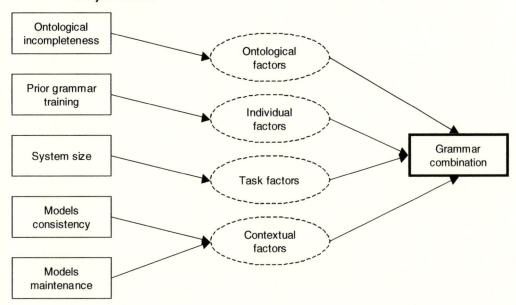

For example, the rules that define the lawful state space, and consequently, the *lawful event space* of a thing are important in the design of an information system. These rules are referred to in the practice of systems analysis and design as *business rules* (e.g., von Halle, 2001). As von Halle (1993) laments, the identification, recording, and integration of the relevant business rules into the design of an information system remain poorly handled issues that manifest themselves in systems poorly received by end users.

Table 9.4 summarizes the results of the full version of the analysis.

Model

The practice of requirements analysis and model creation is complex. Unfortunately, a comprehensive model that describes the critical elements that affect the grammar decisions when modeling the requirements of an information system is not readily identifiable. Some insight can be gained, however, from the work of Ford et al. (1989), who maintain that the cognitive costs and benefits involved in decision making are influenced by individual, task, and contextual characteristics. Based on this work, a cost benefit–based selection mechanism for use in describing the decisions made by analysts (modelers) when choosing grammars with which to represent the requirements of systems can be formulated initially. With the inclusion of ontological factors, this mechanism appears applicable to the decision-making process of analysts (modelers) when using a CASE tool to model and share requirements within a project team.

A vast array of variables could have been selected from the literature as proxies for the task, individual, and contextual factors. Figure 9.1 proposes a small, initial set of determinants selected because they appeared to represent significant costs and benefits underlying the decision by analysts (modelers) whether to use grammars in combination to model user requirements. In particular, the analysts (modelers) will attach expected costs and expected benefits to the CASE tool's repertoire of grammars and their components. At each step of the modeling process, the analysts (modelers) will use those grammars and components that result in the highest net benefit.

Hypotheses

Ontological incompleteness in a grammar is undesirable (Wand and Weber, 1993). Not one of the nine information systems' analysis and design (ISAD) grammars in Excelerator is ontologically complete. Accordingly,

> H1. Because each of the formal graphical ISAD grammars analyzed in Excelerator is ontologically incomplete, analysts (modelers) working in project teams will use two or more grammars in combination when modeling an information system.

Wand and Weber (1993) predict that in a manual environment the use of multiple grammars to produce multiple models will produce inconsistencies and errors across those models. Weber and Zhang (1996) found support for this hypothesis in their limited testing. Consistency of representation across models developed using different grammars here means that a real-world concept represented by a symbol in one technique in a model will keep a consistent meaning when represented by a symbol from another technique in a related model. For example, an entity in an entity-relationship diagram may be consistently represented by a data store or a data flow in a related data flow diagram, but not a process. Therefore,

> H2. Analysts (modelers) working in project teams will use only a combination of grammars in a CASE tool when they perceive that the use of such a combination will cause minimal problems with consistency of representation across the models developed using the various grammars.

Many works emphasize the importance of an individual's prior formal training to the subsequent performance of computer-based tasks (e.g., Amoako-Gyampah and Salam, 2004; Goodhue and Thompson, 1995; Igbaria et al., 1997). Moreover, Tan and Siau (2006) found that training was a significant antecedent of a developer's intention to use object-oriented methods. Therefore,

> H3. Analysts (modelers) working in project teams who have received prior formal training in the use of grammars for the design of an information system will tend to use two or more grammars in combination when modeling an information system within a CASE tool.

One could argue that a combination of grammars would more likely be used to model large situations rather than small, simple situations because analysts (modelers) of the project team would want to ensure that they had a complete understanding of all the important aspects of the large task. The average size of the systems (categorized as large, medium, and small, based on the average number of users who access the systems) is a plausible proxy for this task characteristic. Large organizations are involved typically with large systems and large system developments (Curtis et al., 1998). Prior studies have alluded to the differences encountered in such developments in terms of complexity and sophisticated interfaces (Bansler and Bodker, 1993; Curtis et al., 1998; Kautz et al., 2004). Indeed, Avison and Fitzgerald (2003) suggest that analysts' (modelers') backlash against modeling and methodologies (and the tools they employ) may arise because the methodologies, techniques, and tools are overly complex, usually designed for the largest and most complex development projects. Indeed, strict adherence to the technique may result in developing requirements to the ultimate degree, often over and above what is legitimately required. Technical skills required by developers may be difficult and expensive to acquire, and the associated tools may be costly to implement and difficult to use.

In view of these issues, however, as the size and complexity of the projects increase significantly, an increase in the use of modeling techniques (as they are used in methodologies) and their associated tools by project team analysts (modelers) are expected. However, this situation does not preclude modeling from occurring in smaller organizations involved in smaller, less complex projects. Indeed, a certain level of modeling and simple tool use for requirements analysis is expected.

H4. Analysts (modelers) working in project teams on large information systems will be more likely to use a combination of grammars within a CASE tool to model the information system requirements.

Studies show that maintenance of computer programs, systems, and their associated specifications is a major ongoing problem in the computer industry (e.g., Yourdon, 1989). In this study, maintenance problems across diagrams means that the effects of a change to a diagram developed in one technique can flow through relatively easily and accurately to related diagrams developed using other techniques. For example, deleting an entity from an entity-relationship diagram may require changes to relevant data stores or data flows in a related data flow diagram. It is plausible to expect then that analysts (modelers) would be likely to use combinations of grammars only if they perceived minimal maintenance problems when changes were required to the models in the future.

H5. Analysts (modelers) working in project teams will only use a combination of grammars in a CASE environment when they judge that the use of such a combination will cause minimal problems with the maintenance of the models developed using the different grammars.

Maintaining consistency of representation across a range of models developed by different analysts (modelers) within a project team is a difficult task. Accordingly, this research aims to investigate further the factors that might influence maintaining a high level of consistency among different models within a project team environment. This research argues that the problem of inconsistencies and errors across various models developed using different grammars is minimized in a CASE environment where an automated integrating mechanism is provided. An *automated integrating mechanism* is defined as a feature, or combination of features, supplied in the CASE tool to provide automated support for the use of more than one modeling technique (e.g., repository, extended analysis reporting).

H6. If multiple grammars are used by analysts (modelers) working in a CASE environment within their project team to model an information system's requirements, the problem of resolving inconsistencies between models developed using different grammars will be minimized where an automated integrating mechanism(s) exists.

The concepts of overlap analysis—*minimal ontological overlap* (MOO) and *maximal ontological completeness* (MOC)—were first described by Green (1997); however, they were not fully operationalized and used in an analytical sense until Green et al. (2007) used them to explain how various interoperability candidate standards might best be used in combination to overcome representational deficiencies inherent in the individual standards considered.

Weber and Zhang (1996) provided the insight from their analysis of the Nijssen's Information Analysis Methodology (NIAM) grammar and their subsequent structured interviews with practitioners that grammars will work well together when the constructs they can model have minimal ontological overlap. Their concept of minimal ontological overlap was operationalized by Green et al. (2007) in the following manner:

1. When combined, the grammars need to form combinations that are as ontologically complete as the set of available grammars will allow—a maximally ontologically complete combination. Indeed, as Table 9.4 shows, there are some ontological constructs for which the nine available grammars in the automated tool do not have a representation. Accordingly, any combination of grammars from within the tool can be only maximally complete rather than totally ontologically complete. Of course, depending on the grammars and the tool, for some tool environments, maximal completeness may be the same as total ontological completeness.
2. MOC may be achieved through combinations of two, three, four, and up to the total number of grammars in the tool. The rule of parsimony is used to select the combination of grammars with the least number of different grammars achieving maximal ontological completeness.
3. The grammars in the resultant combination will have minimal overlap in the number of ontological constructs after both the representation and interpretation mappings have been considered.

To construct minimally ontologically overlapping combinations of grammars, for each proposed starting grammar in modeling by the analysts in the team, Table 9.4 is inspected to determine the smallest number of other grammars that need to be combined in with the starting grammar to make it maximally ontologically complete. Where a choice in grammars for the combination is required, only those grammar(s) are selected where the number of construct overlaps between the starting grammar and the other grammars is lowest (or minimal). For example, if the team modeling begins with an ERA, then a STD or a PF or STC could be combined to obtain representations for state, state law, event, process, transformation, and lawful transformation. These alternate combinations would be maximally complete. However, the number of construct overlaps (from Table 9.4) between ERA and STC is 8, while the number of overlaps between ERA and PF, or ERA and STD, is 5. So, ERA can be combined with either PF or STD to form MOO/MOC-compliant sets. While state transition diagram (TRD) only has an overlap count of 3, together with ERA it would not form a MOC-compliant combination as it would not have a representation for state law.

The concepts of minimal ontological overlap and maximal ontological completeness imply that inconsistencies between models developed using different grammars will be reduced if those grammars exhibit minimal ontological overlap (Weber and Zhang, 1996). Accordingly,

H7. If multiple grammars are used by analysts (modelers) working in a project team in a CASE environment, then the problem of resolving inconsistencies between models developed using different grammars will be minimized if the grammars used by the modelers in the team exhibit minimal ontological overlap.

RESULTS

A multiple-method empirical approach was used in the late 1990s to collect data to test the above hypotheses. Moreover, this methodological approach allowed for the minimization of bias problems from using just one method to collect data, in order to provide methodological triangulation of results between methods, and to provide deeper insights into the situation (e.g., Jick, 1979). First, 437 questionnaires were sent to Excelerator users in 174 companies throughout Australia, New Zealand, and Southeast Asia. One hundred and sixty-eight usable responses (a 46.5 percent response rate) resulted. Of the 168 responses, 63 applied to analysts (modelers) who worked in project teams for their ISD work. Second, 34 tape-recorded interviewer-administered structured interviews were performed involving a selected subset of respondents predominantly drawn from those who had completed the original questionnaire.

Again, of these 34 interviewees, 25 were analysts (modelers) who worked in project team environments. Both the survey instrument and the structured interview protocol were pretested and pilot tested before use. Copies of the research instrument, the structured-interview protocol, and the typed transcripts of the interviews are available from the researcher on request.

With regard to the survey respondents, 66 percent had more than five years' experience in modeling. Sixty-six percent also had greater than one year's experience with the specific automated tool environment, while 25 percent indicated they had more than three years' experience with the tool at the time of the survey. Not surprisingly, modelers of commercial systems dominated the responses over modelers of scientific/engineering systems.

Statistical validity tests on the data showed that the results did not display significant monomethod bias or nonresponse bias. When twelve test-retest responses were compared to their original survey responses, confidence in reliability of the instrument was confirmed when not one of the over eighty possible item responses displayed a significant difference (independent samples t-test).

Project Team Survey Results: H1–H5

Hypotheses H1–H5 are tested using the following model:

$$COM\_GRAM = \alpha + \beta_1 ONT\_INC + \beta_2 PFTR + \beta_3 SYS\_SIZE + \beta_4 CONSIST + \beta_5 MAINT + E$$

where   COM_GRAMuse/nonuse of grammars in combination,
ONT_INC   recognition/nonrecognition of ontological incompleteness in each of the grammars available in Excelerator,
PFTR   existence/nonexistence of prior formal training in the use of grammars,
SYS_SIZE   a grouping variable with three levels (high, medium, and low) by the average number of users accessing systems analyzed/designed by the respondent,
CONSIST   perception/nonperception of minimal problems with consistency of representation, and
MAINT   perception/nonperception of minimal problems with maintenance of models as changes occur over time.

The results will be presented here in two ways. First, bivariate chi-square results are presented to establish simple measures of association between the dependent variable (DV) (COM_GRAM) and each of the independent variables (IVs). Second, a logit analysis involving the model with

Table 9.5

Tests of Association with the DV (COM_GRAM)—Projects

	χ^2	df	Signifance (p)	Minimum expected frequency
ONT_INC	3.83772	1	0.05011	9.4
PFTR	1.53000	1	0.21611	5.9
CONSIST	0.79376	1	0.37297	6.6
MAINT	0.12522	1	0.72344	8.7
SYS_SIZE	0.62201	2	0.73271	1.4

the variables measured in project team environments is presented. In the model being tested in this research, all of the variables are either dichotomous or categorical in nature. In particular, the DV (COM_GRAM) is a dichotomous variable. In such circumstances, then, Tabachnick and Fidell (1989) recommend the use of *logit* analysis to analyze the results. In particular, Tabachnick and Fidell (1989, p. 237) explain, "Used this way, multiway frequency analysis (logit analysis) is like a multiple regression or a nonparametric analysis of variance with a discrete DV as well as discrete IVs."

Table 9.5 presents the results of simple bivariate chi-square tests of association between the DV (COM_GRAM) and each of the IVs.

From Table 9.2, the only variable on which the null hypothesis of independence can be rejected is ONT_INC, at the .05 level. All the remaining IVs appear to be independent of the DV (COM_GRAM) from the bivariate perspective. All remaining two-way associations between the IVs were examined. The smallest expected cell frequency was 1.5 within the effect, SYS_SIZE by PFTR. In summary, however, all cells had a minimum expected cell frequency of greater than 1, and 10 percent of the cells had cell frequencies less than 5. This measure is well within Tabachnick and Fidell's (1989) criterion for adequate expected cell frequencies in the design. Accordingly, the expected cell frequencies appear adequate. However, there is not sufficient sample size to ensure nonzero counts in all cells. As noted earlier, however, with adequate expected cell frequencies, logit analysis is reasonably robust in such circumstances (Demaris, 1992).

A nonhierarchical logit analysis was performed with five two-way associations (COM_GRAM by CONSIST, COM_GRAM by MAINT, COM_GRAM by ONT_INC, COM_GRAM by PFTR, and COM_GRAM by SYS_SIZE) and the first-order effect of the DV, COM_GRAM, for the project team data. The model had adequate fit between observed and expected frequencies (likelihood ratio chi-square = 17.59, $df = 18$, $p = .483$). In logit, a nonsignificant chi-square indicating retention of the null hypothesis is the desired result. The adequacy of a logit model suffers only from outliers in the solution or low expected cell frequencies due to an insufficient sample size. The adequate model fit finding was confirmed by a review of the sizes of the standardized residuals of the model. Not one of the 96 cells displayed an absolute z-value greater than 1.96, with the largest standard residual being 1.67. This model has produced reasonable expected frequencies, however; the reduction in uncertainty in the prediction of the use of grammars in combination by the model for analysts/designers working in a project team was poor, with entropy = .10 (similar to R-square). By this measure, there still remains some 90 percent of the dispersion variance attributable to the residuals. A summary of the model with the results of tests of significance (partial likelihood ratio chi-squares) and loglinear parameter estimates in raw and standardized form appear in Table 9.6.

In Table 9.6, the effects (except for the DV) are listed in descending order of z-value. It is

Table 9.6

Summary of Logit Model of Project Team Use of Grammars in Combination (N = 63)

Effect	Partial χ^2 (Significant)		Parameter (λ)		λ/SE (z-value)	
			No	Yes	No	Yes
COM_GRAM			−0.326	0.326	−1.4118	1.4118
COM_GRAM by ONT_INC	4.238	No	0.300	−0.300	2.014	−2.014
	(.0395)	Yes	−0.300	0.300	−2.014	2.014
COM_GRAM by PFTR	1.041	No	−0.164	0.164	−1.058	1.058
	(.3077)	Yes	0.164	−0.164	1.058	−1.058
COM_GRAM by CONSIST	0.884	No	−0.210	0.210	−0.981	0.981
	(.3470)	Yes	0.210	−0.210	0.981	−0.981
COM_GRAM by SYS_SIZE	0.358	<20	0.212	−0.212	0.543	−0.543
	(.8363)	20–100	−0.132	0.132	−0.553	0.553
		>100	−0.080	0.080	−0.010	0.010
COM_GRAM by MAINT	0.016	No	0.033	−0.033	0.167	−0.167
	(.9000)	Yes	−0.033	0.033	−0.167	0.167

interesting to note, however, that the odds of a project team using grammars in combination are approximately 2 to 1 (based on the coefficient for COM_GRAM of 0.326). This ratio is significantly reduced from the 5 to 1 odds of a similar occurrence reported for individual analysts (modelers) who did not work in project teams. This result would seem to indicate that modeling by analysts (modelers) in project teams is inhibited significantly compared to situations where analysts (modelers) are able to conduct their work without the constraints of working in a project team environment.

The only effect that appears to significantly influence use of grammars in combination by members in a project team is COM_GRAM by ONT_INC. Moreover, the effect is in the direction that would be predicted by the theory. Hence, H1 is supported. The remaining effects appear to be insignificant in their influence on the use/nonuse of grammars in combination within project teams.

Accordingly, H2–H5 appear to be unsupported. It is interesting to note, however, that prior formal postsecondary training in grammar(s) (PFTR) appears to have a stronger (albeit insignificant and in the opposite direction) effect on the DV. This result would seem to indicate that the more formal training analysts have in modeling grammar use, the less they appear inclined to use grammars in combination within a project team environment (although not significantly). Moreover, obtaining a high level of consistency among models used within a project team appears to lead analysts (modelers) not to use combinations of grammars (although not significantly). Furthermore, a perception of minimal problems with maintenance (MAINT) appears to have little influence on the decision to use/not use grammars in combination within the project team. Finally, modeling in project teams for small systems (< 20 users) appears to involve single grammar sets while modeling in project teams for medium (< 100 users) and large (> 100 users) systems appears to lead analysts (modelers) in the teams to use combinations of grammars (although not significantly).

Project Team Structured Interview Results: H1–H5

The structured-interview data on the use/nonuse of grammars in combination by project teams within an Excelerator case environment may provide further insight, particularly in light of the fact that 90 percent of the variance in the DV (COM_GRAM) still remains to be explained. Furthermore, such qualitative results may give some confirmatory confidence in the results achieved from the quantitative data. The results of the qualitative data gathered on the project team use of grammars through the structured interviews are summarized in Table 9.7.

In clear confirmation of the quantitative results for project teams, recognition/nonrecognition of ontological incompleteness is the strong influencing factor on the use of grammars in combination in Table 9.6. Apart from system size (SYS_SIZE), not one of the other IVs of the model was mentioned. Some insight into the importance of system/project size for the use of combinations of grammars by the team is given by structured-interview participant 21 (SI21). When asked why combinations of grammars were not used on projects, SI21 replied,

> Because the projects themselves were so small. There was only one analyst on the team. There might be four or five people contracted in to do the coding.

Clearly, the most significant "other" reason for using/not using grammars in combination within the project teams is the need to adhere to some *corporate standard/methodology*. To further investigate this issue, data were gathered in the survey on the existence/nonexistence of corporate standards/methodology for the use of grammars (STAN) by project teams. A logit analysis includ-

Table 9.7

Summary of Structured Interview Responses: Project Team Use of Grammars in Combination

Interview	ONT_INC	CONSIST	MAINT	PFTR	SYS_SIZE	Other
Use grammars in combination						
SI3	X					
SI4	X					Decomposition
SI5						Communication
SI6	X					Documenting
SI7	X					
SI8						Standards
SI10	X					
SI15	X					
SI16						Standards
SI17	X					Specialization
SI18	X					
SI19	X					Specialization
SI22	X					Specialization
SI23	X					
SI24						Standards
SI25						Experience, Standards
SI26	X					
SI30	X					Standards
SI31	X					Specialization, Standards
SI32	X					Standards
SI33						Standards
SI34	X					
Total	16	0	0	0	0	
Do not use grammars in combination						
SI21						
SI27					X	Lack of experience in Excelerator and analysis; lack of training
SI35						Standards
Total	0	0	0	0	1	

ing the additional IV, STAN, was performed. Such a model provided a significantly better fit to the data (Δ likelihood ratio $\chi^2 = 19.6416$, $df = 8$, $p < .02$). The individual effect, COM_GRAM by STAN, however, was not significant with a z-value of 0.543.

Of the remaining "other" factors mentioned, *specialization* is given as a reason/explanation for the use of grammars in combination within a team a number of times. Specialization refers to the situation where a team is constructed of, say, a specialist data modeler, a specialist data flow diagrammer, a specialist in control aspects, and so on. Each specialist brings a different set of skills and grammars to the development process. This factor is very much in line with the findings of Kautz et al. (2007) that one of the major practices for coping with the challenges of ISD is to specialize at, and between, different contextual levels (including the project team).

Project Team Results: H6–H7

Hypotheses H6 and H7 are tested using the following model:

$$CONSIST = \alpha + \beta_1 INT\_MEC + \beta_2 MOO + \varepsilon$$

where

INT_MEC	existence/nonexistence of an automated integrating mechanism for representations across models,
MOO	minimal ontological overlap is/is not exhibited in the combination of grammars used by the analysts (modelers) in the CASE tool, and as before CONSIST perception/nonperception of minimal problems with consistency of representation.

This section discusses the results pertaining to hypotheses, H6 and H7, regarding perceptions by analysts (modelers) working in project teams of problems with consistency of representation when employing a number of grammars for modeling by different members of the development team. Problems with consistency of representation may well be exacerbated where individual analysts (modelers) working as members of a project team must share models developed using different grammars. An automated integration mechanism extending beyond that of the individual CASE tool may be required to minimize problems of inconsistency of representation across the various models used by the team.

Of the original 63 cases relating to analysts (modelers) working in project teams, 18 cases of use of single grammar only by the team were deleted. These modifications left 45 cases in the survey responses for analysis. Unfortunately, the logit analysis performed on these data failed to converge to a result due to the mixture of relatively large and relatively small observed counts in cells caused by the extreme split (93/7) in the MOO variable. Accordingly, the model was tested using bivariate tests of association between each of the IVs and the DV (CONSIST). Table 9.8 presents the results of that test.

From Table 9.8, it is apparent that INT_MEC and CONSIST are significantly dependent at the .005 level, while MOO and CONSIST fail to reject the null hypothesis that they are independent of each other. Accordingly, H6 appears to be supported. By contrast, H7 would seem to be not supported. The fact that minimal ontological overlap of the grammars used by the analysts (modelers) working in teams was not significantly independent of a perception of a high level of consistency among those models requires further investigation. The result points to potential contextual factors,

Table 9.8

Tests of Association with the DV (CONSIST)—Project Teams

	χ^2	df	Significance (p)	Minimum expected frequency
INT_MEC	9.50663	1	**.00205**	5.6
MOO	2.18683	1	.13920	0.9

such as the ones described by Wand and Weber (2002); namely, individual difference factors, task factors, and social agenda factors that could potentially moderate the criticality of the construct deficit in the grammars under observation, and, hence, confound the support of the hypotheses. Indeed, in several qualitative interview situations, modelers had explained they were required to use the two different data modeling grammars (ERA and DMD) in their preferred grammar sets. Such use was required either to integrate designs into the corporate data model repository or because that was the "standard use" set of the organization. Such a grammar combination was not predicted by MOO theory due to the high ontological overlap between the two data modeling grammars. Yet, up to 25 percent of grammar combinations reported by the project teams used the two different data modeling grammars as part of their grammar sets. This situation points to *social agenda factors* in conceptual modeling (Wand and Weber, 2002), such as organizational standards, that can impose restrictions on how grammars are being put to use in organizational environments.

Hence, combining representation theory-based analysis with qualitative inquiry provides an even more fruitful avenue for research into modeling grammar use.

CONCLUSION

This research has demonstrated the application of representation theory to traditional and structured analysis modeling grammars as implemented in an automated tool and used by analysts (modelers) working within a project team environment for ISD. It used data gathered on how analysts (modelers) working in project teams used grammars within a popular automated tool environment at the time—Excelerator—to test a model based on ontological, task, individual, and contextual factors in an effort to explain the decision to use/not use a combination of grammars for modeling. The results found a strong association between recognition of ontological incompleteness in the grammars provided by the tool and the decision to use a combination of grammars. Moreover, the odds of a project team using grammars in combination are approximately 2 to 1, which are significantly reduced from the 5 to 1 odds of a similar occurrence reported for individual analysts (modelers) who did not work in project teams. Furthermore, modeling within project teams for small systems appears to involve single grammars, but for medium and large-sized systems, it appears to require sets of grammar combinations, although not significantly so. This result is in line with the findings of Roberts et al. (2005) in that knowledge sharing using models of single grammars appears to be more prevalent only in less complex projects. Additional qualitative evidence from structured interviews indicated that recognition/nonrecognition of ontological incompleteness is the strong influencing factor on the use of grammars in combination by analysts (modelers) working in teams. Qualitative evidence also highlighted the influence of corporate modeling standards and specialization on the use of sets of grammars within project teams. A model including a variable specifying the existence/nonexistence of corporate standards provided a significantly improved fit of the data; however, the variable was not a significant influence on whether or not the teams used grammars in combination. An integrating mechanism (e.g., central model repository) was seen as highly significant in achieving high levels of consistency among the models generated by the project team. However, the influence of minimal ontological overlap among the grammar sets used by the team was not seen as a significant influence on the decision to use combinations of grammars. Its influence may have been masked by confounding situational factors such as the need to use a particular data-modeling notation for the central corporate repository.

This research suffers from the limitation of a relatively small sample size, and therefore potentially limited generalizability of the results. However, having data from multiple sources (survey and interview) has mitigated these problems to a large extent by being able to cross-reference responses by respondents and check their understanding in many instances. Moreover, it has given us some confidence in the representativeness of the sample responses. The combined use of qualitative and quantitative empirical data has provided some further useful and insightful evidence indicating that representation theoretical analysis provides a fruitful theoretical foundation for advancing the study of modeling grammars.

In conclusion, this chapter has argued that the usefulness of the representation theory and its extensions should be judged on the basis of its insights rather than on the appropriateness of its assumptions. It is on the basis of insights such as these that the debate over the appropriateness of the use of representation theory for the analysis, evaluation, and comparison of modeling grammars can be conducted fruitfully, not on the basis of the underlying assumptions of representation theory.

REFERENCES

Alchian, A.A. 1950. Uncertainty, evolution, and economic theory. *Journal of Political Economy,* 58, 211–221.

Amoako-Gyampah, K., and Salam, A.F. 2004. An extension of the technology acceptance model in an ERP implementation environment. *Information & Management,* 41, 6, 731–745.

Avison, D.E., and Fitzgerald, G. 2003. Where now for development methodologies? *Communications of the ACM,* 46, 1, 78–82.

Bansler, J.P., and Bodker, K. 1993. A reappraisal of structured analysis: Design in an organizational context. *ACM Transactions on Information Systems,* 11, 2, 165–193.

Baskerville, R.; Pries-Heje, J.; and Ramesh, B. 2007. The enduring contradictions of new software development approaches: A response to "Persistent Problems and Practices in ISD." *Information Systems Journal,* 17, 241–245.

Berger, P.L., and Luckmann, T. 1966. *The Social Construction of Reality: A Treatise in the Sociology of Knowledge.* Garden City, NY: Doubleday.

Bodart, F.; Patel, A.; Sim, M.; and Weber, R. 2001. Should optional properties be used in conceptual modelling? A theory and three empirical tests. *Information Systems Research,* 12, 4, 384–405.

Bunge, M.A. 1977. *Treatise on Basic Philosophy,* Volume 3: *Ontology I—The Furniture of the World.* Dordrecht: Kluwer Academic.

Burrell, G., and Morgan, G. 1979. *Sociological Paradigms and Organizational Analysis: Elements of the Sociology of Corporate Life.* Brookfield, VT: Ashgate.

Burton-Jones, A., and Meso, P. 2006. Conceptualizing systems for understanding: An empirical test of decomposition principles in object-oriented analysis. *Information Systems Research,* 17, 1, 38–60.

Butler, T. 2000. Transforming information systems development through computer-aided systems engineering (CASE): Lessons from practice. *Information Systems Journal,* 10, 167–193.

Coad, P., and Yourdon, E. 1990. *Object Oriented Analysis.* 2d ed. Englewood Cliffs, NJ: Prentice Hall.

Curtis, B.; Kellner, M.I.; and Over, J. 1992. Process modeling. *Communications of the ACM,* 35, 9, 75–90.

Curtis, B.; Krasner, H.; and Iscoe, N. 1998. A field study of the software design process for large systems. *Communications of the ACM,* 31, 11, 1268–1287.

Davies, I.; Green, P.; and Rosemann, M. 2002. Facilitating an ontological foundation of information systems with meta models. In A. Wenn, M. McGrath, and F. Burstein (eds.), *Proceedings of the Thirteenth Australasian Conference on Information Systems,* 937–947. Melbourne, Australia.

Davies, I.; Green, P.; Milton, S.; and Rosemann, M. 2003. Using meta models for the comparison of ontologies. In J. Krogstie, T. Halpin, and K. Siau (eds.), *Proceedings of the Eighth CAiSE/IFIP8.1 International Workshop on Evaluation of Modeling Methods in Systems Analysis and Design.* Velden, Austria.

Davies, I.; Green, P.; Rosemann, M.; Indulska, M.; and Gallo, S. 2006. How do practitioners use conceptual modeling in practice? *Data and Knowledge Engineering,* 58, 3, 358–380.

Demaris, A. 1992. *Logit Modeling: Practical Applications.* Newbury Park, CA: Sage.

Faraj, S., and Sambamurthy, V. 2006. Leadership in information systems development projects. *IEEE Transactions on Engineering Management,* 53, 2, 238–249.

Fettke, P., and Loos, P. 2003. Ontological evaluation of reference models using the Bunge-Wand-Weber model. In J.W. Ross (ed.), *Proceedings of the Ninth Americas Conference on Information Systems,* 2944–2955. Tampa, FL: Association for Information Systems.

Fitzgerald, B. 1998. An empirical investigation into the adoption of systems development methodologies. *Information and Management,* 34, 6, 317–328.

Floyd, C. 1986. A comparative evaluation of system development methods. In T.W. Olle, H.G. Sol, and A.A. Verrijn-Stuart (eds.), *Information System Design Methodologies: Improving the Practice,* 19–54. Amsterdam: North-Holland.

Ford, J.K.; Schmitt, N.; Schechtman, S.L.; Hults, B.M.; and Doherty, M.L. 1989. Process tracing methods: Contributions, problems and neglected research questions. *Organisational Behaviour and Human Decision Processes,* 43, 75–117.

Friedman, M. 1953. The methodology of positive economics. In M. Friedman (ed.), *Essays in Positive Economics,* 3–43. Chicago: University of Chicago Press.

Gemino, A. 2005. Methodological issues in the evaluation of systems analysis and design techniques. In P. Green and M. Rosemann (eds.), *Business Systems Analysis with Ontologies,* 305–321. Hershey, PA: Idea Group.

Gemino, A., and Wand, Y. 2005. Complexity and clarity in conceptual modeling: Comparison of mandatory and optional properties. *Data & Knowledge Engineering,* 55, 3, 301–326.

Goodhue, D.L., and R.L. Thompson. 1995. Task-technology fit and individual performance. *MIS Quarterly,* 19, 2, 213–236.

Green, P. 1997. Use of information systems analysis and design (ISAD) grammars in combination in upper CASE tools—An ontological evaluation. In K. Siau, Y. Wand, and J. Parsons (eds.), *Proceedings of the Second CAiSE/IFIP8.1 International Workshop on Evaluation of Modeling Methods in Systems Analysis and Design,* 1–12. University of Nebraska-Lincoln, Barcelona, Spain.

Green, P., and Rosemann, M. 2000. Integrated process modeling: An ontological evaluation. *Information Systems,* 25, 2, 73–87.

———. 2001. Ontological analysis of integrated process models: Testing hypotheses. *Australian Journal of Information Systems,* 9, 1, 30–38.

———. 2002. Usefulness of the BWW ontological models as a "core" theory of information systems. In S. Gregor and D. Hart (eds.), *Information Systems Foundations: Building the Theoretical Base,* 147–164. Canberra: Australian National University.

Green, P.; Rosemann, M.; and Indulska, M. 2005. "Ontological evaluation of enterprise systems interoperability using ebXML. *IEEE Transactions on Knowledge and Data Engineering,* 17, 5, 713–725.

Green, P.; Rosemann, M.; Indulska, M.; and Manning, C. 2007. Candidate interoperability standards: An ontological overlap analysis. *Data & Knowledge Engineering,* 62, 2, 274–291.

Hirschheim, R.; Klein, H.K.; and Lyytinen, K. 1996. Exploring the intellectual structure of information systems development: A social action theoretic analysis. *Accounting, Management and Information Technologies,* 6, 1/2, 1–64.

Howard, G.S., and Rai, A. 1993. Promise and problems: CASE usage in the US. *Journal of Information Technology,* 8, 2, 65–73.

Igbaria, M.; Zinatelli, N.; Cragg, P.; and Cavaye, A.L.M. 1997. Personal computing acceptance factors in small firms: A structural equation model. *MIS Quarterly,* 21, 3, 279–305.

Iivari, J. 1996. Why are CASE tools not used? *Communications of the ACM,* 39, 10, 94–103.

Irwin, G., and Turk, D. 2005. An ontological analysis of use case modeling grammar. *Journal of the Association for Information Systems,* 6, 1, 1–36.

Jablonski, S., and Bussler, C. 1996. *Workflow Management. Modeling Concepts, Architecture, and Implementation.* London: Thomson Computer Press.

Janz, B.; Wetherbe, J.; Davis, G.; and Noe, R. 1997. Reengineering the systems development process: The link between autonomous teams and business process outcomes. *Journal of Management Information Systems,* 14, 1, 41–68.

Jick, T.D. 1979. Mixing qualitative and quantitative methods: Triangulation in action. *Administrative Science Quarterly,* 24, 4, 602–611.

Karam, G.M., and Casselman, R.S. 1993. A cataloging framework for software development methods. *IEEE Computer,* 26, 2, 34–45.

Kautz, K.; Hansen, B.; and Jacobson, D. 2004. The utilization of information systems development methodologies in practice. *Journal of Information Technology Cases and Applications,* 6, 4, 1–20.

Kautz, K.; Madsen, S.; and Norbjerg, J. 2007. Persistent problems and practices in information systems development. *Information Systems Journal,* 17, 217–239.

Keen, C.D., and Lakos, C. 1994. Information systems modelling using LOOPN++, an object Petri Net scheme. In H.G. Sol, A. Verbraeck, and P.W.G. Bots (eds.), *Proceedings of the Fourth International Working Conference on Dynamic Modelling and Information Systems,* 31–52. Noordwijkerhout, the Netherlands: Delft University Press.

Kirsch, L. 1996. The management of complex tasks in organizations: Controlling the systems development process. *Organization Science,* 7, 1, 1–21.

Moody, D.L. 2005. Theoretical and practical issues in evaluating the quality of conceptual models: Current state and future directions. *Data & Knowledge Engineering,* 15, 3, 243–276.

OASIS. 2003. ebXML—Enabling a Global Electronic Market. Available at www.ebxml.org/specs/index.htm (accessed March 26, 2004).

Olle, T.W.; Hagelstein, J.; MacDonald, I.G.; Rolland, C.; Sol, H.G.; van Assche, F.J.M.; and Verrijn-Stuart, A.A. 1991. *Information Systems Methodologies: A Framework for Understanding.* Wokingham, UK: Addison-Wesley.

Opdahl, A.L., and Henderson-Sellers, B. 2001. Grounding the OML metamodel in ontology. *Journal of Systems and Software,* 57, 2, 119–143.

———. 2002. Ontological evaluation of the UML using the Bunge-Wand-Weber model. *Software and Systems Modeling,* 1, 1, 43–67.

Parsons, J., and Wand, Y. 1997. Using objects for systems analysis. *Communications of the ACM,* 40, 12, 104–110.

Recker, J.; Indulska, M.; Rosemann, M.; and Green, P. 2005. Do process modelling techniques get better? A comparative ontological analysis of BPMN. In B. Campbell, J. Underwood, and D. Bunker (eds.), *Proceedings of the Sixteenth Australasian Conference on Information Systems.* Australasian Chapter of the Association for Information Systems, Sydney, Australia.

Rescher, N. 1973. *The Primacy of Practice.* Oxford, UK: Basil Blackwell.

Roberts, T.; Cheney, P.; Sweeney, P.; and Hightower, R. 2005. The effects of information technology project complexity on group interaction. *Journal of Management Information Systems,* 21, 3, 223–247.

Rosemann, M., and Green, P. 2000. Integrating multi-perspective views into ontological analysis. In W.J. Orlikowski, P. Weill, S. Ang, and H.C. Krcmar (eds.), *Proceedings of the Twenty-first International Conference on Information Systems,* 618–627. Brisbane, Australia: Association for Information Systems.

———. 2002. Developing a meta model for the Bunge-Wand-Weber ontological constructs. *Information Systems,* 27, 2, 75–91.

Rosemann, M.; Green, P.; and Indulska, M. 2004. A reference methodology for conducting ontological analyses. In P. Atzeni (ed.), *Conceptual Modeling—ER 2004: Proceedings of the Twenty-third International Conference on Conceptual Modeling,* 110–121. Heidelberg: Springer-Verlag.

Rosemann, M.; Recker, J.; Indulska, M.; and Green, P. 2006. A study of the evolution of the representational capabilities of process modeling grammars. In E. Dubois and K. Pohl (eds.), *Proceedings of the Eighteenth International Conference on Advanced Information Systems Engineering* (CAiSE'06), 447–461. Heidelberg: Springer-Verlag.

Shanks, G.; Tansley, E.; and Weber, R. 2003. Using ontology to validate conceptual models. *Communications of the ACM,* 46, 10, 85–89.

Shanks, G.; Tansley, E.; Nuredini, J.; Tobin, D.; and Weber, R. 2002. Representing part-whole relationships in conceptual modelling: An empirical evaluation. In L. Applegate, R. Galliers, and J.I. DeGross (eds.),

Proceedings of the Twenty-third International Conference on Information Systems, 89–100. Barcelona, Spain: Association for Information Systems.

Sia, S.K., and Soh, C. 2002. Severity assessment of ERP-organization misalignment: Honing in on ontological structure and context specificity. In L. Applegate, R. Galliers, and J.I. DeGross (eds.), *Proceedings of the Twenty-third International Conference on Information Systems*, 723–729. Barcelona, Spain: Association for Information Systems.

Tabachnick, B.G., and Fidell, L.S. 1989. *Using Multivariate Statistics*. 2d ed. New York: Harper and Row.

Tan, X., and Siau, K. 2006. Understanding the acceptance of modeling methods by IS developers: A theoretical model and an empirical test. In D.W. Straub and S. Klein (eds.), *Proceedings of the Twenty-seventh International Conference on Information Systems*. Milwaukee, WI: Association for Information Systems.

Tiwana, A., and McLean, E. 2005. Expertise integration and creativity in information systems development. *Journal of Management Information Systems*, 22, 1, 13–43.

von Halle, B. 1993. The challenges of birthdays and business rules. *Database Programming & Design*, 6, 8, 13–15.

———. 2001. *Business Rules Applied: Building Better Systems Using the Business Rules Approach*. New York: Wiley.

Wand, Y., and Weber, R. 1989. An ontological evaluation of systems analysis and design methods. In E.D. Falkenberg and P. Lindgreen (eds.), *Information System Concepts: An In-depth Analysis. Proceedings of the IFIP TC 8/WG 8.1 Working Conference on Information System Concepts*, 79–107. Amsterdam: North-Holland.

———. 1990. An ontological model of an information system. *IEEE Transactions on Software Engineering*, 16, 11, 1282–1292.

———. 1993. On the ontological expressiveness of information systems analysis and design grammars. *Journal of Information Systems*, 3, 4, 217–237.

———. 1995. On the deep structure of information systems. *Information Systems Journal*, 5, 3, 203–223.

———. 2002. Research commentary: Information systems and conceptual modeling—A research agenda. *Information Systems Research*, 13, 4, 363–376.

———. 2006. On ontological foundations of conceptual modeling: A response to Wyssusek. *Scandinavian Journal of Information Systems*, 18, 1, 127–138.

Wand, Y.; Storey, V.C.; and Weber, R. 1999. An ontological analysis of the relationship construct in conceptual modeling. *ACM Transactions on Database Systems*, 24, 4, 494–528.

Weber, R. 1997. *Ontological Foundations of Information Systems*. Melbourne: Coopers & Lybrand and the Accounting Association of Australia and New Zealand.

Weber, R., and Zhang, Y. 1996. An analytical evaluation of NIAM's grammar for conceptual schema diagrams. *Information Systems Journal*, 6, 2, 147–170.

Wyssusek, B. 2006. On ontological foundations of conceptual modelling. *Scandinavian Journal of Information Systems*, 18, 1, 63–80.

Yourdon, E. 1989. *Modern Structured Analysis*. Upper Saddle River, NJ: Prentice Hall.

Zhang, H.; Kishore, R.; and Ramesh, R. 2007. Semantics of the MibML conceptual modeling grammar: An ontological analysis using the Bunge-Wand-Weber framework. *Journal of Database Management*, 18, 1, 1–19.

CHAPTER 10

ASSIGNING ONTOLOGICAL SEMANTICS TO UNIFIED MODELING LANGUAGE FOR CONCEPTUAL MODELING

XUEMING LI AND JEFFREY PARSONS

Abstract: Although it originated as a language for software modeling, the Unified Modeling Language (UML) is increasingly used for conceptual modeling of application domains. However, due to its origins, UML has many constructs that are purely software oriented. Consequently, it might not be suitable for modeling "real world" phenomena. This chapter aims to assign real-world semantics to a core set of UML constructs. We propose principles for mapping UML constructs to the formal ontology of Mario Bunge, which has been widely used in information systems modeling contexts. We conclude by outlining how the proposed principles can be evaluated empirically in terms of their effectiveness in supporting conceptual modeling using UML.

Keywords: UML, Ontology, Conceptual Modeling

Before developing an information system, the business and organizational domain in which the information system is to be used must be examined and understood. The system analysis phase of information system development focuses on how to represent this domain. Such a description is termed a "conceptual model." Developing a conceptual model that is a good representation of the domain it is intended to represent is critical for successful information system development (Jackson, 1995; Offen, 2002; Sommerville and Sawyer, 1997)—the cost of repairing requirements errors during maintenance may be two orders of magnitude greater than that of correcting them during requirements engineering (RE) (Davis, 1993).

It is widely held that one important advantage of Unified Modeling Language (UML) over other software modeling languages is that it is appropriate both for modeling software and for modeling the problem domain that is supported by a system (i.e., conceptual modeling) (Fowler, 2004). However, since UML was developed in large part based on ideas from the implementation domain, such as object-oriented programming languages and databases, its suitability for modeling real-world domains in the early development phases has been questioned (Opdahl and Henderson-Sellers, 2002). For example, Opdahl and Henderson-Sellers indicate that within requirements engineering, object-oriented (OO) constructs and their use appear less well understood and well defined, and their value is controversial (Opdahl and Henderson-Sellers, 2001). Woodfield (1997) argues that significant impedance mismatches exist between conceptual modeling concepts and the concepts of object-oriented programming. More generally, UML lacks theoretical foundations to support its use for conceptual modeling. While the semantics of its constructs (such as object, class, attribute, link, and association) are clear with respect to software design and coding, they are vague with respect to application domain modeling.

We argue that, to develop a conceptual model that faithfully represents a real world domain, we must understand in advance what exists in the real world. In philosophy, ontology is devoted to the study of the nature and structure of reality. A number of researchers have argued that ontology is an appropriate foundation for identifying the fundamental constructs that need to be supported by a conceptual modeling language and the relationships among them (e.g., Evermann, 2005; Evermann and Wand, 2005a, 2005b; Guizzardi et al., 2002; Opdahl and Henderson-Sellers, 2001, 2002; Parsons and Wand, 1997; Shanks et al., 2003; Wand, 1989; Wand and Weber, 1989, 1990, 1993, 1995; Wand et al., 1995). Our research addresses the question: Can we define a core of UML that has formal ontological semantics and is suitable for conceptual modeling?

ONTOLOGY AND ONTOLOGICAL EVALUATION IN CONCEPTUAL MODELIING

In philosophy, the purpose of ontology "is to study the most general features of reality" (Peirce, 1935). It aims to answer questions such as: what kinds of entities exist in the world? Ontologies have become very influential in the information systems discipline, with research focusing on topics related to system analysis and design, enterprise systems, and Web services. Such research generally follows one of two well-differentiated lines: ontologies as technologies of information systems (covering the ontology-driven information systems that use domain, task, and application ontologies) and the ontological models of information systems (ontologies as abstract models supporting the core of the information system discipline and contributing to the improvement of conceptual modeling techniques). Our research follows the second line.

As noted, various researchers have argued that ontology is an appropriate theoretical foundation for identifying the fundamental constructs and the relationships among them that need to be supported by a conceptual modeling language. Most work has been based on Wand and Weber's adaptation of Mario Bunge's (1977, 1979) ontology for the information systems field. The idea of ontological evaluation of modeling languages developed by Wand and Weber is to find a mapping from ontological concepts into language constructs and vice versa (Wand and Weber, 1993). The first type of mapping shows how ontological concepts can be represented by the language and is therefore called "representation mapping." The second shows how language elements are interpreted ontologically and is called "interpretation mapping."

Based on these mappings, Wand and Weber identify four ontological discrepancies that may undermine the ontological completeness and ontological clarity of constructs in a conceptual modeling language: construct deficit; construct overload; construct redundancy; and construct excess. The mappings between ontological concepts and conceptual modeling language constructs can be used to transfer assumptions from ontology to the modeling language. If there are ontological rules or constraints that relate two or more concepts, then by virtue of the mapping, these same rules or constraints must also apply to the modeling language. Thus, the ontological mappings can lead to modeling rules and guidelines on how to use the conceptual modeling language to model real-world domains (Evermann and Wand, 2001).

Wand (1989) and Parsons and Wand (1997) apply the main concepts of Bunge's ontology to examine principles of object-oriented concepts. They distinguish representation-related constructs from implementation-related ones. Parsons and Wand derive guidelines for using object ideas in systems analysis. They argue that "the key to applying object concepts in systems analysis successfully is viewing objects as representation, rather than implementation, constructs . . . applying them with an implementation focus during analysis may have undesirable consequences" (Parsons and Wand, 1997, p. 105).

More recently, Opdahl and Henderson-Sellers (2001, 2002) analyze and evaluate Open Modeling Language (OML) and UML as languages for representing concrete problem domains using Bunge's ontology and the BWW model. Their analysis and evaluation show that "many of the central UML constructs are well matched with the BWW models" (Opdahl and Henderson-Sellers, 2002, p. 43), and at the same time, they suggest several concrete improvements to the UML meta model. Using UML as an example, Evermann and Wand (2005a) propose a method based on Bunge's ontology to restrict the syntax of a modeling language such that impossible domain configurations cannot be modeled.

Researchers have also employed other ontologies to analyze and evaluate UML. For example, Guizzardi et al. (2002) use the General Ontological Language (GOL) and its underlying upper-level ontology to evaluate the ontological correctness of a UML conceptual model and develop guidelines for how UML constructs should be used in conceptual modeling. They focus on evaluating class, object, powertype, association, and aggregation/composition, and suggest some proposals to extend UML for more satisfactory treatment of aggregation.

Most of the work cited above based on Bunge's ontology evaluates aspects of a modeling language by mapping ontological constructs into those of the modeling language and vice versa in a somewhat inconsistent manner. Also, the equally important mapping of relationships between ontological and modeling language constructs is often ignored. In this chapter, we use Bunge's ontology to establish a more precise and consistent semantic framework of an ontologically grounded UML core for conceptual modeling, which, as shown later in this chapter, can be used to resolve a number of confusions in the UML literature.

CORE CONCEPTS OF BUNGE'S ONTOLOGY

Following is a summary of key elements of Bunge's ontology.

Thing and Construct

In Bunge's ontology, there are two kinds of objects: concrete things or simply things, and conceptual things or constructs. The world is viewed as composed of things. Constructs (e.g., mathematical concepts such as numbers, sets, and functions) are only creations of the human mind that take part in our representations of the real world.

Property and Attribute

All things possess properties. Properties do not exist independent of things; in other words, every property is possessed by some thing or other. Some properties, such as height and age of a person (which is a concrete thing), are inherent properties of things, called "intrinsic properties." Other properties, such as "being enrolled in a university," are properties of pairs (in general, n-tuples) of things, called "mutual properties." A mutual property of a thing is a property that has meaning only in terms of some other thing or things in the world. The scope of a property is the set of things that possess it.

Humans conceive of things in terms of models of things (called "functional schemata"). Such models are conceptual things (thus constructs). Attributes are characteristics assigned to models of things according to human perceptions. We may use different models for the same thing and, therefore, assign different sets of attributes to the same thing. Thus, humans conceive of properties of things in terms of the attributes of their conceptual models, and properties are known to humans only as attributes. In a given model of a thing, usually not every property of the thing will be represented as an attribute. Therefore, every functional schema only reflects partial aspects of a thing. Likewise, an attribute in a given model may or may not reflect a substantial property. For example, the height of a person (which is a model of a concrete thing) is an attribute that reflects a substantial property of the concrete thing. The name of a person (which is a model of a concrete thing) does not represent any specific substantial property of the concrete thing. It is an attribute that stands for the individual as a whole. Sometimes an attribute is used to represent one or more properties. Different attributes may be used to represent the same property.

Composition, Emergent Property, and Hereditary Property

A thing may be composed of other things. A fundamental ontological assumption is that the set of properties of a composite thing is not equal to that of all the properties of its parts. Instead, a composite thing must have at least one emergent property that characterizes the composite thing as a whole. Hence, properties of a composite thing are of two kinds: hereditary properties that also belong to some component thing(s) of the composite thing, and emergent properties that characterize the composite thing as a whole. An emergent property can be either intrinsic or mutual.

Kind

An arbitrary collection of things need not share a given set of properties. When they do, however, and no thing outside the collection has the properties of interest, the collection is called a "kind."

Law, Law Statement, and Natural Kind

A law is any condition or restriction on properties of a thing. A law statement is any restriction on the possible values of attributes of models of things and any relation among two or more attributes. The relation between laws and law statements is similar to that of properties and attributes discussed above: laws restrict and interrelate properties; whereas law statements restrict and interrelate attributes representing these properties, law statements represent laws. Laws are also properties.

A kind of things is determined by a set of properties. A natural kind, however, is determined by the laws the things obey. Indeed, the deepest method of grouping things is by the laws they obey. Note that since a law restricts and interrelates a set of properties and a natural kind of things is determined by a set of laws, then every thing in the natural kind must also obey all the properties restricted and interrelated by the laws. In this sense, a natural kind also determines a set of properties.

State, Conceivable State Space, and Lawful State Space

We do not handle directly concrete things; we handle their models. The attributes of a model (or functional schema, see below) of things represent properties of the things. They are also called "state variables" or "state functions" because their values contribute to characterizing or identifying the states the things of interest can be in. The number of attributes of every functional schema of things is finite.

An ontological hypothesis is that, every thing is—at a given time—in some state or other. There are two kinds of law statements: state law statements, which specify lawful states that a thing could actually stay in, and transformation law statements, which specify lawful transformations of a thing from a lawful state to another lawful state. While state law statements reflect the static characteristics of a thing, transformation law statements reflect its dynamic ones. More precisely, a state law statement can be viewed as a mapping from the possible states of things in a given functional schema into the set {lawful, unlawful}; a transformation law statement can be viewed as a mapping from a set of tuples reflecting lawful states of the things in a given functional schema into {lawful, unlawful}.

Functional Schema

In Bunge's ontology, models of things are called "functional schemata." Any natural kind of things can be modeled by some functional schema. A thing may have multiple functional schemata, reflecting different views of the same thing. Functional schema in Bunge's ontology is a crucial notion because the definitions of other notions such as state, state space, event, and event space of thing(s) depend on the functional schema used to model the thing(s). Since a thing may have different functional schemata, it thus may have different sets of definitions of state, state space, event, and event space.

Event and Transformation

So far we have considered static aspects of thing(s). In the real world, all things are changeable. Change may be qualitative (things acquiring or losing general properties) or quantitative (one or more individual properties of things are changed). Every qualitative change is accompanied by a quantitative change. We may conceive a quantitative change of a thing simply as a transition from one state to another state. The net change of a thing is called an "event." Not all conceivable events are really possible (lawful) because even if the respective states are lawful, the transition between them might not be. We define the notion of lawful event as a transformation of the lawful state space compatible with the law statements of a natural kind.

History and Coupling

Every thing is changeable. Changes of states manifest a history of a thing. The notion of history allows us to determine when two things are interacting with each other, thus bonded or coupled to each other. Intuitively, if two things interact, then at least one of them will not be traversing the same states as it would if the other did not exist.

Postulate 1: Every thing acts on and is acted upon by other things.

For example, consider a husband and a wife who are married to each other. Their histories are not independent; that is, the state history of the husband is not the same as that he would traverse if he were single (and vice versa). As a result, they are coupled.

Couplings are also mutual properties. Two things are coupled if and only if some changes in one are accompanied or preceded or followed by some changes in the other. We call couplings "binding mutual properties" and the mutual properties discussed earlier "nonbinding mutual properties." Note that only a general nonbinding mutual property can be represented by an attribute function in a functional schema.

The interaction between two or more things may give rise to a number of semantically related nonbinding mutual properties. For example, the interaction between an employee and an employer may incur a set of nonbinding mutual properties such as Salary, StartDate, OfficePhone, and so on. Therefore, a binding mutual property between two or more things always implies the existence of some semantically related nonbinding mutual properties shared between these things. The reverse however is not always true; that is, two or more things may share a nonbinding mutual property without being coupled. Examples are all spatiotemporal relations such as "Thing A is five kilometers away from thing B." Here, A and B share a nonbinding mutual property "five kilometers away," but thing A does not act on or is acted upon by thing B; thus they are not coupled. Moreover, the effects of an interaction between two things may be lasting. Thus, if two things interact for a while and then cease to do so, they are still coupled.

Aggregate and System

A composite thing is a thing composed of component things. A composite thing can be either an aggregate or a system. A thing is an aggregate if its history equals the union of the histories of its parts. Otherwise, it is a system.

ONTOLOGY AND ONTOLOGICAL EVALUATION IN CONCEPTUAL MODELING

In this section, we assign to UML ontological semantics for conceptual modeling by mapping ontological constructs discussed above to UML model elements and vice versa, leading to a set of principles for the use of UML for conceptual modeling. It is important to emphasize that we suggest these principles be followed in the early information systems analysis phases when a conceptual model is developed to faithfully represent the domain it is intended to represent. We contend that implementation-oriented considerations should be added only in later system design phases.

UML Object

In UML, "An object represents a particular instance of a class. It has identity and attribute values" (Object Management Group [OMG], 2003, pp. 3–64). Since real-world things are represented in UML conceptual models as objects, we propose that things are modeled in UML as objects, and objects model only things. In software design, not every object corresponds to a thing. For example, as argued in Evermann and Wand, (2005b), Job is a set of mutual properties (Salary, StartDate, and so on) shared by an employee and an employer.

> Principle 1:   In a UML conceptual model, every object models a thing. Conversely, every thing in the domain is modeled as an object.

It is clear from the UML specification that class is a more fundamental notion than object: an object is only a particular instance that originates from a class, and all objects originating from the same class are structured and behave in the same way. This view reflects UML's origin from object-oriented programming languages. In a program, we first have classes. Objects are then created from classes at runtime and behave exactly as specified by classes. Objects cannot move from class to class. In contrast, in Bunge's ontology, things are more fundamental than their classification: they exist in the real world. Things can be classified (into kinds and natural kinds, which are sets) according to some properties or laws they share. Therefore, in any classification of things, every thing has commonalities (the set of shared properties or laws) and idiosyncrasies (the set of unshared properties or laws). Moreover, things can migrate between natural kinds.

UML Attribute

In UML, "An attribute is a named slot within a classifier that describes a range of values that instances of the classifier may hold" (OMG, 2003, pp. 2–24). Since in Bunge's ontology, general (intrinsic and nonbinding mutual) properties are represented by attribute functions, we propose that attribute function is modeled in UML as an attribute, and a UML attribute models an attribute function.

Principle 2:   In a UML conceptual model, every attribute of a class/type models an attribute function representing a general (intrinsic or nonbinding mutual) property. Conversely, every attribute function representing a general (intrinsic or non-binding mutual) property in the domain is modeled in UML as an attribute of a class/type.

Note that, in Principle 2, if attributes of a class/type model attribute functions that represent general intrinsic properties, then that class/type is an "ordinary" class/type, instances of which are objects that model things in the real world; otherwise, if the attributes model attribute functions that represent general nonbinding mutual properties shared by things, then that class/type is an association class, instances of which are links connecting objects modeling those things.

UML Class/Type

In UML, "A class is a description of a set of objects that share the same attributes, operations, methods, relationships, and semantics" (OMG, pp. 2–26). Since a functional schema models things of a natural kind using a set of attribute functions and law statements, we propose that functional schema is modeled as class/type.

Principle 3:   In a UML conceptual model, every functional schema in the domain is modeled as a class/type. However, not every class/type models a functional schema.

For example, Figure 10.1 is a UML conceptual model adapted from Rumbaugh et al. (1998, p. 159). The classes Company and Person model two functional schemata whose natural kinds are sets of companies and persons, respectively. However, association class Job does not model any functional schema because its instances are links, not objects. Instead, the attributes of Job (Salary and StartDate) model two attribute functions representing two general nonbinding mutual properties shared between employees and employers. Salary and StartDate are in fact the only attribute functions owned by functional schemata Employee and Employer, which are represented in Figure 10.1 as named places.

UML Link and Association

In UML, a classifier is a classification of instances describing a set of instances that have structural and behavioral features in common. There are several kinds of classifiers, including class, interface and data type, and so on. Here, we only consider classes.

Figure 10.1   **Attributes of an Association Class**

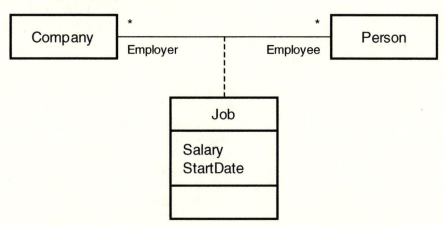

In UML, "A link is a connection between instances. Each link is an instance of an association, i.e. a link connects instances of (specializations of) the associated classifiers" (OMG, pp. 2–110). "An association defines a semantic relationship between classifiers. An association declares a connection (link) between instances of the associated classifiers (e.g., classes)" (OMG, pp. 2–64). Since individual nonbinding mutual property connects things that are modeled as objects in UML, we propose the following principle:

Principle 4:   In a UML class or object diagram, every link between two or more objects models a tuple of values representing semantically related individual nonbinding mutual properties shared between things modeled by these objects. Conversely, every tuple of values representing semantically related individual nonbinding mutual properties shared between two or more things in the domain is modeled in a UML class or object diagram as a link between objects modeling these things.

As a result, instances of an association (i.e., links) in a UML class diagram are more than "a tuple (list) of object references" (OMG, pp. 3–84). Moreover, from Principle 2, each attribute function representing a general nonbinding mutual property is modeled as an attribute of a UML association (or association class); thus we propose:

Principle 5:   In a UML class diagram, every association between two or more classes/ types models a tuple of attribute functions representing semantically related general nonbinding mutual properties shared by things that are modeled as instances of these classes/types. Every association must have at least one attribute. Conversely, every tuple of attribute functions representing semantically related general nonbinding mutual properties shared by things in the domain is modeled in a UML class diagram as an association between two or more classes whose instances model these things.

In a UML class diagram, attributes of an association can be illustrated using an association class attached to this association. Thus in UML class diagrams, association and association class are semantically equivalent.

For example, in Figure 10.1, association (or association class) Job models a pair of attribute functions Salary and StartDate, each of which represents a semantically related general nonbinding mutual property. Therefore, given a specific pair of employee and employer, the instance (link) of association Job is a pair of values that model individual nonbinding mutual properties of Salary and StartDate shared by the pair of employee and employer.

So far, the mutual properties we considered in a real world domain are nonbinding mutual properties.We suggest that, in a UML class diagram, every attribute of an association/association class models an attribute function representing a general nonbinding mutual property. Every association/association class in a UML class diagram must have at least one attribute shared by two or more classes/types because, otherwise, this association/association class is not needed at all. On the other hand, links between two or more objects in a UML collaboration model only binding mutual properties holding between things modeled by these objects. Therefore, links and their corresponding associations in UML class diagrams and collaborations are of fundamentally different ontological natures in that, while links and associations in UML class diagrams reflect static characteristics of a real-world domain, those in UML collaborations reflect dynamic ones. Consequently, we may call associations and their links in UML class and object diagrams "nonbinding associations and nonbinding links," and associations and their links in UML collaborations "binding associations and binding links."

In UML, "A collaboration describes how an operation or a classifier, like a use case, is realized by a set of classifiers and associations used in a specific way" (OMG, pp. 2–117). "A collaboration defines an ensemble of participants that are needed for a given set of purposes. Reasoning about the behavior of an ensemble of instances can therefore be done in the context of the collaboration as well as in the context of the instances" (OMG, pp. 2–124). From the UML specification, it seems that each link in a collaboration is supposed to be an instance of an association in the corresponding class diagram. However, this is a consequence of UML's implementation-oriented origin from object-oriented programming in which links in class diagrams are merely communication passages for sending messages to linked objects.

In fact, this view has given rise to a considerable amount of confusion in the UML literature when considering the relationship between class diagrams and collaborations. For example, in Stevens (2002), in order to remedy the so-called baseless link problem, namely, a link in a UML collaboration may not have a corresponding association in class diagram, Stevens proposes to classify associations in UML into static associations and dynamic associations. An association is static if one of the class definitions includes an attribute that contains a reference to an object of the other class. An association is dynamic if instances of the classes may exchange a message. Although Stevens's classification of associations into static and dynamic associations is somewhat similar to our classification of associations into nonbinding and binding associations, instead of focusing on the correspondence between real-world domain and UML conceptual model, her proposal focuses on the correspondence between UML conceptual model and program code, and is therefore not suitable for conceptual modeling.

Based on the above discussion, we have:

Principle 6:   In a UML collaboration, every (binding) link between objects models a binding mutual property shared between things modeled by these objects.

As a result, in a UML collaboration, a (binding) link is completely determined by the objects it links. Note that, usually, not every coupling or binding mutual property shared between two or more things in the domain is modeled as a (binding) link in a UML collaboration. For example, consider a husband and a wife and the husband's employer. It is reasonable that the state history of the wife is not the same as that she would traverse if her husband's employer has not existed. As a result, the wife and the employer are coupled. However, in a UML collaboration, this (indirect) coupling is usually ignored and not modeled as a (binding) link. Similarly we have:

> Principle 7:   In a UML collaboration, every (binding) association between two or more classes/types models a set of couplings or binding mutual properties shared between things modeled by instances of these classes/types.

Note that the interaction between two or more things (thus their coupling) will most likely give rise to a number of nonbinding mutual properties. Consequently, in a UML collaboration, whenever a binding link (representing a coupling or binding mutual property) exists between two or more objects, there will be a corresponding nonbinding link (representing a tuple of individual nonbinding mutual properties) between these objects in the corresponding class or object diagram. Furthermore, in a UML collaboration, whenever a binding association exists between two or more classes/types, there will be a corresponding nonbinding association between these classes/types in the corresponding class diagram.

On the other hand, although rare, not every nonbinding association/link in a UML class or object diagram corresponds to a binding association/link in the corresponding collaboration. Examples are all spatiotemporal relations such as "Thing A is five kilometers away from thing B." Here, thing A does not act on or is acted upon by thing B; thus they are not coupled.

UML Association Class

In UML, "An association class is an association that is also a class. It not only connects a set of classifiers but also defines a set of features that belong to the relationship itself and not any of the classifiers" (OMG, pp. 2–21).

From Principles 2 and 5, we know that an attribute of an association/association class actually models an attribute function representing a general nonbinding mutual property. Furthermore, an association class does not model any functional schema because its instances are links, not objects that model things in the real world domains. Therefore, as suggested by Evermann and Wand (2005b), an association class cannot have operations or methods. Instead, operations that change attribute values of an association/association class must be placed in participating role classes of the association. This idea has important implications for conceptual modeling (especially role modeling) and system design and implementation, but space precludes discussion of these issues here.

For example, in Figure 10.2 (adapted from Evermann and Wand, 2005b, p. 152), operations RaiseSalary and Terminate must be placed in either Employee or Employer; both are role types participating in the association Job. Note that attributes of Employee and Employer (Salary and StartDate) model only Bunge-attribute functions representing Bunge-general nonbinding mutual properties shared by employees and employers; thus all of these attributes are placed in association/association class Job. As a result, the attribute compartments of Employee and Employer are empty. In system design phases, however, we may treat Job as a "real" class and put implementation-oriented operations such as getSalary/setSalary and getStartDate/setStartDate into it. We may even put an operation Terminate into class Job as long as the semantic difference between Employer. Terminate (which means "lay off employee") and Employee.Terminate (which means "quit job") is not important for the design model.

Figure 10.2   **Operations and Methods of an Association Class**

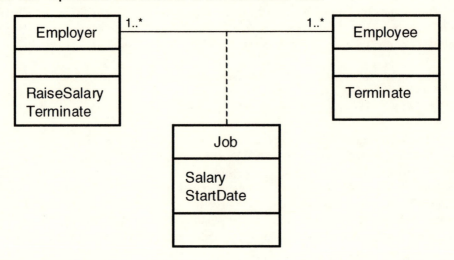

Source: Adapted from Evermann and Wand (2005b).

Moreover, in Figure 10.3 (Rumbaugh et al., 1998, p. 159), association class Job is associated with itself via an association Manages. However, Evermann and Wand (2005b) argue that, since instances of Job are links that model values representing individual nonbinding mutual property Salary, and recall that in Bunge's ontology, a property cannot further have properties, Figure 10.3 is not an ontologically correct conceptual model. In fact, Figure 10.3 suggests that instances of Job that are not objects modeling persons in a domain can play role types Boss and Worker, which do not comply with our intuition.

Based on the above discussion, we have the following principle:

Principle 8:   In a UML class diagram, an association class cannot have operations or methods, cannot be a composite class, and cannot be associated with other class(es).

UML Composition and Aggregation

In UML, "An association may represent an aggregation (i.e., a whole/part relationship). In this case, the association-end attached to the whole element is designated, and the other association-end of the association represents the parts of the aggregation. . . . Composite aggregation is a strong form of aggregation, which requires that a part instance be included in at most one composite at a time and that the composite object has sole responsibility for the disposition of its parts. This means that the composite object is responsible for the creation and destruction of the parts" (OMG, pp. 2–66). "A shareable aggregation denotes weak ownership (i.e., the part may be included in several aggregates) and its owner may also change over time. However, the semantics of a shareable aggregation does not imply deletion of the parts when an aggregate referencing it is deleted" (OMG, pp. 2–66).

It is clear that the distinction between UML composition/aggregation and Bunge's aggregate/ system is along different dimensions. For UML aggregation, components are existentially independent on the composite, and, moreover, they are sharable by other composites. For UML composition, components are existentially dependent on the composite and they are owned by

Figure 10.3 **Ontologically Incorrect Conceptual Model Using UML**

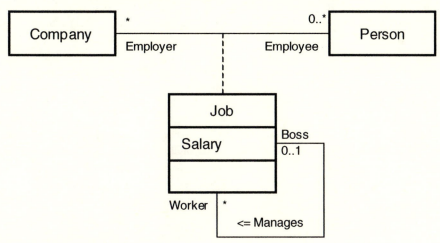

Source: Rumbaugh et al. (1998, p. 159).

the composite exclusively. In contrast, for aggregate, there is no coupling among components of the composite, which is not the case for system.

On page 311, we indicate that a composite thing must have at least one emergent property that characterizes the composite as a whole. Therefore, we have:

> Principle 9: In a UML conceptual model, every composite class/type must own at least one attribute that models an attribute function representing an emergent property.

UML State

In UML, "A state is a condition during the life of an object or an interaction during which it satisfies some condition, performs some action, or waits for some event. . . . Conceptually, an object remains in a state for an interval of time" (OMG, pp. 3–137). Therefore, in UML, there is no precise definition even for such fundamental notion as state. We propose that a UML state models a lawful state and a lawful state is modeled as a UML state.

> Principle 10: In a UML conceptual model, every state of an object models a lawful state of a thing modeled by the object. Conversely, a lawful state of a thing in the domain is modeled as a state of an object modeling this thing.

From Principles 3 and 10, we may conclude that a state of an object in a UML conceptual model is a tuple of values of the attributes of its class/type.

UML State Transition

In UML, "A transition is a directed relationship between a source state vertex and a target state vertex" (OMG, pp. 2–149). "A simple transition is a relationship between two states indicating that an instance in the first state will enter the second state and perform specific actions when a specified event occurs provided that certain specified conditions are satisfied" (OMG, pp. 3–145). We propose that a UML simple state transition models a lawful event and a lawful event is modeled as a UML simple state transition.

> Principle 11: In a UML conceptual model, every simple state transition of an object models a lawful event of a thing modeled by the object. Conversely, a lawful event of a thing in the domain is modeled as a simple state transition of an object.

In UML, "An event is a specification of a type of observable occurrence. The occurrence that generates an event instance is assumed to take place at an instant in time with no duration" (OMG, pp. 2–144). "Event instances are generated as a result of some action either within the system or in the environment surrounding the system" (OMG, pp. 2–155). It is obvious that the notion of event in UML is quite different from that of event in Bunge's ontology, which is simply a state transition.

UML Operation and Method

In UML, "An operation is a service that can be requested from an object to affect behavior" (OMG, pp. 2–44). "A method is the implementation of an operation. It specifies the algorithm or procedure that affects the results of an operation" (OMG, pp. 2–40). Since UML method is merely an implementation construct, it does not have any counterpart in Bunge's ontology. On the other hand, since operation can be requested to affect object behavior, and thus change its state, we propose that an operation models a lawful transformation and a lawful transformation is modeled as an operation.

> Principle 12: In a UML conceptual model, every operation of a class/type models a lawful transformation of a functional schema modeled by the class/type. Conversely, a lawful transformation of a functional schema in the domain is modeled as an operation of a class/type modeling this functional schema.

DISCUSSION

The principles introduced here constrain the use of UML for the purpose of conceptual modeling. Since the principles are based on Bunge's ontology, we expect they will lead to models that more faithfully represent an application domain. However, whether this occurs is an empirical question.

Further research is needed to evaluate the usefulness of the proposed principles for developing good conceptual models of a domain. Such studies could encompass both laboratory experiments and field studies. One line of experiments might involve having participants construct models with or without adhering to the proposed principles, and having independent assessors (domain experts) evaluate the quality of the resulting models. A second line of studies might have participants answer questions about models constructed based on the rules versus not based on the rules. Field studies can be used to evaluate the effect of applying the rules to models constructed for real applications and having developers and users evaluate the modified models in comparison to the originals.

CONCLUSION

In this chapter, we assign ontological semantics based on Bunge's ontology to a core set of UML constructs, namely, UML object, attribute, class/type, association, link, association class, state, state transition, and operation. The choice of these UML constructs is driven by Bunge's ontology. We also analyze consequences for conceptual modeling using UML based on this semantic mapping. For example, we have focused on UML association and link and indicate that links and their corresponding associations in UML class diagrams are of fundamentally different ontological natures from those in UML collaborations. As a result, the so-called baseless link problem disappears naturally. Our analysis suggests that Bunge's ontology is an appropriate foundation for identifying the fundamental constructs and the relationships among them that need to be supported by a conceptual modeling language.

We argue that the proposed principles should be followed when using UML for conceptual modeling purposes. If they are, the ontological semantics of resulting models will be precise, allowing for unambiguous interpretation of a conceptual model expressed in UML. Thus, we argue that the models will more faithfully represent real-world phenomena. In this chapter, we focus on discussing static aspects of UML. In the future, dynamic aspects of UML will be investigated. Research is also needed to determine whether following these rules leads to models that are easier to understand. Such questions are amenable to experimental and field-based empirical research methods.

REFERENCES

Bunge, M. 1977. *Treatise on Basic Philosophy (Volume 3), Ontology I: The Furniture of the World.* Boston: Reidel.
———. 1979. *Treatise on Basic Philosophy (Volume 4), Ontology II: A World of Systems.* Boston: Reidel.
Davis, A.M. 1993. *Software Requirements: Objects, Functions, States.* Upper Saddle River, NJ: Prentice Hall.
Evermann, J. 2005. The association construct in conceptual modelling: An analysis using the Bunge ontological model. In O. Pastor and J. Falcao e Cunha (eds.), *Proceedings of the Seventeenth International Conference on Advanced Information Systems Engineering* (CAiSE'05), LNCS 3520, 33–47. Berlin: Springer-Verlag.
Evermann, J. and Wand, Y. 2001. Towards ontologically-based semantics for UML constructs. In H.S. Kunii, S. Jajodia, and A. Solvberg (eds.), *Conceptual Modeling-ER 2001,* 341–354. Yokohama, Japan. Berlin: Springer-Verlag.
———. 2005a. Toward formalizing domain modeling semantics in language syntax. *IEEE Transactions on Software Engineering,* 31, 1 (January), 21–37.
———. 2005b. Ontology based object-oriented domain modelling: Fundamental concepts. *Requirements Engineering,* 10, 2, 146–160.
Fowler, M. 2004. *UML Distilled: Applying the Standard Object Modeling Language.* 3d ed. Reading, MA: Addison-Wesley.
Guizzardi, G.; Herre, H.; and Wagner, G. 2002. Towards ontological foundations for UML conceptual models. In *Proceedings of the First International Conference on Ontologies, Databases and Application of Semantics* (ODBASE'02), LNCS 2519. 1100–1117, London: Springer-Verlag.
Jackson, M. 1995. *Software Requirements & Specifications: A Lexicon of Practice, Principles and Prejudices.* Workingham, UK: ACM Press/Addison-Wesley.
Object Management Group (OMG). UML Specification 1.5. OMG document number ad/03–03–01 (March 2003) Available at http://www.omg.org/technology/documents/formal/uml.htm.
Offen, R. 2002. Domain understanding is the key to successful system development. *Requirements Engineering,* 7, 172–175.
Opdahl, A.L., and Henderson-Sellers, B. 2001. Grounding the OML metamodel in ontology. *Journal of Systems and Software,* 57, 2, 119–143.

————. 2002. Ontological evaluation of the UML using the Bunge-Wand-Weber model. *Software and Systems Modelling,* 1, 1, 43–67.

Parsons, J., and Wand, Y. 1997. Using objects for systems analysis. *Communications of the ACM,* 40, 12, 104–110.

Peirce, C.S. 1892–93 (1935). *Scientific Metaphysics. Vol. VI of the Collected Papers.* Cambridge, MA: Harvard University Press.

Rumbaugh, J.; Jacobson, I.; and Booch G. 1998. *The Unified Modeling Language Reference Manual.* Reading, MA: Addison-Wesley.

Shanks, G.; Tansley, E.; and Weber, R. 2003. Using ontology to validate conceptual models. *Communications of the ACM,* 46, 10, 85–89.

Sommerville, I., and Sawyer, P. 1997. *Requirements Engineering: A Good Practice Guide.* Chichester, UK: Wiley.

Stevens, P. 2002. On the interpretation of binary associations in the Unified Modelling Language. *Software and System Modeling,* 1, 1, 68–79.

Wand, Y. 1989. A proposal for a formal model of objects. In Won Kim and Frederick H. Lochovsky (eds.), *Object-Oriented Concepts, Databases, and Applications,* 537–539. New York: ACM Press.

Wand, Y., and Weber, R. 1989. An ontological evaluation of systems analysis and design methods. In E. Falkenberg and P. Lindgreen (eds.), *Information Systems Concepts: An In-Depth Analysis,* 79–107. Amsterdam: North-Holland.

————. 1990. An ontological model of an information system. *IEEE Transactions on Software Engineering,* 16, 11, 1282–1290.

————. 1993. On the ontological expressiveness of information systems analysis and design grammars. *Journal of Information Systems,* 3, 4, 217–237.

————. 1995. Towards a theory of deep structure of information systems. *Journal of Information Systems,* 5, 3, 203–223.

Wand, Y.; Monarchi, D.E.; Parsons, J.; and Woo, C.C. 1995. Theoretical foundations for conceptual modelling in information systems development. *Decision Support Systems,* 15, 4, 285–304.

Woodfield, S.N. 1997. The impedance mismatch between conceptual models and implementation environments. In *Proceedings of the ER'97 Workshop on Behavioral Models and Design Transformations: Issues and Opportunities in Conceptual Modeling,* Los Angeles, California, 6–7 November 1997. Springer-Verlag.

CHAPTER 11

META-MODELING TO DESIGN THE STRUCTURED DATABASE SCHEMA

ELVIRA LOCURATOLO

Abstract: A formal meta-model, exploited to define the conceptual model of a database design method named "ASSO," is proposed. The approach integrates features from methodologies of conceptual database design with the formal method B. Starting from a conceptual model based on the notions of class and is-a relationship, two gradual model extensions are considered: the former defines the basic operations, whereas the latter defines the ASSO model, called "Structured Database Schema." The Structured Database Schema permits large conceptual schemas to be specified in terms of class and specialized class and large consistency proofs to be reduced to small consistency proofs. The Structured Database Schema "goodness" is guaranteed by proposing model extensions compatible with the previous models. Both a "qualitative measure" of information implicitly specified within the Structured Database Schema and a "qualitative evaluation" of the consistency costs are provided.

Keywords: Meta-Modeling, Model Evolution, Quality Modeling, Conceptual Modeling, Database Design, Design Methodologies, Formal Methods

MetaASSO (Locuratolo, 2002) is the stepwise approach exploited to define ASSO (Locuratolo, 1997, 2002, 2005; Locuratolo and Matthews, 1999a, 1999b, 1999c), a database design method for quality that achieves:

- *Easiness of use*—the method's ability to provide a conceptual schema that is easy to use.
- *Flexibility*—the method's ability to provide a conceptual schema that is easy to modify.
- *Reliability*—the method's ability to provide conceptual schema consistency and logical schema correctness.
- *Economy*—the method's ability to remove duplication of code that is not necessarily executable and to require low costs for proof processes.
- *Efficiency*—the method's ability to access information using a limited amount of time.

Each step of MetaASSO is composed of an objective, that is, the request for a method that meets some of the listed points; an idea, that is, the proposal of a method that satisfies the objective; and the motivations, that is, the means to validate the proposal. MetaASSO is an informal method that starts from the initial idea to reconcile the flexibility of semantic data models with the efficiency of object-oriented systems, two conflicting quality desiderata. This idea is then refined with more concrete proposals that increase quality and allow the description of ASSO in terms of three components, called "methodological tools." Each methodological tool is a research result that can be used independently of the others.

MetaASSO shows that ASSO has been designed with a quality-oriented approach; that its definition includes those of related methods that can be used in different contexts; and that ASSO can be optimized.

This chapter proposes a meta-model exploited to design a methodological tool—that is, the conceptual model of ASSO, called the "Structured Database Schema." This meta-model refines and formalizes some aspects of MetaASSO: It starts from a conceptual model based on the notions of class and is-a relationship between classes, and proceeds with two model extensions. These integrate formal aspects of B (Abrial, 1996) within the previous conceptual models. Specifically, the former extension adds the basic operations, whereas the latter extension defines the Structured Database Schema, a model at a high abstraction level with respect to the B model (Locuratolo and Matthews, 1999a, 1999c). The Structured Database Schema is seen as a model at a high abstraction level because some details are implicitly specified, whereas the B model is seen as a model at a lower abstraction level because all the details are explicitly stated. Furthermore, the consistency costs of the Structured Database Schema are reduced with respect to the costs of the corresponding B specifications. Structured Database Schema "goodness" is guaranteed by proposing model extensions compatible with previous good models. This approach allows characterization of the specification implicitly stated with the Structured Database Schema, and provision of a qualitative/conceptual evaluation of the consistency costs. The meta-model proposed in this chapter can be compared with the approach described in Locuratolo (2006): both of them integrate database concepts with the formal aspect of B; the approach described in Locuratolo (2006), however, starts from the B formal model, and applies two model contractions in order to generate the Structured Database Schema. In both cases, meta-modeling is seen as a basis for capturing knowledge about engineering methods; a discussion on the two meta-models shows that the approach described in Locuratolo (2006) results in a quantitative evaluation of the consistency costs, whereas the approach described in this chapter results in a qualitative evaluation.

The chapter is organized as follows: background information concerning MetaASSO and ASSO is given in the next two sections. The meta-modeling exploited to design the Structured Database Schema is proposed in the fourth section. A review is presented in the fifth section, and conclusions and further developments, in the final section.

METAASSO

In this section the main objectives, ideas, and motivations of MetaASSO will be given. The initial objective of MetaASSO requires the proposal of a method that is able to combine flexibility in modifying a database schema with efficiency in accessing and storing information, two conflicting quality desiderata.

Conceptual Schema

The initial idea consists in working with two linked schemas: a consistent conceptual schema correctly linked with a logical schema.

Motivations: Conceptual Schema

The following motivations validate this idea: the conceptual schema is a database schema at a high abstraction level, able to guarantee flexibility; the logical schema is a database schema at a lower abstraction level, able to be supported by an efficient system; and mapping is the link to guarantee the achievement of both flexibility and efficiency. Conceptual schema consistency and transformation correctness have been introduced to guarantee idea reliability.

The new objective of MetaASSO requires proposing a consistent conceptual schema that is correctly linked with a logical schema.

Semantic Data Model

The new idea refines the previous one with by proposing a formal semantic data model that is correctly linked with an object model through a formal mapping.

Motivations

The following motivations are given to guarantee idea reliability: semantic data models are promising models to specify database applications in an easy and flexible way; object models are promising models to be supported by efficient systems; and formality of models and mapping are the means for achieving consistency and correctness.

The new step of MetaASSO requires a formal method that is able to correctly transform a semantic data model into an object model.

Revised Partitioning

The proposed idea consists in applying the revised partitioning to extended conceptual classes.

Motivations

Revised partitioning is a formal method that is able to determine all of the classes implicitly specified within a graph of conceptual classes supported by semantic data models. Revised partitioning generates models equivalent to the original graph until an object model is obtained; however, it works only on the structural aspects of a database schema. This proposal suggests extending the model on which revised partitioning works, by designing elementary operations that add objects, remove objects, modify attributes, or leave the class unchanged, in a way that still allows revised partitioning applicability. Revised partitioning defines a method that is able to correctly transform a semantic data model into an object model—that is, a method that achieves flexibility and efficiency linking a database conceptual schema with a database logical schema. However, the model on which revised partitioning works does not permit the declaration of application constraints or the high-level specification of nondeterministic, preconditioned, and partial state transformations similar to those introduced in B.

The new objective of MetaASSO requires the enrichment of the previous semantic data model with application constraints and preconditioned, partial, and nondeterministic state transformations able to establish a relationship between the enriched semantic data model and the model supported by B.

ASSO Components

The proposed idea consists of the following ASSO components, called "methodological tools":

- Structured Database Schema: formal model able to enrich the graph on which the revised partitioning works with aspects of the B formal model in order to ensure consistency between static and dynamics, easiness in conceptual schema specification, and flexibility in modifying the conceptual schema.

- Revised partitioning: formal method designed to combine the flexibility of semantic data models with the efficiency of object systems while guaranteeing correctness. Revised partitioning refines the Structured Database Schema after steps of B behavioral refinements.
- ASSO and B relations: formal link established between ASSO, a method designed at a high abstraction level, and B, a method designed at a low abstraction level. Support tools for B can be used to prove Structured Database Schema consistency; however, low costs of the proof processes can be achieved designing an ASSO toolkit based on support tools for B.

Motivations

The following motivations validate this proposal: ASSO is a formal method that combines features of database design with the formal method B in order to achieve quality. Specifically, it achieves easiness in schema specification, since the conceptual model of ASSO is supported by a semantic data model and formality in ASSO is transparent to the designer until he decides to make proofs; flexibility in reflecting changes occurring in real life on the schema, since the conceptual model of ASSO is supported by an extended semantic data model; reliability in providing conceptual schema consistency and logical schema correctness, since the Structured Database Schema can be translated into the B model and can be correctly refined; economy in requiring low costs of proof processes, since the costs of ASSO proof processes are reduced with respect to the corresponding B costs; efficiency in accessing information, since the logical model of ASSO is an object model.

The next section refines the MetaASSO motivations by describing ASSO.

ASSO

This section outlines the methodological tools and provides a comparison of ASSO with other methods.

Revised Partitioning

Semantic data models and object models (Cárdenas and McLeod, 1990) have similar mechanisms of abstraction; however, while semantic data models have never been implemented efficiently (Nixon and Mylopoulos, 1990), object systems have reached a remarkable level of efficiency. On the contrary, while semantic data models are adequate for conceptual design, object systems can display serious shortcomings in their ability to describe the dynamic nature of real-world entities (Richardon and Schwartz, 1991). Semantic data models enhance flexibility, whereas object models enhance efficiency. The link between semantic data models and object systems is a means to achieve the conflicting desiderata of both flexibility and efficiency.

The differences between semantic and object models are clarified in Figure 11.1, which can be supported by both semantic data models and object systems. The following properties hold:

- Classification: each node of the graph (person, student employee) is a class. A node linked with a higher-level node is a class called a "specialized class." In Figure 11.1, these are the specialized class employee and the specialized class student.

Figure 11.1 **A Graph: Semantic and Object Classes**

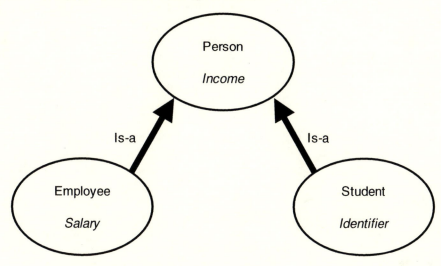

- Attribute inheritance: a specialized class (such as the specialized class employee) inherits all the attributes of the higher-level classes (in our example, the person class) and may have additional attributes.

According to ODMG (Object Data Management Group), the difference between semantic and object models is evidenced by the following properties:

- Semantic data models: each object instance can belong to any class of a graph. This enhances flexibility while limiting efficiency. In our example, the object instances of the specialized class employee are a subset of the person class object instances.
- Object models: each object instance belongs to one and only one class of a graph. This enhances efficiency while limiting flexibility. In our example, the object instances of the specialized class employee and the object instances of person class are disjoint sets.

Object classes limit flexibility in reflecting the changes occurring in real life. Let us suppose that student John becomes an employee. In this case, the corresponding object instance must be removed from the class student and must be inserted into a class student•employee. If John completes his studies later on, the corresponding object instance must be removed from the class student•employee and must be inserted into the class employee. On the contrary, in semantic data models, the object instance corresponding to John can be inserted into the class employee when the student John becomes an employee and can be removed from the class student when John completes his studies.

Structured Database Schema

The Structured Database Schema (Andolina and Locuratolo, 1997; Locuratolo, 1997, 2002, 2006; Locuratolo and Matthew, 1999) is a model that extends the conceptual classes on which revised partitioning works with a notion of behavioral specialization. It has been designed, on the one hand, with the intention of continuing to permit the applicability of revised partitioning and, on the other, with the intention of establishing a relationship between ASSO and B. The Structured Database Schema differs from other models of information systems (Compatangelo and Rumolo, 1998; Kangassalo, 1992/1993) in that it can be refined to be supported by an object system, and differs from other object-oriented approaches (Facon et al., 1996) in that it provides a structuring mechanism that ensures flexibility in modifying the conceptual schema.

In order to design the Structured Database Schema, the following concepts have been introduced:

- Class: mechanism to represent a set of database objects with their attributes, application constraints, and operations, including a special operation called initialization. The operations define preconditioned transformations: that is, state transformation that can be activated only when specified conditions are met; partial transformations, that is, transformations that are not defined on the whole state; and nondeterministic transformations, that is, transformations that can be implemented in different ways.
- Is-a* relationship: is-a relationship extended with a notion of behavioral specialization, which makes uniform modeling of both attributes and operations. Similarly to attributes, the operations are represented as functions, specifically predicate transformers, which preserve the classic is-a constraints.
- Specialized class: concept induced from the is-a* relationships. A specialized class inherits both attributes and operations from a higher-level class and may have other specific attributes and/or operations. If it has specific attributes, it also has two specific operations, called "specializations."

If a class name is in is-a* relationship with a class root, then an inherited operation specified in the specialized class is defined by the parallel composition (Abrial, 1996) of an operation of the class root restricted to the class name, and a correspondent operation defined on variables of the class name. This last operation is called specialization. Only the initialization and the operations that insert objects are explicitly specialized; the remaining operations can be implicitly specialized. The inherited operations preserve the class constraints and the specialization constraints.

The following definitions have been given for the Structured Database Schema:

- connected acyclic graph whose nodes are classes and whose links are is-a* relationships between classes.
- collection of independent classes composed of a root class and specialized classes.

The definition of the Structured Database Schema based on a graph has been given in order to apply revised partitioning after some steps of behavioral refinement (Locuratolo and Matthews, 1999c). The latter definition—that based on independent classes—has been introduced with the intention of decomposing the proof of model consistency into a set of small independent proofs.

A Structured Database Schema is consistent if the root class is consistent and each specialized class is consistent. In our example, the class person, the specialized class employee, and the specialized class student must be consistent. As the operations have been designed in order to preserve the class and the is-a constraints, only the application constraints need to be taken into consideration in proving model consistency. Furthermore, if application constraints involve only class variables, the consistency proofs of inherited operations can be simplified and the proof process is only reduced to class consistency, that is, it is only reduced to the graph nodes.

ASSO-B Relations

The B-Method (Abrial, 1996) is a formal method of consolidating industrial interest. It is based on a model, called *Abstract Machine,* which permits specification of both the static and dynamic aspects of modeling within the same formal framework. Given an abstract machine specification, the mathematical data model defines the static, whereas the operations define the dynamics. The data model is given listing a set of variables and writing the relevant properties of the variables, that is, the invariant. The invariant is formalized using the full notation of the first-order predicate logic and a restricted version of the set theory notation. A data model is animated specifying a set of operations, including an initialization. These are represented as state transitions using generalized substitution language (GSL). A substitution, denoted by "$x: = E$," is a function that transforms the generic predicate R into a predicate obtained by replacing all free occurrences of x in R by the expression E. Functions that transform predicates into predicates are called "predicate transformers." Dynamic modeling is powerful enough to represent preconditioned, partial, and nondeterministic operations. First-order logical formulas, called "consistency obligations," are proved in order to guarantee model consistency.

The B-Method consists of two phases called "specification" and "refinement." A specification is an abstract machine that expresses application requirements. A development process starts from a consistent specification and applies steps of B refinement until an abstract machine near to executable code is reached. At each step, a new abstract machine with more details than the previous one is proposed and proofs are performed to guarantee correctness of the refinement.

The relations between ASSO and B are described in Locuratolo (2002), Locuratolo and Matthews (1999a, 1999b, 1999c), and Locuratolo and Rabitti (1998). The following is the main property establishing relations between Structured Database Schema and abstract machine:

> A class Machine can be identified with an abstract machine whose state variables are constrained to satisfy class-constraints.

The class-machine state is included in the abstract-machine state; thus not all B state transformations are class operations, but only those preserving the class-machine constraints. This property makes it possible to identify the notions of is-a* relationship and specialized class introduced in ASSO, with those of is-a* relationship between class machine and specialized class-machine, respectively.

The following properties hold for a Structured Database Schema:

- A Structured Database Schema can be identified with an acyclic, oriented graph whose nodes are class-machines and whose links are is-a* relationships between class machines.
- A Structured Database Schema can be identified with a class-machine root and a finite set of specialized class-machines.

The next section compares ASSO with related approaches presented in the literature.

COMPARISON

This section outlines the main differences among the conceptual schema supported by ASSO and the correspondent B specifications, as well as among the conceptual schema supported by ASSO and related approaches coming from the database and/or the software engineering areas.

Specifying a database conceptual schema with the *B notation* is a tedious process since many properties implicitly declared within the conceptual schemas must be explicated. Consistency proofs are very expensive because they must be performed with respect not only to the application constraints but also to the conceptual schema constraints. The Structured Database Schema specifications are written using a formal notation that exploits the concepts of class-machine and specialized class-machine, two concepts that enrich correspondent concepts supported by the database conceptual languages. In the Structured Database Schema specifications, many formal details are avoided, and only the state transformations that satisfy the class and the specialization constraints are allowed. This means that the consistency obligations, which must be proved only with respect to the applications constraints, are further reduced since classes are in is-a* relationships.

The data-driven methodologies (Batini et al., 1992) generally consist of two steps: conceptual schema construction and logical schema generation. In order to make the conceptual schema easy to be used, high-level abstraction models, such as *Semantic Data Models* (Cárdenas and McLeod, 1990) or *Entity-Relationship Models* (Chen, 1976), are employed with a diagrammatic representation. The abstraction mechanisms of these models closely resemble those used in describing the applications. In order to represent the complementary dynamic aspects, state-based and data-flow models are employed; however, as the models employed to represent static and dynamics are either informal or have nonintegrated formalizations, it is not possible to prove that the specified operations preserve database consistency. Construction of the conceptual schema is followed by generation of the logical schema. Within this design step, the conceptual schema is mapped to a relational model; however, in the mapping process it is possible to introduce errors. ASSO differs from the above informal approaches, since the ASSO model integrates static and dynamics guaranteeing consistency; further, the conceptual schema is correctly transformed into an object schema establishing a link between flexibility and efficiency.

The object-oriented methodologies (Booch, 1994; Coad and Yourdon, 1991; Rumbaugh et al., 1999) proposed within the software engineering area represent a more natural way to develop object systems, which are very popular today because of the efficiency they provide. These methodologies focus on the identification and organization of the objects that compose an application. The object-oriented methodologies employ the same model along the whole life cycle. This renders the mapping smoother, thus reducing the risk of introducing errors. Object-oriented methodologies, however, have always been very weak when dealing with data design; an example of a methodology that overcomes this problem is IDEA (Ceri and Fraternali, 1997). In this methodology, data design comes first and application design follows. For the generalization hierarchies of IDEA no transformation is required in the passage from analysis to design. The objects of a super-class are partitioned into the objects of the subclasses. This differs from the specialization hierarchy of the ASSO conceptual model, where the objects of a super-class are not partitioned into the objects of the subclasses.

A survey of current database models can be found in Ma (2006). In this chapter, the relationships between conceptual data models and logical database models for modeling engineering information are presented and described from the viewpoint of database conceptual design. Requirements for engineering information modeling have been identified. These include complex objects and relationships, data exchange and data sharing, Web-based applications, imprecision and uncertainty, and finally, knowledge management. The development of some conceptual data models as well as the development of relational and object-oriented databases are presented.

The next section refines and formalizes some aspects of MetaASSO in order to design the Structured Database Schema.

META-MODELING

The meta-modeling approach described in this chapter is based on a sequence of models; these in turn are based on a sequence of notions. A notion is given through a characterization and is introduced through a formal conceptual notation. This notation consists of two parts separated by an equivalence symbol: on the left side are both the name and the specification of the notion, whereas on the right side is its characterization. The same notion can be introduced using more characterizations. In this case, these characterizations are said to be equivalent. A notion can also be given under hypothesis, and its characterization can also be either a conceptual characterization or a formal characterization.

A model M_i consists of a finite number of notions $N_1, \ldots, N_h$, where the characterization of N_1 is given in terms of definitions, whereas the characterization of N_i $i \in \{2, \ldots, h\}$ is given either in terms of definitions or in terms of specified properties. In order to characterize the notion N_i, some of the Notions $N_1, \ldots, N_{i-1}$ can be exploited.

A meta-model consists of a finite number of models $M_0, M_1, \ldots, M_k$, where for each M_j, with $j \in \{1, \ldots, k\}$, the generic notion N_p extends the corresponding notion N_p in M_{j-1}. The notion must be extended in order to satisfy an objective and must exploit a characterization that is compatible with that introduced to extend the notion. In this case, we say that the extension is a "good" extension. The initial model M_0 must satisfy an initial objective Obj_0. Furthermore, each notion must be given with an initial characterization that allows M_0 to satisfy Obj_0. Each of the remaining models M_j must satisfy the objective Obj_j.

In the following, the Structured Database Schema results as the final model of a sequence composed of three formal conceptual models, M_0, M_1, and M_2. We introduce each of them.

M_0

Obj_0:   Formalize the classification and specialization mechanisms of conceptual models with static aspects of the abstract machine in order to guarantee flexibility and to eliminate redundancy of specifications.

[class]: (v, V) is a class $\Leftrightarrow$ 1. v is a term denoting a subset of a given set;
2. V is a finite set of terms denoting functions from v to the powerset of given sets.

[*specialized class*]: If (v, V) and (u, U) are classes, then

class (u, Ue) is the specialized class $\Leftrightarrow$ 1. $u \subseteq v$
2. $Ue \supseteq U$
3. $f \in V \Rightarrow f_u \in U_e$ with f_u restriction of f to the set u
4. $g \in U_e \Rightarrow g \in U$ or $\exists h \in V / h_u = g$

[is-a relationship]: (u, U) is-a (v, V) $\Leftrightarrow$ 1. (v, V) is a class;
2. (u, U) is a class;
3. $\exists$ class (u, Ue).

[conceptual classes]: G_C is a graph of $\Leftrightarrow$ is an acyclic, oriented graph
conceptual classes   1. the nodes are classes
                                     2. the links are is-a relationships between classes

The model M_0 is a formal conceptual model that consists of the following notions: [*class*], [*specialized class*], [*is-a relationship*], and [*conceptual classes*]. Each of them is specified after the : symbol. This specification is given on the left side of the $\Leftrightarrow$ symbol. On the right side of the $\Leftrightarrow$ symbol is the notion characterization.

The [*class*] notion is characterized in terms of definitions: the former is related to the class objects, whereas the latter is related to the attributes associated with the objects. The [*specialized class*] notion is given under a hypothesis and is formally defined in terms of the following properties:

1. the objects of the specialized class $(_{u,}\ _{Ue})$ are a subset of the $(_{v,}\ _v)$ objects;
2. the specialized class $(_{u,}\ _{Ue})$ inherits all the attributes from class $(_{v,}\ _v)$;
3. the specialized class $(_{u,}\ _{Ue})$ includes all the attributes of the class $(_{u,}\ _U)$;
4. no other attributes belongs to the specialized class $(_{u,}\ _{Ue})$. Class $(_{u,}\ _{Ue})$ is an enrichment of class $(_{u,}\ _U)$.

The [*specialized class*] and the [*is-a relationship*] are two equivalent notions. The [*conceptual classes*] notion is characterized by the notions already given—[*class*] and [*is-a relationship*].

The initial model M_0 satisfies Obj_0, since the notion characterizations have been given exploiting the abstract machine formalization. Further, the is-a relationship is the mechanism exploited by semantic data models to guarantee flexibility. This mechanism allows implicit specification of information. Specifically $(_{u,}\ _U)$ *is-a* $(_{v,}\ _v)$ implies that $(_{u,}\ _v)$ is the class representing the implicit information, whereas the couple of classes $(_{v,}\ _v)$ and $(_{u,}\ _{Ue})$ represent all and only the information that can be explicitly specified. These last two classes can be represented without any link; $(_{u,}\ _v)$ results from the attribute difference between $(_{u,}\ _{Ue})$ and $(_{u,}\ _U)$ and represents a "qualitative/conceptual measure" of the implicit information specified with the is-a relationship. Thus, given a graph of conceptual classes, a "qualitative/conceptual measure" of the implicitly declared information can be determined.

M_1

Obj_1: Formalize basic operations in order to eliminate *redundancy* of specifications.

[*extended class*]: (v, V, Op) is an extended $\Leftrightarrow$ 1. v is a term denoting a subset of a given set;
class   2. V is a finite set of terms denoting functions from v to the powerset of a given set;
                                       3. Op is a finite set of basic operations (ADD, REM, SKIP, CHANGE) denoting functions from predicates satisfying the class-constraints to predicates satisfying the class-constraints.

The weakest precondition semantics for a basic operation *op* is the following: $[op\ (v, V)\ (par\_list)]R \Leftrightarrow (class\text{-}constraints(v, V) \Rightarrow class\text{-}constraints(v, V)^*) \wedge R^*$. If v is the set of class objects, A is a given set, $a_1 \ldots a_n$ are the functions representing the attributes and $T_1 \ldots T_n$ define the attribute types, *class-constraints* is the predicate that formalizes the class definition, that is, *class-constraints*$(v, V) = v \subseteq A \wedge a_1 \in v \to T_1 \wedge \ldots \wedge a_n \in v \to T_n$. R is a predicate on the variables of class (v, V) and the star predicates are on the state after the operation.

[*extended specialized class*] If (v, V, Op) and (u, U, Op') are extended classes, then:

(u, Ue, Op') *is the extended* *specialized class*	$\Leftrightarrow$ 1. $u \subseteq v$ 2. $Ue \supseteq U$ 3. $f \in V \Rightarrow f_u \in U_e$ 4. $g \in U_e \Rightarrow g \in U$ or $\exists h \in V / h_u = g$ 5. $op \in OP \Rightarrow \exists op_s \in OP' \wedge op \parallel op_s \in OP_e'$ 6. $op° \in Op_e' \Rightarrow op° \in Op'$ or $\exists op \in OP \wedge \exists op_s \in OP' / op \parallel op_s = op°$
[*extended is-a relationship*]: (u, U, Op') *is-a* (v, V, Op)	$\Leftrightarrow$ 1. (v, V, Op) is an extended class; 2. (u, U, Op') is an extended class; 3. $\exists$ extended specialized class (u, Ue, Op_e')
[*extended conceptual classes*]: G_C *defines extended conceptual classes*	$\Leftrightarrow$ G_C is an acyclic, oriented graph 1. the nodes are extended classes 2. the links are is-a relationships between extended classes

Model M_1 includes the following notions: [extended class], [extended specialized class], [extended is-a relationship] and [extended conceptual classes].

The extended class (v, V, Op) enlarges the couple (v, V) with the set Op of basic operations. The extension is good since the (v, V, Op) characterization is compatible with the (v, V) characterization. Moreover, both attributes and basic operations are defined as functions. Specifically, the basic operations are predicate transformers preserving the class constraints.

The [*extended specialized class*] notion adds properties 5 and 6 to the [*specialized class*] notion making properties 5 and 6 similar to properties 3 and 4. Specifically, property 5 ensures that the extended specialized class (u, Ue, Op') inherits the operations from (v, V, Op). The inheritance consists in the parallel composition of an operation coming from (v, V, Op) and the corresponding specialization. Property 6 ensures that each operation of (u, Ue, Op') is either an operation inherited from (v, V, Op) or an operation of (u, U, Op').

The [*extended is-a relationship*] is given in terms of [*extended class*] notion and requires the existence of an extended specialized class; finally the [*extended conceptual classes*] is given in terms of the [*extended class*] and the [*extended is-a relationship*] notions.

(u, U, Op') is-a (v, V, Op) implies that (v, V, Op) is a "qualitative/conceptual measure" of the implicit information specified with the extended is-a relationship.

M_2

Obj_2: enriches the nodes of the extended conceptual classes with application constraints and preconditioned, partial and nondeterministic operations involving class variables.

[class-machine]: *(v, V, Const, Op) is a* ⇔ 1. *(v, V, Op)* is an extended class
class machine   the generalized substitution language is recursively
                                                     applied to the basic operations
                                                     2. *Const* are application constraints

[specialized class-machines] If *(v, V, Const, Op)* and *(u, U, Const, ' Op')* are class-machines,
then:

(u, Ue, Conste , Op'e) is the specialized ⇔ 1. *(u, Ue, Op' e)* is the extended specialized class
class-machine   satisfying property 1 of the previous notion
                                                    2. *Conste = Const ∧ Const'*

[is-a* relationship]: *(u, U, Const,' Op') is-a** ⇔ 1. *(v, V, Const, Op)* is a class-machine
(v, V, Const, Op)   2. *(u, U, Const,' Op')* is a class-machine
                                                           3. ∃ class-machine *(u, U$_e$, Const$_e$, Op'e)*

[structured database schema]: G_C ⇔ G_C is an acyclic, oriented graph
defines a structured database schema   1. the nodes are class-machines
                                              2. the links is-a* relationships between class-machines.

(u, U, Const,' Op') is-a* (v, V, Const, Op) implies that *(u, V, Const, Op)* is the class-machine
that represents a qualitative/conceptual measure of information implicitly specified within
class-machines in is-a* relationship.

The *Structured Database Schema* is a model that supports ASSO specifications. It is based on
the following notions of *class-machine* and *specialized class-machine*.

A class-machine models both static and behavioral aspects of a set of objects in the database.
The former aspect comprises the set of objects and the set of attributes associated with those
objects. These aspects are formalized using sets and functions, whereas the predicate that formalizes its definition is called a "class-machine constraint." The latter aspect comprises a set of state
transformations, the operations enclosing a distinguished operation, called "initialization," which
defines the initial state of a class-machine. The dynamic aspects are described using predicate
transformers, that is, functions from predicates satisfying the class-machine constraints to predicates
satisfying the class-machine constraints. Each operation is defined by applying constructors to
base operations that preserve the class-machine constraints. For a class-machine $C = (c, C)$ with
attributes $a_1, \ldots, a_n$, the following basic operations are available:

ADD C $(x, v_1 \ldots v_n)$ Inserts the object x with attribute values $v_1, \ldots, v_n$ into C.
REM C (x) Removes the object x from C
SKIP C   Does nothing in class C
CHANGE C a_i (x, v_i) Updates the value of a_i of object x in class C to v_i.

The following constructors can be applied recursively to the basic operations:

PRE *P* **THEN** *op* **C** *(par_\list)* **END**   Preconditioning
P → ? *op* C*(par_list)*   Guarding
CHOICE *op* **C***(par_list)* **ORELSE** *op'* **C** *(par_list)* **END**   Choice
ANY *y* **WHERE** *P* **THEN** *op* **C***(par_list)* **END**   Unbounded-choice

P is a predicate on the variables of class-machine C, op C(par_list), and op' C(par_list) are operations and y is a variable different from the variables of C. Preconditioning specifies the following preconditioned transformation: op C(par_list), for the states satisfying P, and undetermined otherwise. Guarding specifies the following partial transformation: op C(par_list), for the states satisfying P and abort otherwise. Choice specifies a nondeterministic transformation between op C(par_list), or op' C(par_list). Unbounded-choice specifies an unbounded nondeterministic transformation defined by replacing any value of y satisfying P in op' C(par_list). The weakest precondition semantics of these constructors are as follows.

$$[\text{ PRE } P \text{ THEN } op \text{ C } (par\_list) \text{ END }] R = P \wedge [op \text{ C } (par\_list)]R$$

$$[P \rightarrow op \text{ C } (par\_list)]R = P \Rightarrow [op \text{ C } (par\_list)]R$$

$$[\text{CHOICE } op \text{ C } (par\_list) \text{ ORELSE } op' \text{ C } (par\_list) \text{ END }]R = [op \text{ C } (par\_list)]R \wedge [op' \text{ C } (par\_list)]R$$

$$[\text{ ANY } y \text{ WHERE } P \text{ THEN } op \text{ C } (par\_list) \text{ END }] R = y \bullet P \Rightarrow [op \text{ C } (par\_list)]R \text{ if } y \text{ is not free in } R$$

A class-machine can be either the node of an acyclic, oriented graph or a specialized class-machine.

If $C_1 = (c_1, C_1)$ and $C_2 = (c_2, C_2)$ are class-machines with respective constraints:

$$\text{class-machine constraints}_{C1} = c_1 \subseteq U \wedge a_1 \in c_1 \rightarrow t_1 \wedge \ldots \wedge a_n \in c_1 \rightarrow t_n$$

$$\text{class-machine constraints}_{C2} = c_2 \subseteq U \wedge b_1 \in c_2 \rightarrow s_1 \wedge \ldots \wedge b_m \in c_2 \rightarrow s_m$$

and $c1$ and $c2$ are compatible concept, then the constraints of the specialized class-machine are:

$$\textit{class-machine constraints}_{C2} \wedge c2 \subseteq c_1 \wedge C_2 \triangleleft a_1 \in c_2 \rightarrow t_1 \wedge \ldots \wedge C_2 \triangleleft a_n \in c_2 \rightarrow t_n$$

An inherited operation of the specialized class-machine is the parallel composition of an operation on class-machine C1 with the corresponding operation defined on class-machine C2. This latter operation is called "specialization" on class-machine C2. The initialization and the operations on C2 that insert objects are explicitly specialized to preserve the *is-a* constraints, whereas the remaining operations can be implicitly specialized.

The weakest precondition semantics for the inherited operation op of the specialized class-machine is:

$$[op \text{ } C_2 \text{ is-a* } C_1 \text{ } (par\_list)]R \Leftrightarrow [op \text{ } C_1 \text{ } (par\_list)]R1 \wedge [op \text{ } C_2 \text{ } (par\_list)]R_2 \wedge (\text{is-a constraints} \Rightarrow \text{is-a constraints'}) \wedge R_3'$$

where R is a predicate on the variables of the specialized class-machine, R_1 is a predicate on the C_1 variables, R_2 a predicate on the C_2 variables, $R_3 = R - (R_1 \wedge R_2)$, and (*is-a constraints* $\Rightarrow$ *is-a constraints'*) is the predicate that preserves the is-a constraints, that is, the predicate that formalizes the object inclusion and attribute inheritance properties of the *is-a* relationship.

The following syntactic forms are provided to specify the class-machines of a Structured Database Schema:

class-machine *variable* **of** *given-set* **with** *(attr-list; init; oper-list)*

class-machine *variable* **is-a*** *variable* **with** *(attr-list; init, oper-list)*

where *init* and *oper-list* denote the initialization and a list of operations on the specified class-machine state, respectively.

A database application supported by the Structured Database Schema is provided in Appendix 11.1. The database maintains information about a set of persons, their income, a subset of persons in employment, and their salary. The income of each person is greater or equal to 1,000; the salary of each employee is greater or equal to 500:

1. an operation adds information to the database when a person stored in the database is enrolled;
2. an operation partially or completely removes information when a person goes away from the company;
3. an operation removes information related to the employee.

The Structured Database Schema in Appendix 11.1 is composed of two class-machines in is-a* relationship, the corresponding Structured Database Schema with the root class-machine and the specialized class-machine is provided in Appendix 11.2. The class-machine representing the implicit specification within the Structured Database Schema of Appendix 11.1 is provided in Appendix 11.3.

A REVIEW

Meta-modeling is an activity that aims to capture knowledge about methods/models/meta-models. It is the basis for understanding, evaluating, and comparing engineering methods. Among the results obtained by the meta-modeling community, it defines a method as made up of two models: a product model and a process model (Prakash, 1999). A product model, defining a set of concepts, properties, and relationships, is the output of a process. A process model, encompassing a set of goals, activities, and guidelines, supports the achievement of the goal process and the action execution. The construction of methods supported by meta-modeling focuses on the definition of these two models. An approach has been proposed for method engineering that supports the evolution of an existing method, model, or meta-model into a new one satisfying a different engineering method (Ralytè et al., 2005). This approach is helpful for project-specific method construction. The approach proposed in this chapter supports evolution from an initial model to a final model. The initial model includes a paradigm model, composed of the two abstraction mechanisms of classification and specialization (i.e., classes in is-a relationship), and a product model defined by an acyclic oriented graph of conceptual classes. The paradigm model is gradually extended until a class-machine and two class-machines in is-a relationship are defined. Analogously, the product model is gradually extended into an intermediate and a final directed acyclic graph of class-machines. A notion captures only the essential properties of a conceptual specification while generating a description for characterization. Notions are proposed in such a way that, for each specialization mechanism, it is possible to determine a conceptual class/an extended conceptual class/a class-machine/representing the implicit information within the considered specialization mechanism.

Analogously, the consistency cost improvement for a schema composed of two class-machines in is-a relationship with respect to a schema where all the information is explicitly stated consists in the consistency cost of the implicit class machine. This approach is helpful for a conceptual evaluation of the model in terms of implicit information and consistency cost improvement. This differs from most meta-models, which serve as a basis for quantitative evaluations of models. As an example, the meta-model described in (Locuratolo, 2006) is based on an approach that starts from the formal model abstract machine and applies two contractions of models in order to define the Structured Database Schema. The former transformation reduces the abstract machine state defining the structural aspects of the model through specialization, whereas the dynamic aspects are defined as operations on the restricted state, that is, without any mechanisms of specialization.

The latter transformation is based on a notion of behavioral specialization that allows both attributes and operations to be specified similarly. This meta-modeling approach suggests performing a quantitative evaluation of the consistency proofs: a recursive function that computes the correctness cost of a generic operation has been given in terms of variable cardinality (Andolina and Locuratolo, 1997). This function, which can be exploited to compute the correctness cost of an operation in each of the previous models, puts into evidence the reduction of variable cardinality from the former to the latter contracted models. However, in order to compute the cost improvement of a specified operation in these two cases, both proofs must be performed.

In the following, the function correctness cost is given for a generic operation *op* defined on class *C*.

$$cost\ (SKIP) = 0$$

$$cost\ (\text{base } op\ C(par\_list)) = \#\,(Class \wedge Appl)$$

where *base op* is a basic operation not coinciding with SKIP; # (*Class* ∧ *Appl*) is the cardinality of both constants and variables of the predicates class-machine constraints and application constraints.

$$cost\ ([PRE\ P\ THEN\ op\ C\ (par\_list)\ END]\ Appl) = cost\ (op\ C\ (par\_list)]\ Appl)$$

$$cost\ ([P \rightarrow op\ C\ (par\_list)]\ Appl) = cost\ ([op\ C\ (par\_list)]\ Appl)$$

$$cost\ ([CHOICE\ op\ C\ (par\_list)\ ORELSE\ op'\ C\ (par\_list)\ END]\ Appl = cost\ ([op\ C\ (par\_list)]\ Appl) \wedge cost([op'\ C\ (par\_list)]\ Appl)$$

$$cost\ ([ANY\ y\ WHERE\ P\ THEN\ op\ C\ (par\_list)\ END]\ Appl) = cost\ ([op\ C\ (par\_list)]\ Appl)$$
$$where\ y\ is\ not\ free\ in\ Appl.$$

where *P* and *Appl* denote predicates on the variables of class *C*, whereas *op* C (*par_list*) and *op'* C (*par_list*) denote operations.

The meta-model described in this chapter starts from the restricted conceptual notions of an initial model. As reasoning on restricted notions is easier than reasoning on large notions, a "conceptual measure" of the implicit information declared within conceptual classes (as well as of all the explicit information) were given in terms of classes. The restricted notions of the initial model were then extended. Each extension defines notions compatible with previous corresponding notions. This meta-model allows the generalization of the previous conceptual measure, first to evaluate the implicit information declared within extended conceptual classes, then to evaluate the implicit specification within a Structured Database Schema.

Analogously, a conceptual evaluation of the Structured Database Schema consistency cost can be given. In our example, it suffices to prove consistency for each of the class-machines specified in Appendix 11.1. Moreover, the Structured Database Schema company.schema is equivalent to the class-machine person and to the specialized class-machine employee in Appendix 11.2. As the proof of each inherited operation of the specialized class-machine employee is composed of two parts, and one of them has previously been proved, the consistency cost of the whole model is reduced to that of the two class-machines. The cost improvement is provided by the consistency cost of the implicit class-machine in Appendix 11.3. Thus, in order to realize this cost improvement, no proof is explicitly performed.

Let us now suppose that both a constraint, which links variables belonging to the class-machine person and to the class-machine employee such as $\forall e$ $(e \in employee \Rightarrow \exists x(x \in N \land income(e) = salary(e) + x))$, and an operation, which needs to be proved correct with respect to this constraint, are specified within the Structured Database Schema. In this case, the consistency cost of the whole model can be reduced to the consistency costs of both class-machine person and employee plus the consistency cost of a partial specialized class-machine. This partial specialized class-machine encompasses the two attributes income and salary, the above constraint $\forall e$ $(e \in employee \Rightarrow \exists x(x \in N \land income[e] = salary[e] + x))$, and the operation, which need to be proved correct with respect to it. This is because the whole specialized class-machine employee can be decomposed into the specialized class-machine employee in Appendix 11.2, plus the described partial specialized class-machine employee. Also in this case, the cost improvement with respect to a complete specification is given by the consistency cost of the implicit class-machine in Appendix 11.3.

The OMG model driven architecture (MDA) makes models the primary artifacts of software engineering. Fundamentally, MDA concerns a wide variety of models and mappings between models, allowing integration and transformation of those models. Two main categories of mapping can be distinguished:

- refinement or vertical mapping, which relates system models at different abstraction levels;
- horizontal mapping, which relates or integrates models at the same level of abstraction.

Significant attention has been focused on model transformations (Kleppe and Warmer, 2003), in particular, those from platform-independent models to platform-specific models.

The Structured Database Schema is a platform-independent model that raises the abstraction level of the B model. The meta-model language for the Structured Database Schema provides syntactic forms extending those given by the database conceptual languages by means of transactions and application constraints. In the Structured Database Schema specifications, many formal details are avoided with respect to the B specifications, and only the state transformations that satisfy the class and specialization constraints are allowed. The approach described in Locuratolo (2006) is based on a vertical mapping that links the abstract machine to the Structured Database Schema. The meta-model proposed in this chapter relates models at the same level of abstraction. Within the whole formalization of Meta ASSO, the former model extension effects a restricted vertical mapping for linking conceptual and logical schemas of databases in an easy way, whereas the latter extension requires a horizontal mapping, which leaves the state unchanged while modifying transactions. The approach based on notions favors new definitions/good extensions of engineering methods/methodologies.

The importance of meta-models for selecting, comparing, and evaluating ontologies has been proposed in Davies et al. (2005). Ontologies are used for storing and manipulating knowledge, for drawing inferences, for making decisions, or just for answering questions. This is similar to the goal of semantic data models. Abstraction mechanisms, such as the mechanisms of classification and specialization/generalization, are exploited in both semantic data models and ontologies. The use of ontologies can help method engineers to understand the right concepts and to define them in the method under construction.

CONCLUSION

A meta-modeling approach is proposed, the Structured Database Schema, which integrates features from methodologies of conceptual database design with the formal method B. It starts from a conceptual model based on the notions of class and is-a relationship and proceeds with two gradual extensions of models: the former defines the basic operations, and the latter defines the Structured Database Schema. This meta-modeling approach guarantees Structured Database Schema goodness by proposing extensions of models compatible with the previous models. Both a "qualitative/conceptual measure" of the information implicitly specified within the Structured Database Schema and a "qualitative/conceptual evaluation" of the consistency cost are provided. This approach aims at acquiring knowledge for specializing general purpose methods employed at the industrial level for specific areas. The proposed meta-model refines and formalizes some aspects of MetaASSO, the approach exploited to define a database design method for quality. Further developments include the full formalization of MetaASSO.

APPENDIX 11.1. CLASS MACHINES IN IS-A RELATIONSHIP

Structured Database Schema
company.schema
class-machine person of PERSON with (income:N;

$\forall$ p (p $\in$ person $\Rightarrow$ income(p) $\geq$ 1000)

init.person( )=person, income:=$\varnothing$, $\varnothing$;
new.person(*pers,i*)=
       PRE
       pers $\in$ PERSON-person $\wedge$ i $\geq$ 1000
       THEN ADD person(*pers,i*) END
del.person (*pers*)=
       PRE
       pers $\in$ person
       THEN
       CHOICE REM person(*pers*) ORELSE SKIP person
       END
class-machine employee is-a* person with (salary:N;

$\forall$ e (e $\in$ employee $\Rightarrow$ salary(e) $\geq$ 500)
init.employee( )=employee, salary:=$\varnothing$, $\varnothing$;

(continued)

APPENDIX 11.1. *(continued)*

> new.employee(*pers,s*)=
>   PRE
>   s ≥ 500
>   THEN
>   ADD employee(*pers,s*)
>   END
> del.employee(*pers*)=REM employee(*pers*)
> pers(*pers*)=pers ∈ employee ⟹ REM employee(*pers*).
>
> **end.**

APPENDIX 11.2A. ROOT CLASS-MACHINE AND SPECIALIZED CLASS-MACHINE

> **Structured Database Schema**
> company.schema
> **class-machine** person **of** PERSON **with** (income:N;
>
> $\forall$ p (p ∈ person ⟹ income(p) ≥ 1000)
>
> init.person( )=person, income:=,
> new.person(*pers,i*)=
>   **PRE**
>   *pers* ∈ PERSON-person ∧ *i* ≥ 1000
>   **THEN** ADD person(*pers,i*) **END**
> del.person (*pers*)=
>   **PRE**
>   *pers* ∈ person
>   **THEN**
>   **CHOICE** REM person(*pers*) **ORELSE** SKIP person
>   **END**
> **specialized class-machine** employee **with** (income:N; salary: N;
>
> $\forall$ p (p ∈ person ⟹ income(p) ≥ 1000)
> $\forall$ p (p ∈ person ⟹ salary(p) ≥ 500)
>
> init=init.person ‖ init.employee
> new=new.person(*pers,i*) ‖ new.employee(*pers,s*)
> del=del.person(*pers*) ‖ del.employee(*pers*)
> pers(*pers*)=*pers* ∈ employee ⟹ REM employee(*pers*)
>
> **end.**

APPENDIX 11.2B. SPECIALIZED CLASS-MACHINE: EXPLICATED OPERATIONS

---

init=person, income, employee, salary:=,, ,, ,, ,

new=new.employee(*pers,i,s*)=

    PRE

          $pers \in$ PERSON-person $^\wedge i \geq 1000 {}^\wedge s \geq 500$

    THEN

          ADD employee(*pers,i,s*)

    END

del=del.employee(*pers*)=

    PRE

          $pers \in$ person

    THEN

          REM employee(pers)

    END.

APPENDIX 11.3. IMPLICIT CLASS-MACHINE

---

class-machine employee of EMPLOYEE **with** (income:N;

    e (e employee   income(e) 1000)

    init.employee( )=employee, income:=,;

    new.employee(emp,i)=

        PRE

        emp EMPLOYEE-employee $^\wedge$ i 1000

        THEN ADD employee(emp,i) **END**

    del.employee (emp)=

        PRE

        emp employee

        THEN

        CHOICE REM employee(emp) **ORELSE** SKIP employee

        END

end.

REFERENCES

Abiteboul, S.; Hull, R.; and Vianu, V. 1995. *Foundations of Databases.* Reading, MA: Addison-Wesley.

Abrial, J.R. 1996. *The B-Book: Assigning Programs to Meanings.* Cambridge: Cambridge University Press.

Andolina, R., and Locuratolo, E. 1997. ASSO: Behavioural specialisation modelling. In H. Kangassalo, J.F. Nilson, H. Jaakkola, and S. Ohsuga (eds), *Information Modelling and Knowledge Bases* VIII, 241–259. Amsterdam: IOS Press.

Batini, C.; Ceri, S.; and Navathe, S.B. 1992. *Conceptual Database Design: An Entity-Relationship Approach.* Redwood City, CA: Benjamin-Cummings.

Booch, G. 1994. *Object-Oriented Analysis and Design with Applications.* Redwood City, CA: Benjamin/ Cummings.

Cárdenas, A.F., and McLeod, D. (eds.). 1990. *Research Foundations in Object-Oriented and Semantic Database Systems.* Englewood Cliffs, NJ: Prentice Hall.

Ceri, S., and Fraternali, P. 1997. *Designing Database Applications with Objects and Rules.* Reading, MA: Addison-Wesley.

Chen, P.P. 1976. The entity-relationship model: Towards a unified view of data. *ACM Transactions on Database Systems,* 1, 1, 76–84.

Coad, P., and Yourdon, E. 1991. *Object-Oriented Design.* Englewood Cliffs, NJ: Yourdon Press.

Compatangelo, E., and Rumolo, G. 1998. An engineering framework for domain knowledge modelling. In P.-J. Charrel, H. Jaakkola, H. Kangassalo, and E. Kawaguchi (eds.), *Information Modelling and Knowledge Bases* IX, 51–63. Amsterdam: IOS Press.

Davies, I.; Green, P.; Milton, S.; and Rosemann, M. 2005. Analyzing and Comparing Ontologies with Meta-Models In J. Krogstie, T. Halpin, and K. Siau (eds.), *Information Modeling Methods and Methodologies,* 1–16. Hershey, PA: Idea Group.

Facon, P.; Laleau, R.; and Nguyen, H.P. 1996. Mapping object diagrams into B specifications. In A. Bryant and L.T. Semmens (eds.), *Methods Integration: Proceedings of the Second Methods Integration Workshop,* 95–108. London: Springer-Verlag.

Kangassalo, H. 1992/1993. COMIC: A system and methodology for conceptual modelling and information construction. *Data and Knowledge Engineering,* 9, 287–319.

Kleppe, A., and Warmer, J. 2003. Do MDA transformations preserve meanings? An investigation into preserving semantics In A. Evans, P. Sammut, and J.S. Willans (eds.), *Metamodelling for MDA: First International Workshop,* 13–22. Kings Manor, England, Proceedings, November.

Locuratolo, E. 1997. ASSO: Evolution of a formal database design methodology. In *Proceedings of Symposium on Software Technology* (SoST'97), 41–52. SADIO, Buenos Aires.

———. 2002. Designing methods for quality. In H. Kangassalo, H. Jaakkola, and E. Kawaguchi (eds.), *Information Modelling and Knowledge Bases* XIII, 279–295. Amsterdam: IOS Press.

———. 2005. Model transformations in designing the ASSO methodology. In P. van Bommel (ed.), *Transformation of Knowledge, Information and Data: Theory and Applications,* 283–302. Hershey, PA: Information Science.

———. 2006. Database design based on B. In Z. Ma (ed.), *Database Modeling for Industrial Data Management,* 35–61. Hershey, PA: Idea Group.

Locuratolo, E., and Matthews, B.M. 1999a. ASSO: A formal methodology of conceptual database design. In S. Gnesi and D. Latella (eds.), *Proceedings of the Fourth International Workshop on Formal Methods for Industrial Critical Systems,* 205–224. Trento, Italy: STAR, CNR, Pisa, July 11–12.

———. 1999b. Formal development of databases in ASSO and B. In G. Goos, J. Hartmanis, and J. van Leeuwen (eds.), *Lecture Notes in Computer Science, 1708, Formal Methods: Proceedings of the World Congress on Formal Methods in the Development of Computing Systems,* 388–410. Berlin: Springer-Verlag.

———. 1999c. On the relationship between ASSO and B. In H. Jaakkoala, H. Kangassalo, and E. Kawaguchi (eds.), *Information Modelling and Knowledge Bases* X, 235–253. Amsterdam: IOS Press.

Locuratolo, E., and Rabitti, F. 1998. Conceptual classes and system classes in object databases. *Acta Informatica,* 35, 3, 181–210.

Ma, Z.M. 2006. Databases modeling of engineering information. In Z.M. Ma (ed.), *Database Modeling for Industrial Data Management,* 1–34. Hershey, PA: Idea Group.

Nixon, B., and Mylopoulos, J. 1990. Integration issues in implementing semantic data models. In F. Bancilhon and P. Buneman (eds.), *Advances in Database Programming Languages,* 187–217. New York: ACM Press; Reading, MA: Addison-Wesley.

Prakash, N. 1999. On method statics and dynamics. *Information Systems,* 34, 8, 613–637.

Ralytè, J.; Rolland, C.; and Ben Ayed, M. 2005. An approach for evolution-driven method engineering. In J. Krogstie, T. Halpin, and K. Siau (eds.), *Information Modeling Methods and Methodologies,* 80–100. Hershey, PA: Idea Group.

Richardson, J., and Schwartz, P. 1991. Extending objects to support multiple, independent roles. In J. Clifford and R. King (eds.), *Proceedings of the 1991 ACM SIGMOD International Conference of Management of Data,* 298–307. Denver, CO: ACM Press, May 29–31.

Rumbaugh, J.; Booch, G.; and Jacobson, I. 1999. *The Unified Modeling Language Reference Manual.* Reading, MA: Addison-Wesley.

EDITORS AND CONTRIBUTORS

EDITORS

Keng Siau is the E.J. Faulkner Professor of Management Information Systems (MIS) at the University of Nebraska, Lincoln (UNL). He is the director of the UNL-IBM Global Innovation Hub, editor-in-chief of the *Journal of Database Management,* and coeditor-in-chief of the Advances in Database Research series. He received his Ph.D. degree from the University of British Columbia (UBC), where he majored in management information systems and minored in cognitive psychology. His master's and bachelor's degrees are in computer and information sciences from the National University of Singapore. He has over 200 academic publications. His research has been funded by NSF, IBM, and other IT organizations. He has received numerous research, teaching, and service awards. His latest award is the International Federation for Information Processing (IFIP) Outstanding Service Award in 2006. He served as the organizing and program chairs of the International Workshop on Evaluation of Modeling Methods in Systems Analysis and Design (EMMSAD) from 1996 to 2005. He is now serving on the EMMSAD Steering Committee and SIGSAND Advisory Board. He also served on the organizing committees of AMCIS 2005, ER 2006, and AMCIS 2007.

Roger H. L. Chiang is associate professor of information systems at the College of Business, University of Cincinnati. He received his B.S. degree in management science from National Chiao Tung University, Taiwan, M.S. degrees in computer science from Michigan State University and in business administration from the University of Rochester, and Ph.D. degree in computers and information systems from the University of Rochester. His research interests are in data and knowledge management and intelligent systems, particularly in database reverse engineering, database integration, data and text mining, document classification and clustering, domain knowledge discovery, and semantic information retrieval. He is currently the senior editor of the *DATA BASE for Advances in Information Systems,* and the associate editor of *Journal of Database Management, International Journal of Intelligent Systems in Accounting, Finance and Management,* and *MIS Quarterly.* His research has been published in a number of journals including *ACM Transactions on Database Systems, Communications of the ACM, DATA BASE for Advances in Information Systems, Data & Knowledge Engineering, Decision Support Systems, Journal of American Society for Information Science and Technology, Journal of Database Administration, Journal of Management Information Systems,* and *Very Large Data Base Journal.*

Bill C. Hardgrave is the Dean and Wells Fargo Professor at the College of Business, Auburn University. His research on software development (primarily people and process issues) has appeared in *MIS Quarterly, Journal of Management Information Systems, Communications of the ACM, IEEE Software, IEEE Transactions on Software Engineering, IEEE Transactions on Engineering Management, DATA BASE for Advances in Information Systems, Information and Management,* and *Educational and Psychological Measurement,* among others.

CONTRIBUTORS

Steven Alter is a professor of information systems at the University of San Francisco. He received a B.S. in math and Ph.D. in management science from MIT. After teaching at the University of Southern California he served for eight years as co-founder and vice president of Consilium, a manufacturing software firm that was acquired by Applied Materials in 1998. His teaching and research focus on developing systems analysis concepts and methods that can be used by typical business professionals and can support communication with IT professionals. His latest book, *The Work System Method: Connecting People, Processes, and IT for Business Results*, consolidates and extends research that has appeared in many journal articles and conference proceedings.

Dinesh Batra is a Knight-Ridder Research Professor in the Department of Decision Sciences and Information Systems of the College of Business Administration at the Florida International University. He has published articles in journals such as *Journal of Management Information Systems, Management Science, Communication of the ACM, International Journal of Human Computer Studies, Data Base, European Journal of Information Systems, Journal of Database Management, Communications of the AIS, Decision Support Systems, Requirements Engineering, Computers and OR*, and *Information & Management*. His research interests focus on systems analysis and design, and usability issues in systems and databases. He has served as an associate editor for the journal *Data Base*, and is currently on the editorial board of the *Journal of Database Management*, and *Information Systems Management*. He is a co-author of the book *Object-Oriented Systems Analysis and Design*. He has served as the first president of the AIS Special Interest Group on Systems Analysis & Design (SIGSAND).

John Erickson is an assistant professor in the College of Business Administration at the University of Nebraska at Omaha. His research interests include Unified Modeling Language, software complexity, and systems analysis and design issues. He has published in journals, such as the *Communications of the ACM, Journal of Database Management*, and has presented papers at conferences such as AMICIS, ICIS WITS, EMMSAD, and CAiSE. He has also co-authored several book chapters.

Christian Flender is a Ph.D. candidate at the Faculty of Science and Technology, Queensland University of Technology, Brisbane, Australia. He received his MScIS from the University of Bamberg, Germany, in 2006. Since then, he has been conducting research in the area of information systems analysis and design. His main interests comprise conceptual modeling, quantum information, and cognition.

Peter F. Green is professor of electronic commerce and business information systems cluster leader in the UQ Business School at the University of Queensland. He has qualifications in computer science and accounting and a Ph.D. in commerce (information systems) from the University of Queensland. He is a chartered accountant and a fellow of the Australian Computer Society. He has worked during his career as the systems support manager at the South-East Queensland Electricity Board (SEQEB), for a chartered accountancy firm and a Queensland government department. He has researched, presented, and published widely on systems analysis and design, conceptual modeling, information systems auditing, and e-commerce. His publications have appeared in internationally refereed journals such as *Journal of the Association of Information Systems, Information Systems, IEEE Transactions on Knowledge and Data Engineering, Data and*

Knowledge Engineering, Journal of Database Management, Journal of Knowledge Management, and the *Australian Journal of Information Systems.*

Andy Koronios is head of the School of Computer and Information Science at the University of South Australia. He has extensive experience in both commercial and academic environments and has interests in electronic commerce, information security, Internet and Web engineering, data quality, multimedia systems, and online learning systems.

Michael Lane is a lecturer in information systems at the University of Southern Queensland. He holds an Honours degree in information technology and a Ph.D. with a focus in e-commerce development. He has published widely in information systems and electronic commerce but has varied interests in research and teaching, including outsourcing, corporate governance, and the function of the CIO.

Kun-Chang Lee is a full professor in the School of Business Administration, Sungkyunkwan University, Seoul, South Korea. He received his Ph.D. in management information systems and decision analysis from the Korea Advanced Institute of Science and Technology (KAIST), a master of sciences in management science from KAIST, and a B.A. in business administration from Sungkyunkwan University. His research focuses on knowledge management and creativity management from the perspective of decision analysis as well as particle swarm optimization (PSO). His research findings have been published in flagship journals such as the *Journal of Management Information Systems, IEEE Transactions on Engineering Management, Decision Support Systems, International Journal of Production Research,* and the *Journal of the American Society for Information Science and Technology,* among others.

Nam-Ho Lee is a senior consultant at SAP Korea. He received Ph.D. in MIS from Sungkyunkwan University, Seoul, South Korea. His research interests lie in PSO (particle swarm optimization) and its role in IT project management. He has published papers in the *Journal of the American Society for Information Science and Technology.*

Xueming Li earned both his B.S. and M.Eng. from the University of Science and Technology of China in 1997 and 2000, respectively. He was awarded his doctorate from Memorial University of Newfoundland in 2007 and is now working for Consilient Technologies Corp., a leading developer of push e-mail, multimedia, and advertising software for mobile devices.

Elvira Locuratolo is a researcher at the Institute of Information Science and Technologies (ISTI) of the Italian National Research Council in Pisa. She also teaches mathematics and computer science at the University of Pisa. She has collaborated with the Rutherford Appleton Laboratory at Oxford and other foreign institutions. She is the author of numerous articles in journals and books such as *Transformation of Knowledge, Information and Data: Theory and Applications* (edited by Patrick van Bommel, Idea Group, Inc., 2005) and *Database Modeling for Industrial Data Management: Emerging Technologies and Applications* (edited by Zongmin Ma, Idea Group, Inc., 2006). Her research interests include meta-modeling, database design methodologies, formal methods, and reengineering methods.

Fred Niederman serves as the Shaughnessy Endowed Professor of MIS at Saint Louis University (SLU). He has been at SLU since fall 1999. Prior to that he taught for nine years at the University of Baltimore. He earned his doctoral degree from the University of Minnesota in 1990. His primary research areas pertain to global IT, IT personnel, and using IT to support teams and groups. Most recently, he has been investigating the integration of IT functions following a merger or acquisition, preferred leadership characteristics of CIOs from the perspective of followers, and the potential of grounded theory for developing indigenous MIS theory. He has published more than forty refereed journal articles including in *MIS Quarterly, Communications of the ACM,* and *Decision Sciences;* presented at several major conference; and serves as associate editor of the *Journal of Global Information Systems, Human Resource Management, Journal of International Management, CAIS,* and *Database.* Additionally, he has collaborated on special issues of *Communications of the ACM, Human Resource Management, Journal of Global Information Systems, Journal of Database Management,* and currently the *Journal of Organizational Computing and E-Commerce.* He has also served as chair of the ACM special-interest group on computer personnel. Among his proudest recognitions is being selected for membership as a "compadre" for the PhD Project Information Systems Doctoral Student Association.

Jeffrey Parsons is a professor of information systems in the Faculty of Business Administration at Memorial University of Newfoundland. His research interests include systems analysis and design using UML, database management, and the semantic Web. His research has been published in journals such as *Management Science, Communications of the ACM, ACM Transactions on Database Systems, Journal of Management Information Systems,* and *IEEE Transactions on Software Engineering.* He serves as a senior editor for the *Journal of the Association for Information Systems,* is on the editorial board of the *Journal of Database Management,* and is program co-chair of the 2008 Americas Conference on Information Systems (AMCIS).

Jan Recker is senior lecturer at the Information System Cluster in the Faculty of Science and Technology, Queensland University of Technology, Brisbane, Australia. He received his BScIS and MScIS from the University of Muenster, Germany, in 2004 and his Ph.D. in information systems from Queensland University of Technology in 2008. His research interests include BPM standards adoption, context-awareness, and business process flexibility. Findings from his research have appeared in more than fifty research papers. He is also a regular speaker at BPM practitioner conferences as well as manager and regular instructor for the school's Continuing Professional Education offerings.

Alastair Robb is a lecturer in the Business Information Systems Cluster at the University of Queensland Business School. His qualifications are in business and he holds a Ph.D. in commerce (information systems) from the University of Queensland. Previously, he has held positions in the automotive and finance industries. His research interests include IT governance, data quality, deceptive behavior in computer-mediated communications, and e-business.

Michael Rosemann is a professor of information systems and leader of the Information Systems Cluster at the Faculty of Science and Technology, Queensland University of Technology, Brisbane, Australia. He received his MBA (1992) and his Ph.D. (1995) from the University of Muenster, Germany. His main research areas are business process management, conceptual modeling, and enterprise systems. He is the author/editor of six books and more than 140 refereed papers. His books and papers have been translated into German, Mandarin, Russian, and Portuguese. His papers have been published in journals such as *MIS Quarterly, IEEE Transactions on Knowledge and Data Engineering, Information Systems, European Journal of Information Systems,* and *Decision*

Support Systems. He has intensive consulting experience and has provided advice to organizations from various industries including telecommunications, banking, retail, insurance, utility, logistics, the public sector, and the film industry.

Paolo Salvaneschi is an associate professor of software engineering at the University of Bergamo, Faculty of Engineering. Born in 1948, he earned a degree in physics at the University of Milan. He joined the University of Bergamo after spending twenty-five years as a software architect and head of software development groups in industry and research labs. He has been coordinator and scientist responsible for eight research projects funded by the European Community and National Research Bodies. He has published 115 papers mainly in software engineering and artificial intelligence (AI) applications to structural engineering. He is also active as a software engineering consultant. His interests include quality evaluation of software products, software design methods, and AI-based data interpretation.

Glen Van Der Vyver is a senior lecturer in information systems at the University of Southern Queensland. He worked at the "coalface" in IT (mostly) and human resources for about fifteen years before becoming an academic. He teaches courses in the database design and development area and is currently working on research relating to IT careers, outsourcing, offshoring, the function of the CIO, and risk perception.

SERIES EDITOR

Vladimir Zwass is Gregory Olsen Endowed Chair and University Distinguished Professor of Computer Science and Management Information Systems at Fairleigh Dickinson University. He holds a Ph.D. in Computer Science from Columbia University. Professor Zwass is the Founding Editor-in-Chief of the *Journal of Management Information Systems,* one of the three top-ranked journals in the field of information systems. He is also the Founding Editor-in-Chief of the *International Journal of Electronic Commerce,* ranked as the top journal in its field. More recently, Dr. Zwass has been the Founding Editor-in-Chief of the monograph series *Advances in Management Information Systems,* whose objective is to codify the knowledge and research methods in the field. Dr. Zwass is the author of six books and several book chapters, including entries in the *Encyclopaedia Britannica,* as well as of a number of papers in various journals and conference proceedings. Vladimir Zwass has received several grants, consulted for a number of major corporations, and is a frequent speaker to national and international audiences. He is a former member of the Professional Staff of the International Atomic Energy Agency in Vienna, Austria.

INDEX

Page numbers in *italic* refer to figures and tables.